'A ground-breaking book. For years educationists have sought evidence of genuine partnerships between schools and homes - reciprocal partnerships where schools are as keen to foster home practices relating to literacy and learning as they are to tell families "this is what we do" and ask that they should do the same.'

Eve Bearne, Cambridge University, UK

RESEARCHING LITERACY LIVES

In this new media age the potential for mismatch between children's literacy practices at home and at school is considerable. Tensions exist between school conceptions of literacy as a set of self-contained skills and competences, and literacy as social practice. In indicating what families can do to support school literacy, schools often fail to recognise or build upon children's lived experience of literacy, or available parental support for wider learning in the home and community.

Based on the findings of a research project developed in partnership with schools, *Researching Literacy Lives* explores how teachers, positioned as researchers, developed an understanding of the cultural, linguistic and social assets that children bring with them from home. It examines how the practitioners widened their conceptions of literacy, built new relationships with parents and children and sought to develop two-way communication between homes and schools. Key ideas and challenges explored include:

- positioning teachers as learners and researchers
- understanding children's everyday literacy lives and funds of knowledge
- examining teachers' own literacy histories, practices and identities
- creating culturally responsive curricula
- contesting implicit assumptions and deficit discourses about children and families
- developing less school-centric ways of working with parents
- constructing more equivalent, personal relationships with parents, families and children.

Illustrated throughout with examples and case studies of the project teachers, *Researching Literacy Lives* challenges the profession to think more critically about children's out-of-school literacy lives and funds of knowledge, and to invest in cultural change such that curriculum and pedagogy build upon children's assets for learning and new home–school communities are created.

Teresa Cremin is Professor of Education (Literacy), The Open University, UK.

Marilyn Mottram is an HMI and Deputy National Lead for English with Ofsted, UK.

Fiona M. Collins is a Principal Lecturer, University of Roehampton, UK.

Sacha Powell is Professor of Early Childhood Care and Education, Canterbury Christ Church University, UK.

Rose Drury is a Senior Lecturer in Early Years, The Open University, UK.

RESEARCHING LITERACY LIVES

Building communities between home and school

*Teresa Cremin, Marilyn Mottram,
Fiona M. Collins, Sacha Powell
and Rose Drury*

Routledge
Taylor & Francis Group

LONDON AND NEW YORK

First published 2015
by Routledge
2 Park Square, Milton Park, Abingdon, Oxon OX14 4RN

and by Routledge
711 Third Avenue, New York, NY 10017

Routledge is an imprint of the Taylor & Francis Group, an informa business

© 2015 Teresa Cremin, Marilyn Mottram, Fiona M. Collins, Sacha Powell, and Rose Drury

British Library Cataloguing in Publication Data
A catalogue record for this book is available from the British Library

Library of Congress Cataloging in Publication Data
A catalog record for this book has been requested

ISBN: 978-1-138-77717-0 (hbk)
ISBN: 978-1-138-77720-0 (pbk)
ISBN: 978-1-315-77282-0 (ebk)

Typeset in Bembo
by RefineCatch Limited, Bungay, Suffolk

Printed and bound in Great Britain by
TJ International Ltd, Padstow, Cornwall

CONTENTS

FIGURES

AUTHORS' BIOGRAPHIES

Dr Teresa Cremin is a Professor of Education (Literacy) at The Open University. She is a past President of the United Kingdom Literacy Association (UKLA), joint co-ordinator of the British Educational Research Association (BERA) Special Interest Group on Creativity and a member of the Economic and Social Research Council (ESRC) Peer Review College. Teresa is also an Academician of the Academy of Social Sciences, a Fellow of the English Association, a Trustee of UKLA and the Society for Educational Studies, and a Board Member of Booktrust and The Poetry Archive. Teresa's socio-cultural research, teaching and consultancy focus mainly on teachers' literate identities and practices, the pedagogies of reading and writing for pleasure, and creativity in teaching and learning from the early years through to Higher Education. Her recent projects have involved exploring contemporary enactments of Vivian Gussin Paley's work with young children scribing and enacting their own narratives, and the literary discussions of extracurricular reading groups, the members of which were shadowing the Carnegie and Kate Greenaway Medals. She is currently involved in research investigating professional writers' identities and composing practices. Teresa has written and edited over 25 books and numerous papers and professional texts, most recently publishing with Debra Myhill *Writing Voices: Creating communities of writers* (2012, Routledge) and editing with colleagues Kathy Hall, Barbara Comber and Luis Moll *The International Handbook of Research into Children's Literacy, Learning and Culture* (2013, Wiley Blackwell).

Marilyn Mottram was a primary teacher for many years and has taught in a variety of contexts. She has had extensive experience of leadership and improvement work in schools across a number of local authorities. At the time of the project, Marilyn was working as a senior School Improvement Adviser in Birmingham local authority and leading developments in curriculum and pedagogy. She was formerly a Senior Lecturer in Education at Birmingham City University and Head of Primary

English. She works closely with practitioners and pupils and is passionate about offering space for teachers to be researchers of children's learning. Marilyn has been involved in multiple teacher-research projects and her own research interests include exploring the connections/disconnections between literacy practices and events in homes, schools and communities and the implications for literacy pedagogies and approaches. Marilyn is currently HMI and Deputy National Lead for English with Ofsted.

Fiona M. Collins is a Principal Lecturer at the University of Roehampton where she convenes the MA English Education pathway. She teaches on a range of modules linked to English Education and children's literature at both undergraduate and postgraduate level. She has co-edited two books on children's literature: *Historical Fiction: Capturing the Past and Turning the Page* and *Children's Literature in Performance and the Media* and, with colleague Alison Kelly, has been involved in an ESRC series of lectures in which they presented research on student teachers' confidence in using children's poetry in school placements. In recent years Fiona has also been involved in a number of externally funded research projects. These include two EU Comenius funded projects exploring links between creativity and Identity ('Images and Identity' and the current 'Creative Connections') as well as two UKLA/OU research projects: 'Teachers as Readers: Building Communities of Readers' and 'Building Communities: Researching Literacy Lives', on which she is a member of the research team.

Dr Sacha Powell is a Reader in Early Childhood at Canterbury Christ Church University. She currently leads the Research Centre for Children, Families and Communities – a specialist, interdisciplinary unit dedicated to critical, ecosystemic approaches to researching the lives of children and young people using methodologies that foreground participation, co-construction and public involvement. Her own work falls within the broad spectrum offered by the area of Early Childhood studies and in particular focuses on policy and services for children from birth to three with a babies' and young children's rights/agency perspective. Recent studies include The Baby Room Project, which emphasises a dialogic approach to early childhood professional education and practice and the importance of talk in babies' lives. This led to the development of new work which explores and supports practitioners to theorise the role of singing with babies as a component of a pedagogy of care. Both projects have been co-directed with Dr Kathy Goouch and funders include the Esmee Fairbairn Foundation and the Froebel Trust. She is also co-editor with Kathy and Tricia David of the *Routledge International Handbook of Philosophies and Theories in Early Childhood* and *An Introduction to Early Childhood Studies* with Trisha Maynard (Sage, 2013). She lectures on a range of undergraduate and postgraduate programmes in Education and Health and supervises doctoral students from diverse disciplines. Sacha is a convenor of the Parents in Education Research Network and a member of the UK Froebel Research Committee and Executive Committee of TACTYC, the association for early childhood educators.

Dr Rose Drury is a Senior Lecturer in Early Years at The Open University Faculty of Education and Language Studies where she has developed a Foundation Degree in Early Years, teaches on the Masters programme and supervises EdD students. She was formerly Senior Lecturer in Early Childhood Education at the University of Worcester and Principal Lecturer in Early Years Education at the University of Hertfordshire. She worked for the Minority Ethnic Curriculum Support Service in Hertfordshire and has extensive experience of teaching bilingual children in the Early Years. Her research in the field of multilingualism has included a Trentham book, *Young Bilingual Learners at Home and at School*, papers in journals, chapters in books and invitations to speak to practitioners working with young bilingual learners. In recent years she has been involved in researching 'A day in the life of a bilingual practitioner' and 'Ethnography of an early years teacher – superdiversity in a London nursery class'. Rose is currently undertaking a study of the early years services (nidi and scuole d'infanzia) in Pistoia, Tuscany – to illuminate the unique quality of nurseries in Pistoia and their documentation of young children's learning.

ACKNOWLEDGEMENTS

The project team would like to acknowledge and thank both the Esmée Fairburn Foundation and the UK Literacy Association (UKLA) for their generous funding of this work, without which the project *Building Communities: Researching Literacy Lives* would not have taken place. In addition, the team are indebted to a number of colleagues: the many teachers, headteachers and children involved; the local authority co-ordinators who facilitated this research in five authorities in England; the partners from other agencies who worked alongside the co-ordinators and teachers; the members of the project's Steering Committee, and the external evaluator Dr Judy Durrant from Canterbury Christ Church University who so perceptively analysed the work of the project. In addition, and significantly, the team want to recognise the rich and time intensive contribution made by Dr Eve Bearne – who contributed as an independent researcher to the moderation of the findings, and through ongoing dialogue and debate to the study itself.

1

INTRODUCTION

Setting the context

Teresa Cremin and Fiona M. Collins

The significance of home as an influential feature in children's literacy and learning development is widely recognised (e.g. Heath, 1983; Nutbrown *et al.*, 2005), yet frequently home–school literacy relationships are framed around notions of school-based literacy. Such notions, underpinned by an 'autonomous model' of literacy (Street, 1998; 2008), conceive of it as a set of self-contained and transferrable skills and competences. Popular in educational regimes driven by market-based notions of accountability, this conception fails to take account of difference and can, with its emphasis upon predetermined sets of knowledge and skills, lead to judgements and the labelling of some children and families and teachers as 'deficient' in various ways (e.g. insufficient conversation or books at home). Tensions between school literacy, with its more limited sanctioned and individual performances, and more open and inclusive views of literacy as multiple, contextual and situated, (Street's (ibid.) 'ideological model') persist. Mottram and Hall (2009) argue that 'the current language of schooling is sharply focused on deficit and on oversimplified, easily measurable notions of attainment' (109). They further assert that this language has had a homogenising effect, since 'children's literacy development is discussed according to levels and descriptors, rather than in the context of the child's home and family history' (ibid.: 109). Research evidence suggests that there is a significant mismatch between literacy practices at home and school and that teachers, unaware of children's out-of-school literacy and learning experiences are not in a position to acknowledge and validate them in schooling (Cairney, 2002; Larson and Marsh, 2005; Thomson and Hall, 2008). Additionally, despite the reality of living in this technological age, school and societal conceptions of literacy remain somewhat print-oriented and book-bound (Marsh, 2003). Furthermore, schools frequently indicate what families can do to support school literacy and frequently fail to recognise or build upon parental support for wider learning in the home and community. Indeed many schools see parents' roles as being to support what is done in class, rather than seeing them as a source of different and/or complementary literacy and learning experiences (Cairney, 2003; Crozier and Davies, 2007). Thus, as Feiler *et al.* (2006) argue, the traffic between home and school is traditionally conceived and one-way in nature.

The project *Building Communities: Researching Literacy Lives (BC: RLL)* on which this book is based sought to enable teachers, positioned as researchers, to develop new knowledge about children's everyday literacy practices and widen their own conceptions of literacy. It also sought to develop two-way traffic between homes and schools and new teacher–child and teacher–parent relationships. The UK-based project was a collaborative university, local authority (LA) and school partnership study that sought to explore children's everyday literacy practices in the twenty-first century. It was undertaken by a team comprised of five university-based researchers, five LA co-ordinators, and 18 participatory teacher-researchers from 10 schools (for children aged between 4 and 11 years). In an attempt to avoid the 'cheery, unfailingly positive tone' (Vincent, 1996: 74) of some project reporting, this text explores the challenges which emerged during the course of the project; the dilemmas and difficulties the teachers faced, as well as the rich insights gained when they were invited to reposition themselves as learners and researchers. The project team recognised the challenge of teaching in this new media age in which multimodal literacy practices, located in the lived social realities and everyday experiences of children, are rarely acknowledged or built upon in school. The team also appreciated the pressure of teaching in a culture of accountability which tends to sideline important questions such as:

- How can teachers develop their understanding about children's uses and meanings of literacy in the communities in which they live?
- How can they find the time to engage in more meaningful interaction with their children's families?
- How can they develop teaching repertoires that help diverse individuals make progress?

The project *BC: RLL* reasserted the importance of asking these questions. It involved teachers stepping away from officially endorsed literacy practices and the more commonly employed uni-directional and often transmissive approaches to parental participation. It sought to help teachers develop an understanding of the cultural, linguistic and social assets children bring with them from home and to connect these vitally to their work in school, affording new opportunities for learning. Through undertaking Learner Visits to children's homes and through classroom practices which aimed to enable children to consider, capture and share their out-of-school literacy practices, it was expected that teachers would become insiders in their pupils' social worlds and cultures. The teachers were also involved in reflecting upon their own literacy histories, practices and identities and sharing more of their lives and home literacy practices with the children. It was expected that as a consequence of new knowledge and understanding, shifts in pedagogy would occur that would enable children to 'unpack their virtual school bags' so that home knowledge and tools for thinking could be recognised and utilised in school (Thomson, 2002). However, this required a shift in mindset, openness to learning and a willingness to change and challenge existing perspectives, positions and agendas on the part of all involved: teachers, headteachers, LA co-ordinators and the team of university-based researchers. The project team, acutely conscious of the challenges of working in a culture of 'performativity' (Ball, 1998), recognised that the high profile focus on raising literacy standards in ways defined and delineated by government, had constrained practitioner research (Kemmis, 2006), prompting a focus on enhancing teaching techniques or assessing new programmes. As a consequence, the project team, drawing on the work of Luis Moll and his colleagues, designed a new study focused on children's lived experience of literacy in the world beyond school (Moll *et al.*, 1992; González *et al.*, 2005). They sought to provide space and time for teachers to develop researcher dispositions, and to use the tools of ethnographers as a way of finding out what literacy resources (skills, knowledge and attitudes) children bring to school. The teachers were also encouraged to consider what counts as literacy in their schools, potentially coming to question, challenge and reconsider this.

In the late eighties and early nineties, Moll and his team of researchers (González, Greenberg, Velez Ibanez and Amanti, a teacher researcher) working in Tucson, Arizona had sought to offset the consequences of pervasive deficit views about particular groups of children and families. They established an approach that enabled teachers to learn more about their students' home lives in order to connect home–school knowledge production and impact upon the young people's education and later prospects. Premised on the belief that 'people are competent, they have knowledge, and their life experiences have given them that knowledge' (González *et al.*, 2005: ix–x), Moll's team identified strategic practices which they named 'funds of knowledge' associated with different households. Their approach involved teachers, supported by anthropological researchers, visiting homes to learn about, acknowledge and later celebrate and use the rich and diverse funds of knowledge documented within the Hispanic families and communities in school (Moll *et al.*, 1992; González *et al.*, 2005).[1] Since then, this term and the original research has not only been adapted and developed by Moll's team, but also by multiple other researchers (see Hogg, 2011 and Rodriguez, 2013). It was in this tradition that the *BC: RLL* project was conceived; indeed the challenge of creating more informed professionals who would recognise children's and families' funds of knowledge and view these as rich resources for constructing school literacy curricula was a core part of the English project.

While the project drew upon the empirically grounded funds of knowledge framework, it was not explicitly framed within the social justice agenda which underpins this approach. The new project acknowledged the presence of persistent deficit views regarding economically, linguistically or socially diverse children and families, but did not focus specifically upon marginalised groups or communities. Rather its focus was upon helping teachers to reconceptualise literacy in the twenty-first century and legitimise a wider conceptualisation of literacy in school, based on new knowledge gained in large part from observations and conversations in their 'Learner Visits' to children's homes. The team coined the term 'Learner Visits' in order to foreground the teachers' positions as learners and researchers; they visited homes not to inform parents about their children's school literacy attainment, but to find out about the young people's home literacy practices. In the project the teachers visited a broad range of children's families, selected by the practitioners for multiple reasons; these included families that might be described as 'mainstream' as well as others from more marginalised communities and the teachers sought information from all the children in their classes. Thus, in the tradition of studies which have explored children's and families' funds of knowledge, a broader than usual focus was adopted as it was believed that all children have funds of knowledge that could and arguably should be energised in the classroom. Additionally the teachers visited homes alone; they were not, as in Moll's work, accompanied by anthropological researchers. This was because the team sought to explore a possible model for future LA or school use. The project did, however, in line with Moll's early studies, include a focus on the development of more responsive and connected classroom practices, that in the case of *BC: RLL* involved the teachers in exploring ways to validate and build upon the children's concrete life experiences of literacy and linked to their learning at home (Cremin *et al.*, 2012; Cremin, 2013a). At the outset and through the project a number of taken-for-granted assumptions about children and their families, about perceived literacy 'levels' and the extent of parental support were voiced. The project sought to enable all those involved – the university-based researchers, the LA co-ordinators, the teachers and headteachers – to question their own tacit assumptions and explore the consequences of their new understandings about children's lives and out-of-school literacy practices. As Moll and Cammarota (2010) claim, from a professional perspective:

> Such work, done as learners entering households with an ethnographic eye toward documenting knowledge, provides teachers with an important cultural framing of families and students, with implications for the teaching of literacy as meaningful practice.
>
> *(Moll and Cammarota, 2010: 289)*

The *BC: RLL* team perceived that coming to view all children and their funds of knowledge as resource rich, would contest deficit discourses or mistaken assumptions about them, their families and communities, and that observation and an increased understanding of language and culture would be a necessary precursor to more active social justice practices of a transformational nature. Consequently, the team sought to help the teachers question the dominant discourse about school literacy and reshape their school literacy practices in ways that built upon the children's lived experience of literacy.

The project was not only framed by Moll's work (González *et al.*, 2005) but was also linked to an earlier one undertaken by a similar project team: *Teachers as Readers: Building Communities of Readers* (2007–8). This focused on reading for pleasure and was also funded by the Esmee Fairbairn Foundation and the UK Literacy Association

(Cremin *et al.*, 2008a, b; Cremin *et al.*, 2009; Cremin, 2010a, b, c; Cremin, 2013b; Cremin *et al.*, 2014). A key strength of the earlier project was the way in which it helped schools turn the rhetoric of personalised learning into a reality. Practically, this started with the teachers finding out more about the realities of children's reading lives, yet although new teacher–child and child–child reading relationships were brokered and reciprocal classroom reading communities established, relatively few teacher relationships stretched beyond the schools. At the outset of this earlier work classroom reading relationships were virtually absent, so schools prioritised their internal relationships before turning their attention to those in the wider community. Those schools which did seek to extend relationships beyond the classroom, tended to lean on traditional ways of working which frame teachers as 'all-knowing' and parents as 'needing to be told'. However, the 43 project teachers from 23 schools across England involved in the building reading communities project did begin to recognise the diverse nature of reading in the twenty-first century, and as a consequence new understandings began to emerge. There were signs in the classrooms of those who developed as Reading Teachers — teachers who read and readers who teach (Commeyras *et al.*, 2003) of boundaries beginning to blur between children's home and school reading lives. This encompassed a lessening of the boundary 'authority' and hierarchical structures around reading and made a marked impact on teachers' conceptions of reading and children's growth as readers. It also influenced some parent's perceptions of the nature of reading (Cremin *et al.*, 2009; Cremin 2010a). The new project *BC: RLL* sought to build upon the insights gained, in particular those around the significance of the positioning of the teacher, awareness of their adult reading practices, and knowledge of the children's everyday reading lives. In the earlier project, whilst the reading communities created rarely stretched beyond the classroom, the external evaluator recognised there was potential:

> There is still much to do to reach many families that cannot readily engage. It is therefore important to examine models where parents have been involved successfully. A teacher from one Birmingham school described a whole range of strategies involving libraries, the police, trained volunteers, buddies across year groups and 'Dads and Lads'. Here there has been a noticeable increase in families using the library over weekends and holidays, which is particularly significant where children usually show a marked dip in reading level over the summer. Parents have developed confidence and reading at home has massively increased. This example shows what can be achieved when particular focus is given to building communities of readers beyond the school.
>
> *(Durrant, 2008: 15)*

The project *BC: RLL* took a wider focus than reading and explored children's everyday literacy lives with a view to building new, more connected classroom practices, new relationships and home–school communities. In order to establish genuinely reciprocal partnerships with parents, it was recognised that the project teachers would need to credit the parents as genuine partners in children's literacy learning and development. In their US research, Hughes and Kwok (2007) suggest that alongside teacher–pupil relationships, the relationship between parents and teachers is the fulcrum in the home–school interface and that the emphasis on parental 'involvement' in schooling is too often at the expense of developing better home–school relations. They argue it is crucial for the profession to explore strategies for enabling teachers to make more personal connections with parents and children. Endorsing this point, Muschamp *et al.* (2007, 2010), in their international Cambridge Primary Review Research Survey on parenting, caring and education, observe that:

> Whilst policy has shifted from viewing parents as problems, to parents as customers and more recently to parents as partners, the home-school relationship is really between individual parents and individual teachers who both have the interest of an individual child at heart.
>
> *(Muschamp* et al., *2010: 93)*

Although governments worldwide espouse the value of home–school partnerships, home–school relations between parents and teachers are often shaped by unequal power relations and historically set roles (Crozier, 2000) and may be underpinned by deficit assumptions which disadvantage certain families and communities. The prevailing model suggests that children from at risk or 'hard to reach' backgrounds bring linguistic and cultural resources to school, but that these remain unrecognised or are misrecognised (Luke, 1997), and that schooling systematically rewards those with the most mainstream/middle-class and dominant language practices and backgrounds. Pervasive deficit discourses have grown up in classrooms and staffrooms which conceive of some families, particularly minority ethnic groups, as lacking; they are not widely credited as having valuable literacy experiences in relation to the school's language and literacy practices (Comber, 1997; 1998; Cairney, 2002; Thomson, 2002; Larson and Marsh, 2005; Lingard and Keddie, 2013). The literacies that young people from marginalised communities bring to mainstream schools from their home communities have often been considered non-traditional, denounced as inferior, or seen as impeding children's progress in acquiring school literacy. The families and communities of those young people who do not come to school with the purportedly 'right' set of literacy practices, understandings and classroom behaviours are thus often perceived as 'deficient' (Comber, 1997). This deficit view appears not only to be dismissive of difference, but perceives difference as difficult, yet as Meek (1991: 21) argued, 'difference is at the heart of what it means to be literate'.

In discussing the 'circularity and persistence of deficit discourses', Comber and Kamler working with teachers in Australia (2004) argue:

> We seriously question how, as a teaching profession, we can move out of this dead end, while also addressing wider challenges of ageing teacher populations,

increasingly culturally diverse student populations and more overt divisions between the affluent working class and the poor. The teaching profession at present, lacks serious mechanisms for change.

(Comber and Kamter, 2004: 293–4)

In perceiving difference and diversity as a strength and people as individuals not as homogenous groups, the *BC: RLL* project hoped to challenge this perception of difference as difficult by helping teachers recognise, value and work with the children's diverse literacy lives, building new relationships and home–school communities in the process. It sought to help teachers make connections between children's different social and cultural experiences as they moved between school and home.

The concept of community at the core of this project was of something not fixed but fluid, organic and complex, with many connections and relationships; one that holds at its heart 'the quality of human relationships – communitas – rather than systems or structures' (Williams, 1976). As Mercer (2000) also acknowledges, 'today, community membership can be distributed, multiple and complex, and based as much on common interests as common locality' (105). This is well aligned to the underlying project assumption that children move in and out of many different social spaces and learn in a range of situations, which not only transcend school and classrooms, but also involve virtual and on-screen experiences in rich and diverse social and cultural contexts. While a child may be a member of a community defined (by some) in terms of ethnicity or social class, they will also move through and be part of many other communities every day.

Findings from the earlier project on building reading communities identified a set of core values and principles that were key to the growth of successful, new learning communities. The most significant of these, common to all examples, were those of reciprocity and interaction, equivalence and diversity (Cremin *et al.*, 2014), echoing the concept of 'confianza en confianza' (trust in mutual trust) inherent in the work of Moll's team (González *et al.*, 2005). Such reciprocity has the potential to address inequality and create possibilities for home–school relationships. As Cairney *et al.* (1997) argue, 'it is the development of reciprocal relationships between home and school which offers simultaneously our greatest challenge, and yet our greatest possibility of breaking down educational inequities' (70). The project *BC: RLL* therefore sought to promote approaches based on reciprocity and interaction, where no one party was seen as the 'all knowing authority' but where all parties were seen as learners. This involved a philosophical shift: the teacher would no longer be the exclusively privileged holder of knowledge about literacy, transmitting this to the home by way of the child. It also involved a shift in power relations. González *et al.* (2005), Thomson (2002) and Nespor (1997), among others, propose that real changes in education will only take place when teachers make it a priority to know the communities they work with and when the voices of parents and local community members are heard in school. This raises profound questions around the current highly centralised, standards-driven and bureaucratic model of schooling that prevails in many countries. It also raises questions about how educators use their time, and what their professional priorities and pedagogic practice look like.

Teachers, Muschamp *et al.* (2007, 2010) argue, need to establish new links between home and school, links which build on the practices and understandings that already exist in homes and communities; they state that 'research as to *how* this can happen would be helpful' (92). The project *BC: RLL* responded to this agenda and call for action by inviting teachers to identify and begin to unlock children's and their families' funds of knowledge and to make connections between these and their lives in school. In particular, the project aimed to: support teachers as researchers, documenting and understanding children's literacy lives; extend teachers understandings about twenty-first-century literacy identities, habits and cultures; and enable teachers to create innovative classroom approaches that build on children's literacy lives and foster positive literacy identities. Teachers were also supported to explore their habits and beliefs and implicit assumptions and perceptions about children and parents. Positioned as researchers, they undertook Learner Visits to children's homes and in local and national meetings supported by readings and focused dialogue explored their emergent understandings about children and their home literacies. They also reflected upon their own literacy histories, practices and identities as adults. Over time the practitioners became increasingly aware of the inherent tensions between different conceptions of literacy and the discourses and dispositions commonly associated with their roles as teachers in an account-ability culture. While their journeys as learners, researchers and teachers were not without challenge, many came to question the institutional framing of literacy and the impersonal imperatives of the audit-driven agenda and all made new relationships with parents and children.

Note

1 Many of the original funds of knowledge publications (previously published in journals) are drawn together in the compilation edited by González *et al.* (2005).

2

LAYING THE FOUNDATIONS

Teresa Cremin and Rose Drury

This chapter explores the underpinning principles and research base upon which the project *Building Communities: Researching Literacy Lives (BC: RLL)* was based. It considers the team's conception of community and sociocultural approach, and foregrounds the view that learning, embedded in social and cultural contexts, occurs through participation in practice. It explores research documenting children's language and literacy learning in the home, children's contemporary digital practices and the wealth of assets for learning that they can bring to school. Studies of the continuities and discontinuities of home and school practices are also considered as are the extent to which children's home knowledge and cultural practices are built upon in educational settings. Additionally there is a focus on parental involvement and research examining home–school partnerships. Finally, attention is paid to teachers' literate identities and conceptions of literacy, and to research relating to teachers' roles as pedagogues and as researchers. In this way the chapter lays the foundations of the work developed with teachers in the *BC: RLL* project and seeks to contextualise it within the wider research literature.

Conceptions of community

In seeking to build new home–school communities as part of the project, the team recognised that the word community carries many shades of meaning. Williams (1982) describes it as 'that difficult word' and points out that, unlike other terms of social organisation, such as the state, nation or society, it tends to be used favourably. However Watson (2014), writing more recently, recognises this 'apparently comfy concept is not without its downside' (25). In the context of exploring the development of 'effective' professional learning communities, Watson argues that the 'co-existence of justified competing/conflicting values' are rarely recognised or fostered within such communities, although they may serve as a driver for change and development. He also highlights that ironically an 'as an inclusive body a community necessarily excludes' (ibid.: 26). This is linked to Fendler's (2004) concerns: she perceives the concept of professional learning communities has become a 'mechanism of governance and a forum for specifying norms and rules of participation', and suggests this legitimises organisational control.

The *BC: RLL* team, while acknowledging a role for conflict and negotiation/ re-negotiation of positioning within communities, took an alternative view of the concept. Connecting to their previous research, *Teachers as Readers: Building Communities of Readers*, the team focused upon the core values that were identified as underpinning the rich classroom reading communities that were fostered in that project, namely: reciprocity and interaction; equivalence and diversity (Cremin *et al.*, 2008a, b, 2009; 2010a, b, c; 2014). The new project work was also informed by Williams' (1976) interpretation of community as centred on the notions of equality and the quality of human relationships – communitas – rather than systems and structures. This links to the distinctions noted by Alexander (2000) who, drawing on Tonnies' (1887) Gemeinschaft/Gesellschaft continuum (community/society), highlights the differences between the notion of society – based on organisational structures, and community – based on effect. For the purposes of the *BC: RLL* project, this distinction was important. The goal of community creation that lay at the heart of this work was seen not as consciously organised, but as fluid, organic and rooted in affect. As Williams' argued:

> The making of a community is always an exploration, for consciousness cannot precede creation, and there is no formula for unknown experience. A good community, a living culture, will, because of this, not only make room for but actively encourage all and any who can contribute.... *Wherever we have started from we need to listen to others who started from a different position.*
> *(Williams, 1982: 334)[Our emphasis]*

This notion of community as something that individuals create in different contexts links to post-structuralist theories of identity; in these identities are seen as multiple in the same way as communities are multiple. Language plays a central role in this as children's lives and identities are bound up with the cultural contexts they inhabit; different children and adults bring different kinds of language resources and preferences into the classroom and these influence their identities and position them in particular ways (Heath, 1983; Gregory and Williams, 2000; Gregory *et al.*, 2004). The project *BC: RLL* sought to help teachers to extend their understanding of the multiple communities of which children and their families were members and to develop more inclusive and responsive classroom pedagogies as a result, creating a sense of community in their classrooms as well. It was also expected that as teachers began to draw on the social and cognitive contributions that parents and other community members made – and that they had become party to – new identities would be shaped and new more equivocal relationships formed.

This emergence of new social relationships within and beyond the classroom supports the links between community, culture and learning, since as Bruner (1986) claims 'most learning in most settings' is 'a communal activity, a sharing of the culture' (127). As he asserts: 'the language of education is the language of culture creating, not of knowledge consuming or knowledge acquisition alone' (ibid.: 133). The project *BC: RLL* was concerned with the making and remaking of classroom cultures and involved an exploration of the teachers' perceptions and understandings of children, their families and communities, as well as the roles that teachers, children and families might play in the social process of cultural re-creation. It was recognised that to adopt a view of culture that attributes regularities to groups of individuals (often minority groups) and assumes homogeneity in all group members was inappropriate. Rather, the diverse cultural practices in which people engage – as members of different and changing communities – needed to be acknowledged. Thus the children's cultural experiences, their repertoires of cultural practices were foregrounded and seen as dynamic, hybrid and emergent (Gutiérrez and Rogoff, 2003). Studies of children and young people's everyday lives affirm the heterogeneous and fluid nature of cultural practices (Rogoff, 2003; Hall, 2008), and that 'individuals both participate in and constitute multiple practices and communities at the same time' (Gutiérrez and Rogoff, 2003: 22). The importance of recognising the complexity of community membership and the value of studying lived experience is asserted by González *et al.*, who observe:

> The border between knowledge and power can only be crossed when education institutions no longer reify culture, when lived experiences become validated as a source of knowledge and when the process of how knowledge is constructed and translated between groups located with nonsymmetrical relations of power is questioned.
>
> *(González et al., 2005: 42)*

In a not dissimilar manner, Wenger (1998) recommends that members of different communities, such as the teachers and parents in the *BC: RLL* project, should not seek to protect or defend their domains of expertise (as educators or parents for example), nor to blend these with each other's in an attempt at some form of homogenisation, but that they might more fruitfully manage their boundaries as learning assets. He suggest that the borders between domains of expertise can become spaces of renegotiation, in which new learning and new meanings can be shaped and new communities formed. The project *BC: RLL* rather than expressing power relations as traditionally conceived between parents and teachers, sought to give rise to new and stronger more equivalent relationships between these two groups. It was also an opportunity to shape and be shaped and it included, as will be seen, 'all kinds of relations, conflictual as well as harmonious, intimate as well as political, competitive as well as cooperative' (Wenger, 1998: 116).

A socio-cultural approach to language and literacy

Linked to the project's conceptualisation of communities, the team took a social practice approach to literacy, perceiving literacy as defined within the context of its use. Literacy practices were recognised as: 'the general cultural ways of uti-lising written language which people draw upon in their lives. In the simplest sense literacy practices are what people do with literacy' (Barton and Hamilton, 1998: 3).

To see literacy as an everyday and localised practice is in tune with the wealth of ethnographic and anthropological studies which have demonstrated the situated nature of literacy practices in contexts, such as the home, the school, the workplace, and the community (Brice Heath, 1983; Barton and Hamilton, 1998; Barton et al., 2000). These studies reveal a wide range of reading and writing practices in parti-cular social contexts, and highlight that children's 'literacy practices', such as the routine use of texting friends or reading for homework, are undertaken in parti-cular 'domains' – in this case in the home – and are particularised as specific 'literacy events'. For example, composing a specific text to arrange a place to meet or reading a particular reading scheme book. Literacy events may well be repeated and are arguably 'particular activities in which literacy has a role', while literacy practices are 'the general cultural way of utilising literacy that people draw on in a literacy event' (Barton, 1991: 5). Significantly though, as Barton et al. (2000), and many others observe, some literacy practices are rendered more visible and dominant than others due to social organisational patterns. Some of the ways in which literacy is used outside education, in homes and communities for example, have been sidelined, while others have been reified and positioned as more highly valued.

This understanding of literacy practices is situated itself within the work of the New Literacy Studies (Street, 1984), which argues against a view of literacy as a set of decontextualised self-contained skills or sub-skills and for a multi-literacies approach which recognises literacies as situated in different domains. The *BC: RLL* project team, in adopting a view of literacy as a situated social construct, eschewed the 'autonomous' model of literacy as articulated by Street (1984; 2008). This model is prevalent in accountability cultures that measure progress against sets of normal-ised sub-skills and seek to prescribe approaches to teaching literacy. Such a model of literacy fails to take account of difference. Instead the project team adopted a view of literacy as richly embedded in social and cultural practice, and saw literacy activities and the social structures in which they are embedded as inextricably linked. That is, they perceived children develop literacy knowledge, skills and under-standing through their immersion in and engagement with a multitude of everyday literacy practices that vary from one context to another. Street (1984; 2008) has termed this context-dependent notion of literacy, the 'ideological' model. This conceptualisation recognises the diversity and complexity of children's literacy practices, that they are everyday, situated, multiple, and that they make use of a range of tools (pencils, paper, touch screens, keyboards) and multiple modes of expression (e.g. words, spoken and written, drawings, digital designs and so forth).

Acknowledging that literacy is not a single entity but is multiple, multimodal and context dependent prompted questions to be asked in the *BC:RLL* project about the value afforded different literacy practices within and across home and school, and about teachers' and parents' beliefs and attitudes towards these different practices. The team viewed literacy as considerably broader than reading, writing, speaking and listening, which was and still is predominantly the framing of schooled literacy in England, (DfE, 2104) where the project was situated. They sought to help the project teachers find out about the children's lived experience of literacy, consider their own conceptualisations of literacy, and question the continued dominance of school literacy activities framed around an autonomous model.

Children's language and literacy learning in the home

Working from this sociocultural perspective, the *BC: RLL* team viewed learning as occurring through participation in practice in different social and cultural contexts. As Rogoff (2003) observes: 'humans develop through their changing participation in the sociocultural activities of their communities, which also change' (11).

Children's first learning community is their home: a space and place of significant participation. As Mayall (2007) notes, 'studies of home learning conceive of the home as a social construct that is almost synonymous with family. Home/family provides structures and continuity, rooted in past time – for eating, division of labour, routines, celebrations, contacts with wider kin' (8). Across these studies, children are viewed as both apprentices and active participants in their families' and communities' social practices. Through their involvement they learn ways to make meaning and co-construct their identities as learners. Studies have shown that toddlers and children from a variety of communities all have opportunities to learn, though different socialisation practices exist (Heath, 1983; Rogoff, 1993). From birth, children in different cultures learn to participate in different environments and in diverse social relationship networks (Rogoff, 1993; Volk and de Acosta, 2004). As a consequence, through their families and the communities in which they live, the young have access to different 'funds of knowledge' (González *et al.*, 2005), though research suggests such assets for learning are not always recognised or legitimated in school (Comber and Kamler, 2004; Comber, 1997; 1998; 2007; Thomson and Hall, 2008; Lingard and Keddie, 2013). A point revisited throughout this chapter.

Studies of bilingual and multilingual learners also highlight the wealth of learning opportunities and language practices in their homes and communities. In Gregory and Williams' (2000) ethnographic study for example, children from British-Bangladeshi families in contrast to their monolingual peers, were observed to experience a range of formal learning outside school; regularly attending both Bengali classes and Qur'anic school. In their homes, they read aloud to siblings from school reading books and mixed and blended practices from home and school; 'syncretising' their home–school learning. The work of Robertson (2004) and Drury (2007) also demonstrates that even very young bilingual learners syncretise their home–school literacy learning. As Gregory *et al.* (2004) observe, syncretic literacy studies:

> go beyond issues of method, materials and parental involvement towards a wider interpretation of literacy, including what children take culturally and linguistically from their families and communities . . . and how they transform existing languages, literacies and practices to create new forms (syncretism).
>
> *(Gregory* et al., *2004: 5)*

However, children's proficiency in their home language and their ability to operate simultaneously in English and mother tongue is not always fully recognised or fostered in educational settings (Kenner, 2000; Drury, 2007). As Volk (2004) argues, the education profession needs to view literacy practices in all homes as 'people rich', with substantial funds of knowledge relevant to both children's home and school literacy learning. In *BC: RLL,* the project teachers were supported in finding out about the children's linguistic, cultural and historical assets developed and practised in their homes and communities. They were also supported in widening their conceptualisations of literacy learning.

The foundations of literacy are laid in the home and the earliest conceptual understandings of literacy are established in this context (Hannon, 1995). As research has demonstrated, toddlers begin to interact with print and display early reading behaviours at a very young age (Crago and Crago, 1983; Minns, 1997). They acquire knowledge about texts from early exposure to and immersion in stories and texts of diverse kinds, including for example written tales (Wells, 1987), oral tales (Fox, 2004), televisual and digital tales (Marsh, 2000; Hill, 2010) and begin to experiment with communicating through drawing and writing using different multiple media. However, despite the fact that reading and writing are fundamental characteristics of children's everyday lives, each child's experience of literacy is different and unique. The children from the monolingual families in Gregory and Williams (2000) study for example, experienced literacy differently from their multilingual peers. A substantial part of their home reading was 'unofficial', closely linked to popular cultural texts and the 'emergent' alternate tradition of literature (Luke, 1988). This was not, Gregory and Williams argue, likely to be perceived as appropriate literature in school. Additionally, this research highlighted the role of grandparents as literacy brokers in the monolingual homes, contrasting this with the role of siblings as literacy supporters in many of the bilingual learners' homes.

Children also participate in multiple digitally related literacy practices at home (Marsh, 2005; Hill, 2010). Their use of social networking and online games communities are increasingly characterised by more diverse social relationships around literacy events (Carrington, 2007; Dowdall, 2009), and their home-based knowledge of popular cultural texts gives them the basis for critically understanding both texts and the contexts in which they are produced (Marsh, 2004; Vasquez, 2005). However, while the social and cultural context makes a difference to text production, the metaphorical, conceptual and physical spaces, sometimes referred to as 'third spaces', in which texts are experienced, are also influential (Moje *et al.*, 2004; Leander and Sheehy, 2004). These spaces allow learners to negotiate between 'different discourse communities' in which their identities and literate practices are realised (Moje *et al.*, 2004: 44). Central to this view is a sense of the possibility for change through 'conversations' between different funds of knowledge.

However children's experiences of digital and multimodal texts seem rarely to be acknowledged or built upon in the classroom, creating 'dissonance between home and school experiences from children's first years of schooling' (Larson and Marsh, 2005: 70) and potentially beyond. Although technology is available for use in classrooms, multiple challenges remain (see Levy *et al.*, 2013 for a recent review). Abrams and Merchant (2013) argue that primary phase educators appear to privilege traditional literacy in school, perceiving digital technology as supplementary to this. Alongside teacher confidence and comfort with technology, they also note policy-framing, infrastructure, and time limitations are common concerns. As a consequence, it is suggested that practitioners tend not to use digital texts as part of their daily teaching, and children experience few opportunities to engage in autonomous text production or reconstruction. Additionally, inequality of opportunity in access to technology at home and schools exists, with studies showing that children with lower socioeconomic status are disadvantaged compared to their more affluent peers (Livingstone and Helsper, 2007; Dwyer and Harrison, 2008). Though studies working with learners on the margins have shown the power of technology to engage, motivate and challenge children (e.g. Walsh, 2007). This has implications for teachers' awareness of children's funds of digital knowledge and for professional practice (Bearne, 2009; Dwyer, 2013). In order to understand children's digital worlds, Lankshear and Knobel (2006) suggest that teachers should research their digitally mediated social practices.

Through undertaking Learner Visits, many of the teachers in the *BC: RLL* project came to recognise the children's multiple digital competences, passions and practices and some, in tune with Hedges (2011), came to perceive the young people's expertise in and experience of popular cultural texts as funds of knowledge. But as Chapter 6 highlights, the teachers did not find it easy to take the next step and capitalise upon the children's interest and expertise in media-based culture in the classroom.

Home and school

The diversity documented in different community contexts (Scribner and Cole, 1981; Taylor and Dorsey-Gains, 1988; Rogoff, 1993) led to an interest in whether such diversity is reflected in the context of schooling. Research studies in many countries have revealed that for children coming from cultural and minority group environments, their ways of making meaning and elaborating on knowledge, and their use of language and discourse styles used at home, differ markedly from those predominantly emphasised in school (e.g. Brice-Heath, 1983; Cairney *et al.*, 1997).

In Brice-Heath's (1983) seminal American study, it was evident that different communities' sets of literacy practices created different challenges for children from non-mainstream groups when they entered schooling. In highlighting the mismatch between the ways language is used in linguistically and culturally diverse families and in schools, Brice-Heath (1983) identified this as the cause of the underachievement of some minority groups in schooling.

Deficit discourses about various children's ability to achieve in schooling were in evidence in this study (Brice-Heath, 1983), acting to lower teachers' expectations and arguably remain prevalent in classrooms and staffrooms today (e.g. Thomson, 2002; Cairney, 2002). The deficit model suggests that children from low-income groups and those from minority and immigrant families have limited resources and come from 'literacy impoverished' homes (Auerbach, 1995: 13). The 'taken for granted' assumption is that in such homes, the parents may not read themselves or read to their children and may not value or support literacy learning. Seen in this light, parents from particular groups may be viewed by educators as in need of being taught white, middle class values and practices, and homes may be viewed as places to be co-opted to the mainstream school agenda (Crozier, 2000). Causal assumptions appear to underlie simple home–school mismatch theories, which make presumptions about the common experiences of groups of individuals. Yet as Reese and Gallimore (2000) argue, based on their work with Latino families, 'some home-school discontinuities may diminish or increase over time as parents adaptively respond to new and changing circumstances' (105). In response to the complexity of the continuities and discontinuities between home and school, Volk (2004) suggests that teachers may be led 'to approach children's learning at home with a school-based model of valued learning interactions and, as a result, judge homes to be deficient when their expectations are not met' (37). Children may be seen to lack appropriate skills and experiences; their cultural capital and 'habitus' (Bourdieu, 1990) – their lived experienced handed down over generations – may remain unrecognised or be misrecognised in schooling (Luke, 1997). As a consequence, underperformance is often seen as a problem vested in individual learners and their families, not in schools and teachers' expectations and the pedagogy and curriculum on offer.

> Rather than reflecting deficits in skills and experiences, differences in school literacy achievements seem to have more to do with some students' lack of familiarity with the literacy practices of schooling and schools' failure to recognise and build on the literacy practices children bring with them from home.
>
> *(Cairney, 2003: 89)*

The early studies of Luis Moll and his colleagues undertaken in working class Hispanic families in Tucson, Arizona (Moll and Greenberg, 1990; Moll *et al.*, 1992; 1993; Gonzales *et al.*, 1993; Gonzales and Moll, 2002; Gonzales *et al.*, 2005) suggest that variations across families need to be seen as a rich resource for learning rather than a set of factors that determine literacy success. While children in the homes visited in this work were commonly considered 'disadvantaged', as their families were reputed not be able to provide the rich and engaging environments offered by other more 'advantaged' families, Moll's research showed that in reality these families and their communities contain extensive 'funds of knowledge'. He uses this term to refer to the skills, strategies and information utilised by households, which may include information, ways of thinking and learning, approaches to learning, and practical skills. Examples given include knowledge related to farming, construction, and household maintenance, such as shopping, meal preparation, gardening, and socialising with wider family and community members. Thus 'funds of knowledge' are described as: 'those historically accumulated and culturally developed bodies of knowledge and skills essential for household or individual functioning and well-being' (Moll *et al.*, 1992: 133).

Significantly it is recognised that this concept is dynamic not static; families' funds of knowledge alter over time, in response to changed circumstances and cultures. Most recently Moll and colleagues have summarised the concept in the following manner, noting that:

> Families, especially those in the working-class, who have been our particular focus of study, can be characterized by the practices they have developed and knowledge they have produced and acquired in the living of their lives. The social history of families, and their productive or labour activities in both the primary and secondary sector of the economy, are particularly salient because they reveal experiences ... that generate much of the knowledge household members may possess, display, elaborate, or share with others.
>
> *(Moll et al., 2013: 172)*

This work provided the conceptual basis of the project *BC: RLL* and contributed to its practical framing. Working with anthropological researchers, the teachers in Arizona visited homes as participant-observers to carry out ethnographic research and find out about the lived experience of children and their families (González *et al.*, 2005). The project in the UK sought to emulate these visits, though as discussed further in Chapter 3, in order to establish a possible model for future school use, the teachers undertook their Learner Visits without being accompanied by members of the university-based research team or their LA co-ordinators. Significantly too, the project *BC: RLL* did not just focus upon visiting children from minority groups or those in danger of being marginalised in schooling, but encompassed a broader range of learners from 'mainstream' contexts as well. Though in the UK, as in Arizona, the research team sought to enable the teachers to recognise and legitimate the children and their families' diverse funds of knowledge pedagogically, as cultural resources for teaching and learning.

In her earlier ethnographic work, Brice Heath (1983) had also considered how teachers' knowledge of children's ways of learning in their homes and communities might enable young learners to bring these ways into their classrooms. She provided teachers with a framework for raising their awareness of the resources non-mainstream children brought to school and helped practitioners consider how to adapt their teaching approaches and literacy curricula in response. More recent empirical studies that connect the domains of home and school and formal and informal literacy have also sought to support teachers in recognising children's life experiences and knowledges and in developing related classroom approaches (Comber and Kamler, 2005; Lingard and Keddie, 2013; Rosemberg et al., 2013; Thomson and Clifton, 2013). These studies undertaken in different contexts tend to suggest, as Thomson and Hall (2008) also assert, that children's funds of knowledge 'might be changing, but also that they are likely to be different for different children in different locations, communities and networks' (88). Research into children's funds of technological and popular cultural knowledge (e.g. Hill, 2010; Hedges, 2011) also affirm this as does the work of Rosemberg et al. (2013).

Researching indigenous communities in Argentina, Rosemberg and colleagues (2013) endorse Moll's arguments about the funds of knowledge, patterns of interaction and language variety into which young children are socialised. Their work in particular demonstrates the potential of creating 'ethnographic reading books' which encompass the 'speech, customs and daily lives of the children who belong to social groups that don't share the linguistic dialect or types of knowledge most frequently valued at school' (70). The books' events are based on their teachers' observations, knowledge of local issues and children's interests, as well as awareness of the experiences that shape the young learners' lives and cultural norms. These researchers suggest that such ethnographic reading books can serve to 'increase children's personal growth by capitalising on, rather than denying their linguistic and cultural heritage' (Rosemberg et al., 2013: 72). Developing such responsive pedagogic instruments is important to enable children to employ their funds of knowledge and embedded ways of making meaning in school. However, in her review of studies linked to families' funds of knowledge, Rodriguez (2013) suggests that the extent to which families' funds of knowledge as pedagogical resources are used to affect teaching and learning is both unpredictable and contingent on local contexts.

Other scholarly work investigating teachers' roles in enabling children to transition home knowledge into school ranges from implementing specific sets of pedagogic practices, to documenting more general changes in teachers' attitudes and assumptions (see Compton Lily, Rogers and Lewis, 2012 for a recent related review). In the UK, Thomson and Hall (2008), in their research into schools engaged in working in the creative arts, often with creative partners from beyond the school's boundaries, show that while examples of children's funds of knowledge 'leaking' into English classrooms exist, they represent 'wasted opportunities'. The pedagogues, largely unaware of the value and relevance of the children's experiences and expertise from beyond school and often challenged by their own moral positions in relation to what the children produced (especially in the currently market-driven education system) did not capitalise upon these opportunities. Indeed they were marginalised. Nonetheless as they assert:

> The affirmation of home and community practices ... builds positive social identities for students and sensitises their teachers to the myriad ways in which the mandated curriculum excludes some and privileges others.
>
> *(Thomson and Hall, 2008: 88)*

In the *BC: RLL* research, the team sought to encourage teachers to recognise the limited nature of school literacy, to find out about and build respectfully upon children's diverse funds of knowledge – the resources and strengths they possess – developing more culturally relevant pedagogies that fostered positive literacy and learning identities for the young people. The team also sought to help the teachers consider their perspectives and attitudes towards children, their parents and families' home and community practices. Chapter 6 details the pedagogical shifts made by some of the teachers and the very considerable challenges they experienced in bringing locally-based literacy practices into school, while Chapters 7 and 8 consider the data with regard to the development of new relationships with parents and families.

Parent and school partnerships

Historically, in the UK, where the *BC: RLL* project was based, home and school have been positioned as two distinct and separate realms of a child's life. The role of parents in children's learning has however risen to the top of the political agenda in the last three decades. This is in part because research evidence suggests that parental influence via the home learning environment is a more powerful predictor of attainment at primary school than measures of school 'quality' (Desforges and Abouchar, 2003). As a consequence, a much higher profile has been afforded parent–school relationships and as Selwyn *et al.* (2011) argue, the 'notion of the "engaged parent" has become a key element of governmental policy efforts to improve educational standards and reduce inequalities' (314). However, policies intended to improve parents' engagement have served to alienate some families while privileging others (Hallgarten and Edwards, 2000) and have arguably led to surveillance of parenting by the school or/and the state (Gewirtz, 2001). Some attempts to increase parental involvement amount to little more than 'a form of cultural imperialism, devaluing the practices and value of families who may already be marginalised' (Dyson and Robson, 1999: 3). Indeed, while some parents have labelled in the UK education system as 'hard to reach', research reveals this may more aptly describe some schools (Harris and Goodall, 2007). Thus 'partnership' claims need to be treated with caution. As Muschamp *et al.* (2007) note in their review of parenting, caring and educating: 'The policy rhetoric speaks of a changing relationship between parents and schools, but the reality may be somewhat different, there is little evidence of real change' (14).

Parents and teachers themselves hold diverse views on what the parent–school relationship might encompass, and within different ethnic and class groups, parents may have very different understandings/perceptions of appropriate involvement. For example, Crozier (2000) found that middle class parents tended to be viewed as more 'involved' by teachers as they ensured their children remained in tune with school values and expectations, though they were also perceived as more intrusive, with high expectations that put teachers under pressure. Lareau (1987; 2000) found that middle class parents appear to have access to a wider range of resources than working class parents to influence their children's educational experiences and some working class parents believe it is the teachers' role to educate their children and feel intimidated by teachers' professional authority. More recent research into the relationships between black middle class parents and schools suggests that while these parents behave in similar ways to white middle class parents, they perceive that racist attitudes and behaviours limit their potential involvement (Ball *et al.*, 2011; Maylor and Williams, 2009). Recognising these and other differences is important since parents are often represented as homogenous, and government policies tend to homogenise class, race and gender differences (Williams, 2009). Additionally, research evidence suggests that power differentials between parents and teachers/ schools are not always recognised (e.g. Crozier, 2000; Hallgarten and Edwards, 2000) and that schools tend to have very stereotypical expectations of parents (Griffith and Smith, 2005). Furthermore, there are significant social and economic factors that prevent many parents from becoming more involved in schooling, even though they may wish to do so. Peters *et al.* (2007) showed in their study that the desire to get more involved tended to be stronger among 'disadvantaged' parent groups, for example those in lower socioeconomic groups, from minority groups or those with a long-term illness or disability. In another study, Woods *et al.* (1999) also found differences; parents of young bilinguals expressed concern about home–school practices in relation to the loss of the home language and maintenance of cultural identity.

Even when parents, teachers and pupils all perceive parental involvement positively, they may have different perspectives about the purpose of such engagement (Harris and Goodall, 2008). Differentiating the ways that parents become involved, Tveit (2009) notes that many attempts at parent partnerships have been based on school-centric models, models that imply what parents should do to support their children's school learning. These tend to diminish the value of children's learning in home and community contexts. Tveit (2009) notes that parents undertake roles to support school learning in two main ways: through home-based and through school-based activities. The former include activities such as: checking a child's progress, helping with homework, discussing school issues with the child, augmenting school activities, and talking to the teacher. The latter encompass activities such as accompanying pupils on trips, volunteering at school, and participating in parents' meetings. Such involvement is not only potentially limiting but is framed from the school's perspective around what parents 'should do' to, particularly in relation to school literacy tasks. In the *BC:RLL* project, the asymmetry in this relationship was brought into question and the teachers, supported to visit homes to find out about the children's cultural, linguistic and social resources, opened themselves to new and deeper relationships with parents. In some instances this fostered different kinds of parental involvement and in several schools, new perceptions and partnerships with parents and families developed. These are discussed in Chapters 7 and 8.

Teachers' conceptions of literacy and literacy identities

Recognising the multiplicity of literacies across the different realms of life, home, work and school, the project *BC: RLL*, also acknowledged the significance of identity in literacy practices. How identity is viewed will, Moje *et al.* (2009) argue, influence the way literacy is viewed and vice versa. The project's conceptualised identity as positional and thus multiple, enacted in interaction (Holland *et al.*, 1998; Holland and Lave, 2001). This metaphor acknowledges that:

> Subjectivities and identities are produced in and through not only activity and movement in and across spaces, but also in the ways people are cast in or called to particular positions in interaction, time and spaces and how they take up or resist those positions.
>
> *(Moje* et al., *2009: 430)*

Underpinning this positional view of identity is awareness that positioning is relational such that when teachers discursively construct their literate identities, they do so in relation to others – children, other teachers, teaching assistants and parents for example. Though the ways in which teachers negotiate and enact their identities in relation to parents has received less attention in research. Based on past and present experiences, such identity positions are constantly enacted and performed and are context-dependent, maintained by individuals through their interaction with others (McCarthey and Moje, 2002; Alsup, 2005; Hall, 2008).

Teachers' identities as literate individuals and in particular their conceptualisations of literacy are significant. Evidence suggests that their identities and conceptualisations not only shape what counts as literacy in their classrooms, but also influence children's literacy and learning identities (Cremin *et al.*, 2014; Hall *et al.*, 2010). For example, Hall and colleagues show how teachers' conceptions of reading identities frame and frequently limit children's identities as readers. In Hall's study, which revealed the significant role that literacy plays in young people's identity construction, the language the teachers used served to convey specific qualities associated with being 'good' or 'poor' readers to the children. As these dominant identity positions were not open to question, children ascribed themselves accordingly and accepted their assigned identities (Hall *et al.*, 2010). Other studies show, for example, that teachers' book choices and mediation of them in the classroom have a profound effect on 'how [children] see themselves and who they want to be' (McCarthey and Moje, 2002: 237).

The earlier research project *Teachers as Readers: Building Communities of Readers* from which the study *BC:RLL* developed, highlighted the value and consequences of teachers widening their conceptions of reading, recognising its diversity in the twenty-first century and its inherently social nature (Cremin, 2010b; 2013b; Cremin *et al.*, 2014). The practitioners also reflected upon their own reading identities, habits and preferences and explored children's everyday reading practices. As a consequence some also developed as reflective 'Reading Teachers' and took up dual identity positions as both teachers and readers (Cremin *et al.*, 2014). These teachers in particular came to recognise the significance of difference and diversity in texts, contexts and the social and cultural aspects of their own and the children's lives. They also implicitly adopted a more ideological model of literacy (Street, 2003) and began to recognise that reading and literacy practices are interwoven with identity and social interactions. Their own re-positioning as readers in the classroom and related pedagogic shifts appeared to positively influence the young people's emerging identities as readers (Cremin, 2010a; Cremin, 2013a; Cremin *et al.*, 2014).

In *BC: RLL*, the team sought again to enable the teachers to consider their practices and identities, not only as readers but more broadly as literate individuals. Scholars have also suggested that teachers' reflective engagement in writing and recognition of their identity positioning as writers in the classroom has implications for their practice and for the identity positions afforded younger writers (Cremin, 2006; McKinney and Giorgis, 2009; Cremin and Baker, 2010). However, some research studies suggest that teachers are neither as keen nor as assured writers as they are readers, and that many do not view themselves as writers (Peel, 2000; Gannon and Davies, 2007), and that reading, not writing, forms the backbone of teachers' literacy experiences (Yeo, 2007). If this is the case, it is likely to influence teachers' identities as literate individuals and impact upon classroom practice.

Additionally, research has documented pre-service teachers' digital practices and identities (Burnett, 2011) and a professional identity crisis around the digital divide which it is claimed has been triggered by the changing face of literacy (McDougall, 2009). Graham (2008) argues that teachers need to be given opportunities to consider their digital literacy histories and identities and to make connections to their own funds of knowledge in this technological world.

> Playful social teachers have much to share with colleagues; made explicit, their digital literacy stories enable them to draw on their own "funds of knowledge" about digital worlds (González et al., 2005, p. ix). Shared with others, these experiences might well help develop understandings about the digital worlds of their pupils.
>
> *(Graham, 2008: 17)*

Recognising that funds of knowledge can derive from a variety of sources, and that they are 'not possessions or traits of people in the family, but characteristics of people-in-an-activity' (Moll and Greenberg, 1990: 326), it is possible to refer to teachers' funds of knowledge. Greenhough *et al* (2003) suggest that these are made manifest though events and activities within school and beyond. In the Home School Knowledge Exchange (HSKE) project in the UK, the term funds of knowledge was used to describe 'the knowledge, skills and strategies, both implicit and explicit, which teachers draw on in their classroom practice' (Andrews *et al.*, 2005: 78). In HSKE, the teachers' funds of knowledge were seen to extend well beyond the professional knowledge associated with being a teacher; they drew upon their experiences as parents, as members of different ethnic and faith groups, and as local community members (Andrews *et al.*, 2005). However, while the teachers implicitly drew upon their lived experience in the classroom, there are almost no examples given in this project of teachers sharing their funds of knowledge with learners or of linking these to their own or others identity positioning.

In contrast in *BC: RLL*, the teachers, encouraged to reflect upon their literacy histories and identities, were also encouraged to share self-chosen aspects of their literacy lives and identities in the classroom. In so doing they arguably positioned themselves overtly as co-readers for example, as challenged writers or in some cases as 'digital immigrants' (Prensky, 2001). In addition, the identity positions adopted by the teachers and the funds of knowledge upon which they drew, when visiting homes and meeting parents and other family members, were considered by the teachers and the project team. These are discussed further in Chapter 7.

Teachers as researchers

Historically, teachers positioned as the objects of literacy research have found their practice and perspectives documented and analysed by university researchers: typically minimally involved, they merely provided access to research sites or responded to questionnaires for example. In recent decades however, the involvement of teachers in research related practices has diversified, with many researchers demonstrating the value of collaborating with practitioners and designing literacy projects that either position them as the lead researchers in their own inquiries (Bearne *et al.*, 2007; Hattam *et al.*, 2009) or as co-participants in university-led, but locally developed inquiries (Comber and Kamler, 2005; Grainger *et al.*, 2005; Kwek *et al.*, 2007; Cremin *et al.*, 2009; Hill, 2012). Additionally, practitioners have undertaken their own classroom-based research, framed around self-identified literacy-focused questions, both individually, often as part of credit bearing courses (Walsh, 2007) and collectively as part of teacher research networks (Bearne and Kennedy, 2009). Predominantly teachers have been involved in action research undertaken in own classrooms and schools. As a form of practitioner research, action research is arguably about improving practice rather than producing new knowledge, although debates about its aims and purposes abound (Cochran-Smith and Lytle, 2009). It is argued that the ultimate goal of teachers' inquiries is to transform children's life chances (Lytle, 2008), and as such it is often oriented towards contributing to the quality of teaching and learning. It is also recognised that such research can be a strategic 'methodology for confronting deficit thinking and more fully engaging students as literate learners' (Walsh and Kamler, 2013: 499–500). Additionally, it is posited that it can enhance teachers' sense of their professional roles and identities (Fishman and McCarthy, 2000).

In the UK, however, Kemmis (2006) suggests that harnessing teacher research, specifically teacher action research, to the school improvement agenda, has diluted its critical transformative potential. He suggests that this has prompted a focus on improving teaching techniques or evaluating new programmes or practices, without sufficient attention to the 'social, cultural, discursive and material–economic historical consequences' of such practices (ibid.: 460).

In *BC: RLL*, which was a research and development project, the teachers were involved as insider-researchers, but they were not engaged as action researchers making interventions in their classroom, rather they were positioned as researchers with an 'ethnographic eye' (Gonzales *et al.*, 2006). They undertook Learner Visits to children's homes alongside other data-gathering practices, such as observations and conversations in class with their case study children. Although the interpretative ethnographic research tradition is well suited to teacher research, there are surprisingly few published accounts of teachers undertaking data collection beyond the bounds of their schools as they did in this work. The work of Comber and Kamler (2005) has led the way in publishing teachers' accounts of their insights and understandings developed within and beyond the classroom, through their involvement as researchers in an intergenerational funds of knowledge project. These Australian practitioners worked to create responsive curricular that altered the literacy performance of their most 'at risk' students from marginalised and low–socio-economic groups. The teachers in *BC: RLL* also sought to develop their pedagogic practice in responsive ways, building on and connecting to the new knowledge about children's everyday literacy lives they developed as researchers, both in their classrooms and on the Learner Visits. Their journeys as researchers are discussed in Chapter 4.

Teachers as pedagogues

In the 'turn-around pedagogies' research (Comber and Kamler, 2005; Kamler and Comber, 2008) the Australian teachers were supported to explore how school literacy teaching might encompass the knowledge, skills and experiences children already have – their funds of knowledge. In 'turning around' to their least experienced students and getting to know them and how they operated, they began to redesign aspects of their practice and in so doing repositioned their students as active learners. While few of the teachers made visits to homes, they observed and listened carefully in their classrooms, documenting the learners' involvement. They challenged themselves and each other to recognise that the 'problems children encountered were not just attributed to the individual, but seen in relationship to the structure and design of the teacher's curriculum and pedagogy' (Comber and Kamler, 2005: 9). For example, one pair of teachers, working together from different schools successfully reshaped their early writing curriculum to maximise two Greek boys' engagement, response and production (Moreau and Sharrad, 2005). Through close observation these teachers came to appreciate that the boys 'were more interested in being social than in being literate', and as a consequence they turned their pedagogy around (ibid.: 36). They changed their solitary, teacher-focused, often silent writing workshops and encouraged dialogue and collaborative writing instead. This pedagogic shift, which also encompassed an emphasis on sharing student work in class and the establishment of free choice writing corners, afforded the boys some control over the writing process. As a consequence these young people, and many other reluctant writers in their classes, became more enthusiastic and involved; their expertise and self-esteem as writers was enhanced. However, such work requires teachers to:

> Deeply understand their changed pedagogies at multiple levels: not just to focus on relevant topics or new technologies or writing buddies from year seven, but on the significant repositioning of children with respect to the production and consumption of texts. These changes allowed children to do significant identity work at the same time that it allowed them to acquire new repertoires of practice.
>
> *(Comber and Kamler, 2004: 307)*

In the UK, linked to such funds of knowledge work, the Home School Knowledge Exchange (HSKE) project also sought to help teachers alter their pedagogy, through building on children's home practices (Hughes and Pollard, 2006; Hughes and Greenhough, 2006). Somewhat differently though, this work involved the literal transfer of artefacts such as photographs and toys brought from home to school and there was less documented evidence that this fully transformed pedagogic practice (Feiler *et al.*, 2006). Curriculum constraints were reported as being the reason for teachers not developing more work around children's out-of-school interests (Hughes and Greenhough, 2006). Additionally, it appeared that though the teachers made use of the toys or 'personalised shoe boxes' (with items of significance to the learner) from home, these were almost exclusively harnessed to the purposes of school literacy. To an extent the teachers in HSKE appeared to perceive 'home knowledge' as framed by these objects and artefacts. They did not perhaps recognise or seek to acknowledge the social context and use of these artefacts – the social practices around them – in the children's homes. Although Hughes and Greenhough (2006) note that conversations about such artefacts were fostered and school writing ensued, their significance and use in particular families and communities is not discussed. In contrast, the project *BC: RLL* sought to enable teachers through their Learner Visits to observe in situ some of the social practices in which the children and their families engaged at home. They were able to enquire about these literacy events and practices in which the children's funds of knowledge were made manifest and then sought to connect to these and reshape their pedagogies.

In the US, earlier research by Au (1993) working with pupils of native Hawaiian ancestry, showed that when teachers (particularly those of European ancestry), sensitively adapted their interactions in response to the children's ways of debating issues, there were gains in both attitudes and attainment. Ladson Billings (1992) too found benefits when teachers' knowledge about African American students and their local communities was used to create 'culturally relevant pedagogy'. This approach, which prompted teachers to recognise 'the existence of an African connection and consciousness' (Ladson Billings, 1992: 379), used cultural referents to impart knowledge, skills and attitudes in order to empower the young 'intellectually, socially, emotionally, and politically' (ibid.: 382). Different manifestations of this work have developed (Stein, 2004) which seek to enable teachers to make connections between learners' lives, their communities and larger historical, national and global issues.

These studies highlight ways of building on children's experiences of life and everyday practices constructing 'pedagogies of reconnection' (Comber and Kamler, 2005). As a result of developing new knowledge about learners, teachers may come to think differently about the literacy curriculum, and may make changes to their pedagogic practice and the positions made available to children within it. As Thomson (2002) argues, it is insufficient merely to start where the children are at in order to enhance success in school literacy and learning, or for teachers to simply add funds of knowledge connections to mainstream schooling. She suggests that what counts as important knowledge or, in the case of *BC: RLL* what counts as literacy, needs to be questioned, challenged and broadened such that more inclusive models of literacy and of learning are recognised, validated *and* taught in schools. In the project, while teachers did widen their conceptualisations of literacy and many also sought to broaden their pedagogic practice, in the light of tight curriculum framing in England, this represented a significant challenge as this book testifies (see Chapters 6 and 8 in particular). Recognising children's strengths and resources derived from their lived experience of literacy may be a first step, moving to altered responsive practice may be a second, but unless the dominant discourses around literacy are disrupted within schools and more widely, then children's cultural, social, and linguistic assets will remain sidelined, with significant consequences for children's learning.

Conclusion

Regardless of ongoing changes to primary curricula across the world, developing knowledge about children and their parents and communities and building new more reciprocal relationships with children and parents remains a critical issue for the profession. Deficit discourses have long existed in the UK and internationally, yet there have been relatively few UK studies that have sought to disrupt teachers and schools 'taken for granted' sets of assumptions and stereotypes which operate and impact on achievement. It is also argued that the profession needs to recognise the diversity of children's literacy practices in the twenty-first century and legitimate as valid their pupils' experiences and practices, thus enabling their classroom practice to build on the familiar and the known, and challenge the dominant discourse with its limited conceptions of school literacy.

This chapter has offered a synthesis of the research literature undergirding the project *BC: RLL*, noting its conceptualisation of community and the sociocultural approach adopted in the context of ongoing debates about home–school partnerships and parental 'involvement' in education. Much of the literature, as already noted, is concerned with the ways in which parents are positioned and expected to support their children's learning in the 'basic skills' of literacy, much less attends to the need for teachers to develop a rich understanding of the learning assets and funds of knowledge children bring to school and which they are rarely enabled to utilise. The synthesis has also highlighted the diversity of children's contemporary literacy practices and considered the influence of teachers' literate identities and their experience as pedagogues and researchers. It sets the scene for a more detailed exploration of the project and its findings in the chapters which follow.

3

THE PROJECT METHODOLOGY

Sacha Powell and Teresa Cremin

This chapter describes and reviews the project's design and the methodology employed for researching literacy lives within and beyond the contexts of the schools involved in the study. The chapter begins by explaining the rationale that under-pinned the overall design, which involved a combination of research and professional development activities; the strategies for sampling and recruiting participants; the methods, used for collecting, analysing and interpreting data; and the nature and intended purposes of the incorporated professional development activities.

The challenges presented by the project's complexity are highlighted, both in terms of the organisation and management of a multi-site, multi-method strategy and the diverse epistemological and ontological perspectives that (perhaps inevitably) emerged across a team comprising several researchers working alongside multiple participants. The strengths and weaknesses of the project's design and methodology are reflected upon with particular reference to its similarities and differences to Moll and his colleagues' funds of knowledge approach (González *et al.*, 2005), which influenced the research and the project's theoretical orientation.

Aims and rationale

The project *BC: RLL* sought to enable and support a group of English primary school teachers' explorations and understandings of twenty-first-century literacy constructs as situated and practised within the classrooms, homes and communities of children they taught. It also sought to help the teachers review their under-standings and assumptions about children and families and about literacy and to consider the consequences of any new insights for classroom practice. The work was undertaken against a landscape of educational discourses that have contributed to the construction of school experiences and roles for teachers and their pupils and by extension the children's families.

The design of the project was significantly influenced by the work of Luis Moll and his colleagues who developed the concept of households' funds of knowledge and supported teachers' explorations and use of these (Moll *et al.*, 1992; González *et al.*, 2005). Aligning to the values and principles that Moll and colleagues espoused for their studies, the *BC: RLL* project was grounded in a view of learning as a social process, occurring through participation in practice in different social and cultural contexts; and bounded within wider socio-cultural, historical and political-ideological frameworks; and where all learners are viewed as competent with resources (or funds) of knowledge (González *et al.*, 2005). As discussed in Chapter 2, these funds of knowledge may be recognised and valued in school or – crucially – overlooked or dismissed as irrelevant to school-based learning and teaching (Thomson, 2002; Marsh, 2003; Thomson and Hall, 2008; Hedges, 2011).

Although there are similarities between Moll's studies and the study reported here, there were also differences. Moll's original research focused on working class Hispanic (mainly Mexican) communities in Arizona in the late 1980s and early 1990s while the *BC: RLL* project involved five local authorities in England in 2010, and parents and families in each of these (from majority and minority groups); the research team expected more heterogeneity. Moll's research team encompassed teachers and university researchers, and his university team drew on both anthropological and educational perspectives. The *BC: RLL* project involved a more layered structure of support with a national research team, comprised of researchers drawn from universities and local authorities, that is LA co-ordinators, and partners from external agencies such as the Minority Communities Achievement Service (MCAS) and specialist family support workers from voluntary or community organisations. Moll's researchers and teachers visited local communities together while in the *BC: RLL* project, the Learner Visits were usually undertaken by teachers going alone to families' homes and data were collected by the teachers themselves. This was in order to foster a model for possible future use and because the team were committed to a co-participative design which fully engaged the actual users of the research (though in some cases the project teachers visited in pairs or were accompanied by others, such as an interpreter). The close partnership between the university researchers and the teacher–researchers reflected a commitment to supporting the development of the teachers as researchers through this collaborative endeavour. Moll's team documented and conceptualised households' funds of knowledge (see Chapter 2) which this project also connected to but did not examine in as much detail. The *BC: RLL* project team more explicitly focused on children's funds of knowledge – their lived experience particularly in relation to their everyday literacy lives and worked to support teachers not only in becoming aware of these, but of connecting to them overtly in a planned manner in the context of curriculum design and pedagogic practice. Thus the *BC: RLL* project teachers sought information about the children's interests, strengths and literacy practices. While these are perhaps less classically termed funds of knowledge in Moll's terms, they are an important part of their identities and as Greenhough *et al.* (2003) recognise, funds of knowledge can derive from a variety of sources. In a review of the funds of knowledge literature, Hogg (2011) notes that different researchers have adopted the term and have employed it flexibly within their own work to refer to the content and forms of knowledge identified from homes, often with a view to emphasising the potential of this content and knowledge in relation to the school curriculum. Thus in tune with Moll's work, many studies focus their attention on accessing *and* using the funds of knowledge and resources children bring with them to school (for example, Lee, 1995; Dyson, 1997; McIntyre *et al.*, 2001; Greenhough *et al.*, 2003; Thomson and Hall, 2008; Hedges, 2011) and in this regard *BC: RLL* was no exception. Finally, the project placed an emphasis on the importance of teachers sharing their own literacy lives with the children, which was not a focused feature of Moll's work, although in the account in González *et al.* (2005) it is noted that the teachers were encouraged to make connections with their own lives and histories as they elicited narratives and engaged in conversation with families in their homes. Thus the key differences were the profile and attention afforded children's literacy and learning lives rather than their families or households' funds of knowledge (though it was clear children drew upon these as young learners), and their teachers' literacy practices and histories, as well as more layered organisational structure across five different areas of England and the breadth of homes visited included both majority as well as minority groups.

In sum, as noted in Chapter 1, the project encouraged the teachers involved to reflect upon their assumptions constructed in part by the available discourse, and invited them to identify and begin to unlock the potential assets for learning that are accessible in the diverse social and cultural contexts of children's lives, making connections between these and their lives in school. In particular, it aimed to:

- support teachers as researchers, documenting and understanding children's literacy lives;
- extend understandings about twenty-first century literacy identities, habits and cultures;
- create innovative classroom approaches that build on children's literacy lives and foster positive literacy identities.

The specific research questions which drove the project and its design were developed from these broad aims and the relevant research literature. They included the following:

1   What were the challenges involved in teachers as researchers undertaking Learner Visits?
2   Did the Learner Visits influence the teachers':
    - knowledge of children's everyday literacy practices?
    - knowledge and understanding of children and families' learning beyond school?
    - attitudes towards the children and their families?
    - relationships with the children and their families?
    - perceptions of themselves and their professional roles and relationships?

3   What (if any) new knowledge (and understanding) was developed as a result of the research?
4   What were the consequences for the teachers' pedagogic practice?
5   Were the LA co-ordinators involved in professional learning and if so what did this comprise?

Project structure and organisation

The design incorporated an amalgam of research, professional development and curriculum design activities, which fed into and from each other. While some of this fusion was planned, some was incidental, occurring as a consequence of the teachers' and researchers' discoveries and their altering (sometimes faltering) perceptions and understandings.

The relationship between research, professional development and school improvement has long been established in the field of education and many teachers have become proficient in 'action research'. Influenced by Lewin in the 1940s in the US and Stenhouse in the 1970s in the UK, this approach to studying and articulating one's own role and its impact in teaching and learning has been shown to be an effective vehicle for professional learning, leading to many benefits for teachers and pupils (Cordingley *et al.*, 2003). Although the *BC: RLL* project did not adopt an action research strategy, it had a common aim to transform educational practice using research as the basis for professional development and understanding. Other similarities included: the teacher taking on a researcher role; willingness and a capacity to be self-critical; and a belief that inquiry, reflection and dialogue can improve education practice, experiences and outcomes (see for example, McNiff, 2010). The project was also underpinned by a set of core values and principles related to community construction: reciprocity and interaction, equivalence and diversity, which had emerged from an earlier study on building communities of readers within and beyond school (Cremin *et al.*, 2008a, b; 2009; 2010a, b, c; 2014). The project's emphasis on the relevance and importance of children's literacy lives outside school meant that school-based action research offered an insufficiently broad scope. Consequently, the project incorporated exploratory 'Learner Visits', which teachers made to children's homes for which the teachers were encouraged and supported to adopt an ethnographic stance. This approach was intended as a means to enable the teachers to reposition themselves as learners and researchers; gathering data while situated in the unfamiliar territory of children's homes (see Learner Visits sub section below).

Participants in the project

The project involved a range of professionals, although eighteen teachers from ten schools located in five LA areas in England formed the core group of participants. The additional participants were five advisory teachers who worked for the local authorities of Barking and Dagenham, Birmingham, Kent, Lambeth and Medway, representatives of a range of agencies who had an interest and/or involvement with families and education, and the headteachers of the participating schools. In total, the project involved 43 professionals working with the 5 members of the research team. A cumulative 'snowball' approach was used for the recruitment of participants, all of whom got involved on a voluntary basis, although arguably some of the headteachers and teachers *may* have felt obliged to participate once they had been approached by the LA co-ordinators (see Ethics below).

Local authorities and their project co-ordinators

Initially, the UK Literacy Association provided a means of publicising the project's aims and inviting partners from local authorities (LAs) to get involved. Five LAs in England responded to the opportunity and agreed to participate in the project. Each LA allocated a member of its schools advisory service to be designated as 'local authority co-ordinators' for the project. All but one were literacy consultants working under the remit of the (former) Primary National Strategy. This was a government-led strategy focused on raising standards in literacy and mathematics through detailed curriculum specification and guidance (DfEE, 1998; DfES, 2007) and an extensive programme of accompanying training. The project's LA co-ordinators were invited to recruit two infant and/or primary schools per LA to join the project. In each case, the LA co-ordinators approached headteachers in schools that were well-known to them through their work in the LA advisory service. The research team provided the LA co-ordinators (and subsequently the headteachers) with information that stipulated the conditions of schools' involvement. These were that the school should have both the capacity and desire to engage with the developmental research project; have identified a need and commitment to finding new ways of building relationships with parents, families and communities (recorded in their school evaluation or development plans); be prepared to explore ways that the work could support community cohesion and the broader learning outcomes of the 'Every Child Matters' agenda (DfES, 2004 – an overarching government policy at the time); be committed to research as a way of developing professional learning communities and moving the school forward; be able to identify two teachers who were willing to try new and innovative ways of working with a range of partners and to consider and value children's learning experiences outside school; be prepared to develop sustained inter-agency partnerships and produce evidence of the impact of their project involvement and be willing to collaborate and share effective practice with other professionals within and beyond their own LA/school. Visits were made to interested schools by the LA co-ordinators and ten schools were identified.

Each of the LAs was allocated a research team member, known as their 'linked researcher' who attended most if not all of the LA group sessions and was the main point of contact for the LA co-ordinator. The linked researcher also visited the schools for the data analysis meetings with the teachers (see below).

Schools

The project focused on schools for children aged between 4 and 11 years. Ten schools were recruited to the project. Eight were primary schools, and two were infant schools. All were in the state schools sector, two had integral nursery provision and five had an affiliation to a particular faith – three were Church of England and two were Catholic, but all the schools included the study of many faiths in their curriculum. Across the ten schools there was a wide range in terms of pupil demographics: several had many children who were eligible for free school meals (52 per cent in one school, less than 1 per cent in another). Three of the schools recorded few or no minority ethnic backgrounds and languages other than English among their pupils, but the other seven schools showed high proportions of children from minority ethnic groups and whose first languages were not English (as high as 90 per cent in one school). The schools' populations also varied, the smallest having 119 pupils on roll, the largest having 670 at the time of the project. This diversity provided a rich and interesting multi-site context for the study.

Headteachers and teachers

The ten headteachers who took part were not simply 'gatekeepers'. Each headteacher was asked to agree to be interviewed twice by a member of the research team and to attend at least one of the professional development days (see below). Therefore, their voluntary, informed consent was also sought as project participants. Once the schools' details were received from the LA co-ordinators, each headteacher was contacted directly by the research team. The headteachers subsequently used staff meetings to publicise the project and to ask for volunteers from their teaching staff to take part in the project. In this way, 18 members of staff – two per school in most cases – agreed to get involved. Some of the teachers who participated were the literacy co-ordinators for their schools. They too received information about the project directly from the research team, which also provided an opportunity to opt out. Each teacher was asked to participate on the basis of voluntary informed consent. Collectively, these teachers were working with children across the whole primary-school range from 4 to 11 years of age. Two had slightly different advisory roles as teachers and were working alongside teachers in particular schools as part of an Education Action Zone programme. Only two of the teachers lived in the local community in which they taught, most travelled to and from school by car, underground or bus as they lived some distance away.

Children and their families

Each teacher was invited to select up to three children. These children were invited to be part of the study for various reasons, all of which were chosen through discussions between the teachers, the LA co-ordinator and the LA's link researcher.

The children's participation was voluntary, although it is possible that some may have felt unable to decline because most of the activities in which they were involved in Term 1 and 3 took place during curriculum time. Parents' consent was gained for the teachers' Learner Visits to their homes in Term 2 and the parents were asked to discuss these with their children and to agree only if the children were also happy for the visits to take place (see Ethics). There were no prescribed criteria for selecting case study children and the teachers' reasons for choosing them were multiple and diverse. But there were some common themes among the reasons they gave for their choices.

Of the 44 children identified by the teachers, 18 spoke English as an additional language, with 13 different first languages covered and this was often a factor in the selection. Knowledge or perceptions of family circumstances and characteristics were also cited as reasons for choosing particular children to case study. It seemed that the teachers knew more about the children's mothers than the fathers and phrases such as 'Mum is the key', 'Mother is concerned', 'Mum spends a lot of time reading with him but his dad never does' were given as part of the reasons for their choices. Features of some children's home lives were also given as part of the justification for choices: for instance, two of the children's fathers were working away in Malaysia and Nigeria and this was seen to be of importance in relation to the teachers' choice; both boys were perceived to have behaviour issues that the teachers believed stemmed from this circumstance. Other reasons included being a recent arrival in school, a 'looked after' child or being in receipt of free school meals, which one teacher rather contentiously perceived 'tells you everything really'.

The teachers were particularly clear about their chosen children's reading habits and abilities *in school* and this was also a commonly mentioned factor in their choice of children to case study. Several children were chosen because they were 'not making any progress' with literacy and their teachers felt there was no explicit reason for this. The children's attainment and their attitude to reading was a significant reason for some who felt that the children either loved reading but made less progress than teachers expected, or they seemed to dislike reading. Children who were learning English as an additional language were often chosen as case study children and their relative fluency in English noted as a reason for selection, though the teachers did not all know the children's mother tongue nor what languages were spoken in their homes. Most of the teachers voiced the view that they wanted to find out more about their case study children and acknowledged that they knew very little about them outside of the school environment, as discussed in Chapter 5.

Having identified their case study children, each teacher then approached one or more of the children's families to ask permission to make Learner Visits to the home or a 'neutral' location, outside school. No pressure was put on the families to take part. They did not have to give reasons for choosing not to participate and two families declined, another did not reply and was thus assumed to have declined. If a family declined to be involved, the teacher approached the next potential case study child's family. All the teachers succeeded in recruiting at least two families, most met three. The families were informed about the project and the purpose of the teachers' visits and gave their consent to the visit and to their views being used as research evidence, which would be shared with the research team.

Partners from external agencies

One of the project's aims was to develop models of effective working practices that enhance school–community relations. It was therefore decided to include partici-pants from agencies and organisations that were involved in the local community and that might help the schools to develop better understandings of the children's (and families') literacy lives outside school. Since each school's local community differed from the next and their links with other agencies also varied, the decisions about whom to invite to participate in the project as 'agency partners' were led by the teachers, headteachers and LA co-ordinator working collaboratively with the linked researcher. For example, in one case (Lambeth), the ethnic background of the majority of the families steered the decision about the involvement of the Portuguese Outreach worker from a local Children's Centre. In another (Kent), historically strong relationships with the Library Service, built during the previous research on building communities of readers (Cremin *et al.*, 2014) fostered con-tinued involvement and in addition a colleague from the Minority Communities Achievement Service (MCAS) was involved, as her expertise and knowledge of local traveller and Polish communities was desired. In all cases, the suggested agency partners were approached directly by the research team and invited to take part on a voluntary basis.

Professional development activities

The planned professional development activities constituted a series of gatherings where all the participating teachers, LA co-ordinators and agency partners were invited to come together over the course of one academic year. On six occasions these day-long events happened in London, drawing together the groups of participants from five different local authority areas in England. These sessions were known as the project's 'national meetings' and were convened by the research team who attended them all. In between these sessions, the five local groups of teachers, LA co-ordinator and partner(s) met on several occasions in a mutually convenient location, such as one of the project schools. These local project sessions, known as 'LA group sessions', were intended to help to maintain the project's momentum and coherence and to provide additional support and dialogic oppor-tunities; they varied in number but each LA co-ordinator organised a minimum of six meetings across the year. This dual approach of national and local meetings were highly responsive in nature and provided the teachers with an active role in questioning, exploring and testing alongside the research team in a way that

Stenhouse believed to be crucial for a more critical and equitable development of the profession:

> The crucial point is that the proposal [in this cases the existence and value of 'funds of knowledge'] is not to be regarded as an unqualified recommendation but rather as a provisional specification claiming no more than to be worth putting to the test of practice. Such proposals claim to be intelligent rather than correct.
>
> *(Stenhouse, 1975: 142)*

The local and national meetings focused on engaging and supporting the teachers as researchers, enabling them to research the children's literacy lives *and* consider their own literacy histories, practices and identities and also consider the consequences for classroom practice. At the day-long national meetings methodological issues such as stance, perspective, reflexivity, ethics, data collection and interpretive analysis were all examined and related international research papers were read and discussed. These included papers by: Comber and Kamler (2004); Marsh (2003); Moll *et al.*, (1992); and Mottram and Hall (2009), and chapters from González *et al.* (2005), as well as papers relating to the previous project *Building Communities of Readers* (Cremin *et al.*, 2008a; 2009). These introduced teachers to the concept of funds of knowledge, gaps between home and school practices, twenty-first-century literacy practices, building classroom communities and potential ways to ameliorate home–school mismatches through attention to children's lived experience of literacy. Each of the sessions included time for participants to re-read, to discuss and debate their views, to reflect, to record their thoughts and air their concerns or anxieties. In line with reviews of research that highlight the salient and common features of effective professional development, the national meetings incorporated content focus (literacy/funds of knowledge and research methodology), active learning, coherence and collective participation in whole day sessions spread across a year (Desimone, 2009). With contributions from experts, these facilitated access to research, placed value on teachers' knowledge and expertise, and helped to structure teachers dialogue and encourage to embed ideas in the real world contexts of classrooms (Yoon *et al.*, 2007; Cordingley, 2011). During the LA group sessions, these activities were extended and followed up within the smaller groups and augmented by particular research team support for processes such as designing questions and prompts for Learner Visits and collectively analysing data gathered during those visits. These multiple professional development sessions were in principle not dissimilar to the study groups which Amanti, one of the teacher researchers in Moll's study, discusses as a pedagogical model (González *et al.*, 2005). Locally and nationally and in the data analysis meetings held in schools with one or two teachers and the university-based researcher, the university researchers and LA co-ordinators sought to open spaces for discussion, spaces that built upon the teachers' emerging understandings gained in the home, spaces that encouraged the teachers and all present to voice their tentative thoughts and explore possibilities for pedagogical action together.

Practically, the work was organised across a school year from September to July: in Terms 1 and 2 (September to December and January to April), the teachers worked with the children to explore their literacy lives beyond school and the teachers considered their own literacy histories and shared their home literacy practices with their classes. In Term 2, the teachers also undertook Learner Visits (see below) and sought to analyse their new knowledge and understanding with support from their linked researcher. In Term 3 (April to July), they were challenged to build on this in the context of their classroom practice and home–school relations.

The research design and methodology

The project's professional development activities were intended to support the participating teachers in adopting an ethnographic stance and engaging in exploratory enquiries in children's home and community contexts. None of the teachers was familiar with ethnography as an approach or strategy for gathering research data prior to their involvement in the project. For many, although they had been told about the project's aims and proposed methods, it seemed that the realisation that this was not a home–school literacy intervention came about during the initial national events. It was through discussion at national and local events and through their engagement as researchers that the teachers' conceptions of literacy were widened, supported by their reading and reflection on their own literacy histories and identities. It was in the national events that the teachers were introduced to interpretive research.

The ethnographic stance sought was indicative of the interpretive orientation of the study. Like the studies conducted by Moll and colleagues (González *et al.*, 2005) the project sought to understand how different cultures (on small and large scales) shape people's interpretations and understandings of their worlds and influence their beliefs, attitudes and actions. Where dominant discourses within education pose a particular form or forms of literacy and designate particular standards as 'the norm', different interpretations can become marginalised and constructed as deviant or deficient, rather than being accepted as viable and valid aspects of a much richer literacy tapestry. Hammersley (2012: 22) suggests that an interpretivist would argue, 'that we cannot understand why people do what they do, or why particular institutions exist and operate in characteristic ways, without grasping how those involved interpret and make sense of their world'. For researchers to inhabit this world of others' meaning-making they must be willing to suspend their own cultural assumptions. Consequently, the project's national meetings challenged participating teachers to adopt the interpretivist position, to begin to recognise their own cultural assumptions concerning literacy, learning and the families with whom they came into contact through their work, and to find ways to suspend those beliefs so that they might find ways to look differently at their own and others' literacy identities and practices. Each teacher had chosen children about whom their enquiries would focus and broadly they sought to understand the children's literacy identities, habits and cultures as described and demonstrated within family contexts outside the schools. The project foregrounded literacy learning as social practice, imbued with cultural and historical characteristics, although this perspective was not necessarily shared by the teachers particularly in Term 1.

Moll and colleagues (Moll *et al.*, 1992; González *et al.*, 2005) sought to highlight how difference portrayed both as deviance and as a normalising representation of particular social or cultural groups results in discriminatory practice and in so doing their approach resonates with critical ethnography. Similarly, the *BC: RLL* project sought to unsettle taken-for-granted positions, beliefs and assumptions and to throw a spotlight onto the barriers and disadvantages experienced by children and families for whom a dissonance existed between their home and the school's sociocultural norms and practices or whose literacy habits and accomplishments – their literacy funds of knowledge – were unacknowledged in school contexts. Both acknowledge Carspecken's (1996) view that a critical epistemology is one that sees links between power and thought and between power and claims of what constitutes truth. Since power relations between schools and parents/families have underpinned or emerged from many studies concerned with subjects such as partnerships with parents, home–school relations or policies and parental involvement in education (see for example Desforges and Abouchaar, 2003); the attention to power distribution inherent to a critical perspective was highly relevant to the *BC: RLL* project. Arguably taken for granted assumptions about different children's ability to achieve in literacy and in schooling remain widespread. These conceive of some families, particularly minority ethnic groups and white working class, as lacking; they are not widely credited as having valuable literacy experiences. Such notions are likely to lower teachers' expectations of different groups of learners.

Although the families visited in *BC: RLL* may have become accustomed to particular notions of literacy that they had learned through contact with the school and these may have been re-enacted through the identities and practices they described during the teachers' enquiries (see Chapter 4), the Learner Visits offered scope for different conceptualisations of literacy to emerge if the families decided to share these with the teachers. Therefore, despite the teachers' and the families' shared history of school literacy practices (which were normally discussed at parents' evenings), the ethnographic approach adopted for the Learner Visits sought to allow families' everyday practices to be noticed by the teachers or described by the families. As discussed in Chapter 7, it was found that when teachers opened up and offered something of their own lives and literacy identities, they families reciprocated. The Learner Visits approach differed from that which Moll and colleagues had used in their study because those teachers had been accompanied and supported by anthropologists when they visited the local Hispanic communities. In the *BC: RLL* project, the teachers mostly made their Learner Visits alone, although the research team offered support while they prepared for these visits and they met the teachers to help them reflect on and analyse their data after the visits had taken place; these were initially referred to as 'debrief' meetings and later came to be known as the 'data analysis' meetings, though such analysis also occurred in local and national group meetings and independently by the teachers.

The research team sought to explore whether and in what ways the teachers, positioned as researchers, developed new understandings about the children's everyday literacy lives and the extent to which any new understandings had consequences with regard to the curriculum and/or home–school relations. Consequently, a multi-layered study was designed, which was intended to capture data at individual, school and local authority levels and to compare the findings across the whole sample. In contrast with much school-based research, with which some of the teachers were familiar, the project required an approach that was less structured, with learning being reflective, cumulative and largely unpredictable. A qualitative ethnographic approach (Denzin, 1997; Denzin and Lincoln, 2000) as the basis for data collection and analysis was therefore well-suited to the work; it should be acknowledged, however, that the timeframe of the project created challenges in terms of using an ethnographic approach to open up possibilities for attitudinal change. It was important that the project set about providing a conceptual framework for the research within which the teachers could explore different conceptions and constructs of literacy and literacy identities beyond school as well as literacy as social practice. This fundamental detail provided the basis from which the teachers could explore children's literacy identities and habits at home and the team believed it was more likely to have a lasting impact than explorations which had not started with the sociocultural theorising of literacy. Even though the Learner Visits were reasonably brief and intermittent, akin to Jeffrey and Troman's (2004) description of 'selective intermittent' ethnography, the teachers' opportunities to explore different constructions of literacy and their researcher roles were intended to empower them: armed with their new knowledge and insights they might recognise and resist, if they so chose, the dominant discourses and 'what works' agenda surrounding school-based literacy (Kincheloe, 2003). The teachers' ethnographic stance was accompanied by encouragement from the research team to be open, avoid critical judgements and to engage in reflexivity. This stance was pivotal in enabling the teachers' development of dispositional shifts (see Chapter 4), challenging them as it did to depart from the more traditional types of practitioner research and safe boundaries of their classrooms (Somekh, 2006).

Central to the project's design were the teachers' Learner Visits to homes or other contexts outside school. In England, home visits are not common beyond the Reception year. During the Learner Visits, the teachers were re-positioned, not as holders of knowledge about the child's literacy, but as learners and researchers with an 'ethnographic eye' (González et al., 2005). They sought to find out, to listen, to remain open, to observe from an emic perspective (Schieffelin and Cochran Smith, 1984) and to learn without judging. For practical reasons, although they all happened within the second and/or third terms of the school year in which the project took place, the frequency and timing of the Learner Visits was flexible. This made allowances for the teachers' busy professional and home lives and enabled them to respond to the families' preferences for scheduling the visits. This pragmatic approach with research enquiries occurring at intervals includes a key criterion, which Jeffrey and Troman (2004) describe as 'depth of study, entailing progressive focusing' for which 'time in the field is determined by decisions as to whether the analytical categories have been saturated' (540). Within the BC: RLL project, the teachers were encouraged to engage in progressive focusing as far as was possible within the scope permitted by their involvement in a time-limited project. They did so by making return visits to the families' homes and to alternative families, by talking further with family members when they came to the school and/or through the deeply iterative process of data analysis and interpretation in which they engaged.

Data sources and methods

The methods employed included:

- A series of semi-structured interviews (three each with teachers, headteachers, LA co-ordinators and agency partners, carried out by the linked researcher) which were transcribed from audio recordings.
- Learner Visit conversations (usually two or three per family), all transcribed from audio recordings, field notes made by the teachers, pre- and post-visit reflective writing by the teachers.
- Learner Visit 'debrief'/analysis meetings, with the linked researcher (one per teacher or pair of teachers following visits). During these the teachers selected episodes from the Learner Visit transcripts to analyse and interpret with the support of the university-based researchers; a selection of these meetings were transcribed from audio recordings.
- Teachers' Professional Learning Journey Portfolios. These included a wide range of documentation, some focused on the case study children e.g. observations, notes from conversations, children's written work or literacy and some focused on the teacher, e.g. reflective journals, literacy histories, related teaching plans and materials.
- National Day proformas and other written evidence, such as teachers' expectations prior to undertaking Learner Visits and summaries of their insights from Learner Visits.
- Teachers' PowerPoint presentations and researchers' notes made during the teachers' presentations at the final National Day.
- Researchers' field notes made during National Day meetings.

In addition, the LA co-ordinators' ongoing progress reports (five) and reflective journals as well as email correspondence and notes made at local meetings were a source of research evidence, with the LA co-ordinators' consent. Thus the project was multi-layered in terms of research activity with evidence being gathered by the teachers and the research team. This layering and ongoing reflective approach meant that the team could explore their own, the teachers' and the LA co-ordinators' developing roles as ethnographic researchers within a discursive frame.

Data analysis

Analysis of the research evidence was cumulative; each university-based researcher worked independently using the iterative process of categorical analysis (Coffey and Atkinson, 1996) to draw out patterns and themes from their assigned local authority/schools context across the year. Each focused on one LA co-ordinator, two headteachers, and four teachers and drew across this dataset to identify questions and themes. These were discussed and debated by the wider team with constant feedback from the data informing the ongoing analysis. Additionally, in order to afford 'thick descriptions' which Geertz, describes as 'our own constructions of other people's constructions of what they and their compatriots are up to' (1973: 9), one teacher from each school was studied in more depth. For these teachers, the debrief meetings were also transcribed and their portfolios and other written evidence were subject to closer scrutiny. To support the trust-worthiness of the findings, the themes and case accounts were cross-checked by an independent researcher and adjustments and new categories created and debated where appropriate.

The teachers' Learner Visits were pivotal in the project's data collection activities. Examples from these visits are described throughout subsequent chapters of this book. The call to teachers to employ an interpretive, ethnographic approach to their explorations of children's literacy lives asked them to reposition themselves as learners, to strip away and make transparent their own assumptions about families and to look through a different lens. Erickson (1984: 121) described the process of interpretive research as 'to make the familiar strange and interesting again'. While Hammersley and Atkinson (1995) assert that, 'We see the term [ethnography] as referring primarily to a particular method or set of methods'; they also describe the role of reflexivity (and values) of the researcher in the process of exploring and creating knowledge. As such, they position themselves and other ethnographic researchers as actors in a world in which knowledge is constructed and reconstructed. The critical ethnographer plays a role in deconstructing taken-for-granted beliefs and practices that may serve to dominate. This positioning was described to the teachers and discussed by them as an ethnographic stance.

The methods adopted for the Learner Visits leant upon the ethnographic tradition. Firstly, the teachers sought to understand children's literacy funds of knowledge in unfamiliar territory – the children's homes or community contexts, which in some cases included journeys from school to home. Secondly, they generally approached their visits with unstructured or semi-structured guides for what they intended to ask or to do, although all had an overarching question concerning the children's and families' literacy identities, habits and practices. Thirdly, all the teachers were aware of the need to explore their own cultural assumptions and did so in collaboration with the researchers and other participants through structured dialogue in national meetings and LA group sessions before and after their Learner Visits. Fourthly, the teachers documented their visits as richly as they could. Most used the digital voice recorders which they had been loaned; some also took photographs and all wrote copious field notes about what they did, what the families did, what they discussed and noticed and how they felt before, during and after the visits.

In addition to being linked researchers supporting specific small groups in their LA group sessions, each university researcher was also assigned to a group for the purposes of core research enquiries and documenting and advising on the teachers' data collection and initial analysis. Thus they not only worked to support the teachers emerging analyses and insights, but were also arguably co-analysts. Positioned as outsiders, in the data analysis meetings held in schools after the Learner Visits, they asked questions of the teacher-researchers to prompt reflection upon the data, raising issues such as the noises in the background and the additional voices on the tape as they sought to understand more of the context. In this way they worked to help the teachers question their own descriptions and explanations and examine the theoretical assumptions which underpinned them. Although the teachers were supported in analysing the data, the arms-length approach to data collection by inexperienced teacher-researchers represented a risk to the project. Many of the teachers were anxious about the visits and analytical processes and needed regular reassurance and support. This was provided in the form of discussions at national meetings and LA group sessions as well as ongoing contact by email or telephone. This guided participation in the ethnographic enquiries proved fruitful but the robustness of the analysis across all the teachers' data could not be guaranteed despite the team's best efforts to help the participants in this process. The university-based researchers were involved, for example, in working alongside the teachers, offering and discussing relevant readings, providing a framework for beginning to analyse their field notes, observations and transcripts from Learner Visits and revisiting the data repeatedly during various group sessions. The analysis of the Learner Visit conversations was iterative and thematic but was based in part on an 'interview as research instrument' rather than 'interview as social practice' perspective which, Talmy (2011) argues, may fail to acknowledge the co-constructed ebb and flow that occurs between interviewer and interviewee. However, the team, listening to the transcripts alongside the teachers, did highlight the socially situated nature of the Learner Visits discussions and sought to help the teachers in recognising how their status (as teachers and researchers), and their questions, prompts and responses to the families generated a particular conversation.

Ethics

Throughout the project and particularly during discussions at national meetings, the research team was eager to highlight research ethics, but also to move beyond a procedural approach. So, while samples of consent and information letters were provided for the teachers and the project as a whole was subject to scrutiny by the Open University's Ethics Committee, discussions also centred on ethicality (Solvasson, 2013). That is, thinking and behaving in an ethically responsible manner and conducting research in which an ethic of respect and associated responsibilities permeated throughout. This involved respect for all the people involved in the research as well as for knowledge, democratic values, the quality of the research and academic freedom (BERA, 2011). This principled approach was adopted to help steer the research procedures. Issues of confidentiality and anonymity were discussed in detail at the national meetings attended by all the teachers and where particular concerns were raised, these were examined collaboratively in detail during these sessions, local group sessions and in email correspondence with the research team. A similarly collaborative approach was adopted for the development of the information for children and their families and consent letters for parents/carers. The core information was created through discussions at the national meetings. All the teachers then modified their own letters to make sure that these would be appropriate in style/language for the families they wished to involve. In some cases, the teachers chose to talk through the information and letters with the families in person rather than send the letters home via the children or by post. This method helped to ensure that the information would be appropriate in content and tone and the activity itself provided an opportunity for the teachers to identify and reflect on the ethical issues involved in their role as teacher-researchers.

The research team gained permission from all those involved in the project for the data to be included in a range of dissemination activities, such as publications and conference papers. Underpinning this request was an assurance that the outputs from the project should ultimately serve a beneficial purpose. That is, to share the experiences and findings from the project as widely as possible while protecting the anonymity of participants and matters of confidentiality, where appropriate. While the LAs involved were comfortable being named, all the schools, teachers and agency colleagues involved have been given pseudonyms, as have all parents and children.

An additional aspect of the ethical approach within the project was the caution employed when working with a wide range of theoretical perspectives and professional experiences. All contributions were of value even where discussion and debate might challenge opinions and care was taken to ensure that all the members of the project felt that they were working within safe parameters with supportive colleagues despite taking what sometimes felt like risks, particularly in rejecting dominant discourses and adopting novel Learner Visits.

At the end of the project, the research team was also concerned that the teachers, LA co-ordinators and external partners should not feel that their involvement had reached an abrupt end and so all were encouraged to join the UK Literacy Association, which had supported the project. In this way, it was hoped that the participants would continue to access networks of similarly research-active and research-informed colleagues across the UK. Each headteacher and LA co-ordinator was also helped to develop a strategy for embedding learning from the project within their schools and LA teams and all the participants had access to printed and electronic copies of the project report, as well as the Executive Summary (Cremin et al., 2011), which had been written by the research team. Since the research team never learnt the real identities of the families involved in the study (they were known only by their pseudonyms) reports were not sent directly to them, but the teachers and headteachers were encouraged to share the project's findings with the families. In addition, in several LAs, the local team of teachers shared their insights at LA events and led professional development work in their own and other LA schools.

The organisational challenges

This project presented many organisational challenges for the research team. In addition to working with numerous participants from different schools, agencies and local authorities (as well as the team members being from different institutions), the practicalities of organising simultaneous and integrated research and professional development were complex. The content of national meetings was partially pre-planned but also required flexibility to allow for responsiveness to the teachers' developing questions and concerns over the course of the year.

The Learner Visits were orchestrated centrally by the research team but carried out in practice by individual teachers operating independently. This approach required constant alertness and sensitivity on the part of the research team to ensure that the teachers felt confident and competent to carry out their Learner Visits and had addressed all the necessary procedural matters relating to research ethics (such as informed consent and the teachers' own safety). The linked researchers' visits to LA group sessions and regular email contact with the LA co-ordinators and teachers in between sessions were helpful in this respect.

The multi-layered nature of the data sources and multiple data collection methods required careful organisation. Each national meeting provided an opportunity to gather responses to specific questions from the participants and for recording discussion groups systematically. The teachers were provided with guidance on recording their thoughts pre-and post-Learner Visits and these thoughts and other commentaries, field notes about their observations, photographic evidence and diary-style entries were gathered in project portfolios, which were leant to the research team for analysis at the end of the project. This made the collection and analysis of diverse data sets more accessible and manageable. The series of interviews with teachers, headteachers, LA co-ordinators and agency partners was also pre-planned and despite being semi-structured, key areas for discussion meant that the interviews covered similar issues and topics without preventing participants from discussing matters that were of particular interest or concern to them. Recording and transcribing all the interviews and most of the Learner Visits (where families gave permission) allowed the research team to gain a first-hand insight into the teachers' experiences of visiting the families' homes, as well as hearing about them from the teachers' written reflections and verbal reports during the debriefing sessions. This also helped to minimise potential tensions from the dilemma of wishing to give the teachers a relatively free rein in conducting their Learner Visits. They were asked, for example, to record particular memories retrospectively (immediately after the Learner Visit), such as how they had felt just before and during the visit, how they perceived the families had responded to their presence, what they had noticed and whether there was anything they felt they might have forgotten to do or say. In addition, several teachers also kept their own project journals which again were leant to the team.

The philosophical challenges

The study *BC: RLL* sought to accommodate professional development, research and curriculum change within one project design. This composite aim led to some philosophical dilemmas. At the heart of the project was an ethnographic approach to exploring the literacy lives of children beyond the realms of school and this interpretive perspective is inherently indeterminate (Hammersley and Atkinson, 1995). The lack of delineated outcomes that might arise as a consequence of their research was troubling for most of the participating teachers and LA co-ordinators who had become accustomed in their professional lives to itemising the expected outcomes of particular efforts (their own and children's). It was simultaneously risky for the research team since the project rested on an assumption by these participants that their involvement would be rewarded by something advantageous happening – being a 'better' teacher, getting 'improved' results from the children they taught, developing 'stronger' relationships or 'increasing' parents' participation in their children's learning. Coupled with the uncertainty that was demanded by the adoption of an ethnographic stance and mode of enquiry, was the necessity to structure a plan for the project as a whole and for the integral professional development sessions. The participants were advised that they would be involved in a project in which they would undertake independent research in Terms 1 and 2, which would be followed by changes to their classroom practice/curriculum design in Term 3 based on their learning during the first two terms. This consequentialism was troubling for the research team members and was regularly debated during team meetings: how could curriculum change be planned when it was not known what the teachers might learn and how they might interpret their learning? (How) could potential attitudinal or dispositional change be translated into alterations to practice? Would this compromise the principles of ethnographic enquiry at the heart of the project? The content of the national meetings was only partly pre-planned and flexibility was essential. This space enabled responsiveness to the evolution of the project, particularly to the teachers' questions, concerns and emerging insights and a compromise was found.

Some of the teachers were clear about the changes they wished to make to their practice as a consequence of the findings from their enquiries; others were more hesitant or unsure. The opportunities for collaboration and dialogue with the other teachers during the national meetings and LA group sessions helped some to recognise how their learning might be developed into plans for change in their own classrooms. Though the project team and the LA co-ordinators as well as some teachers were concerned that this should not reduce the project to a focus on technical teaching issues which Kemmis (2006) warns against. The emphasis within the *BC: RLL* project on shifting perspectives rather than change in technical (or indeed, technicist) terms was finally agreed among the team to be sufficient justification for the design, which was ultimately reminiscent of a communities of practice paradigm; that is,

> Consistent with pragmatist philosophy but accommodates variations and inconsistencies that prevail within mixed research by promoting a diversity of researchers, allowing paradigms to operate at different levels, incorporating group influences on methodological decisions, shifting debates about paradigms to level [sic] of practice and research culture and allowing methods to be chosen on their practical value for addressing a research problem.
>
> *(Denscombe, 2008 in Onwuegbuzie et al., 2009: 134)*

Conclusion

Despite the philosophical and organisational challenges involved, the multi-layered nature of the data collection and analysis within the interpretive paradigm selected for the *BC: RLL* project, sought to gather and re-present the voices of the teachers whose perspectives examined and challenged dominant discourses of literacy and in some cases deficit discourses in relation to children and families. The professional development meetings provided a crucial space for the participants to seek the company of colleagues experiencing similar dilemmas and anxieties and equal excitement at the opportunity for collaboratively exploring their own and the children's identities and practices concerned with twenty-first-century literacy as social practice. The 18 teachers played an active role in all aspects of the project and were centrally positioned and supported as ethnographically styled researchers. The ethnographic stance adopted by the teachers represented an important means by which to encourage dispositional and attitudinal change as well as offering the possibility for teachers to step outside their comfort zones physically and intellectually. Though this was not without difficulties – these are explored in more detail in Chapter 4.

The project did not seek to measure the teachers' learning or to document changes or improvements in children's attitudes and achievements in school-based literacy. As such, it cannot claim to contribute to the literature that seeks to quantify the effects of teachers' professional development, particularly that involving teachers in research activities. But subsequent chapters of this book highlight many of the aspects of the processes involved in becoming a researcher and the *BC: RLL* project teachers' learning about research, literacy, children's lives beyond the school and themselves as teachers and as learners.

4

EXPLORING RESEARCHER DISPOSITIONS

Sacha Powell and Teresa Cremin

As the teachers on the project *BC: RLL* were invited to take on an ethnographic research stance, this necessarily generated tensions and challenges as the work evolved. However, these also opened up possibilities for new ways of thinking. In ordinary circumstances the teacher role is characterised by planning ahead, knowing what aspects of the curriculum are to be taught and having a sense of what the pupils should learn. The ethnographic researcher role is deliberately much less confident of its outcomes; it is characterised by observation, gathering and sifting information and generating ideas about what is under scrutiny as the research progresses. Shifting from one discourse to another is likely to be (even temporarily) destabilising, leaving the individual somewhat unsure of what is expected. As a consequence, the teachers raised many concerns and voiced their anxieties, but as Kemmis (2006) observes, such insecurities can indicate 'gaps to be explored' in the research process and 'openings for new conversations' (463).

This chapter seeks to highlight the challenging and sometimes uncomfortable process experienced by project teachers as they moved from the relative safety of their habitual teaching practices and contexts into unfamiliar terrain as novice researchers working independently beyond the school gates. The chapter also considers the benefits that the teachers reported as a consequence of their involvement and ultimately how they believed that these far outweighed the difficulties they had faced. Mirroring the work of González *et al.* (2005), who offer a framework for teacher involvement, the UK study also recognised the critical role of relationships among the university-based researchers, the LA co-ordinators and the teacher researchers and these are also considered. Connecting to Bourdieu (1977), the development of new actions, new perceptions and new appreciations on the part of the 18 teacher-researchers are examined. A case study is also offered to illuminate one teacher's experience of developing a researcher's disposition.

The start of the journey

While some of the teachers had taken part in action research focused on classroom practice in an effort to raise standards prior to this work, they were in the minority; none had undertaken ethnographically styled research. To work as researchers in the tradition of ethnography the teachers were asked to accommodate to a mind shift about the different positions taken by research (in particular ethnography) and practice and to reconsider their values and behaviours in relation to families. In so doing, they were encouraged to scrutinise the situated nature of their own professional identity, their role within the educational establishment, their expectations of children in the classroom and assumptions about the children's home lives. This meant, in Homan's (2001) words, 'trying to see others as they are, rather than imposing one's own ideas and biases on them' (37). By problematising the value judgements inherent in their comparisons of the perceived richness or deficiency of learning environments and interactions, they experienced discomfort as unconscious bias and prejudice were exposed. Furthermore, the teachers were challenged to translate new knowledge and understanding, new sensitivities and perspectives into classroom behaviours without compromising the integrity of their research endeavours or implanting tokenistic activities. The fundamental change in terms of practice was to work as a researcher, gathering and analysing original data and to acquire a 'researcher disposition'. This meant relinquishing the power and positionality of school–home relationships where the teachers tend to dictate the terms of engagement.

Most of the project teachers' experiences of interactions with parents had been those taking place on school territory during formal events such as parent consultations about children's educational progress or consisted of brief conversations at the school gate. Very few project teachers were experienced in making home visits of any kind during their teaching careers. The two exceptions were within the minority who had worked with very young children (in Foundation Stage classes) where home visits are more common – but not universal – as part of a child's induction to statutory schooling in England. As Munn (1993) acknowledges, opinions vary regarding the value of teachers' visits to parents' homes; some see this atypical practice as valuable, offering increased understanding of the home environment, while others view it as an invasion into parents' personal life. One other teacher had undertaken home visiting as part of a previous job. For virtually all the project teachers, the prospect of visiting a child's home was entirely novel and several acknowledged their fear, with one admitting to feeling 'physically sick' at the thought of the first Learner Visit. The teachers' knowledge about families' everyday lives, life histories, resources or funds of knowledge was, by their own admission, extremely limited at the start of the project (see Chapters 5 and 8). Yet the importance of parental 'involvement' or 'partnership' has long prevailed in educational policy and practice, and as discussed in Chapter 2 the traffic between home and school is traditionally conceived (Feiler *et al.*, 2006; Harris and Goodall, 2007); schools tend to explicate what parents are expected to do to support school literacy, and rarely recognise their contribution to wider literacy and learning (Cairney, 2003). The teachers' minimal knowledge and paucity of experience of visiting homes perhaps reflected adoption of a professional distance between teacher and student (and family) so that they might be 'at all times observing proper boundaries appropriate to a teacher's professional position' (DfE, 2013:14). Their involvement in the project national meetings provided teachers with an opportunity to consider where those boundaries might lie, why and with what effects and implications. The requirement to visit family homes extended the physical boundaries beyond the school gates and legitimised for many teachers, mostly for the first time, the possibility of entering a pupil's home environment.

The intention of the teachers' visits was to develop a richer, more nuanced understanding of children's out-of-school literacy practices, but they were also seeking to build relationships, and entered the homes as learners for the purposes of research. To distinguish between home visiting and these research visits, the project team coined the term 'Learner Visits' to highlight that the teachers were entering as 'investigators'. Arguably, this involved a not inconsiderable positional shift; repositioned as researchers, rather than 'all-knowing educators', the teachers engaged in an ethnographically styled inquiry, and sought to be open to new learning, and willing to consider and challenge existing perspectives, positions and the often school-framed partnership agenda (see Chapter 9).

Conceptualising researcher dispositions

The aim to support teachers as researchers drew on the ethnographic work of Moll and colleagues (Moll *et al.*, 1992; González *et al.*, 2005), who posited that learning and development can be enhanced if teachers, positioned as researchers, investigate children's funds of knowledge to make learning more socially and culturally meaningful. The call to teachers to engage as researchers and, in so doing, to adopt a different role and – more importantly – a different perspective was underpinned by an assumption that there exist both a teacher disposition and a researcher disposition and that the two are not necessarily similar or the same. Furthermore, these dispositions are not necessarily fixed, but can also be viewed as evolving or fluctuating (Diez, 2007). In the *BC:RLL* project there was an assumption that teachers could develop a researcher disposition through interaction in a 'social environment that supports and challenges their growth' so that the 'organizing principles, reasons and affect people use in interpreting their experiences [become] more complex, integrated, and principled over time' (Oja and Reiman, 2007: 93 in Diez 2007: 390). Bourdieu (1977) understood disposition to be the 'matrix of perceptions, appreciations and actions' that influence practice (83). His concept of 'habitus' (a system of dispositions) highlights the power invested in patterns of lived experience, handed down over generations:

> Habitus is neither a result of free will, nor determined by structures, but created by a kind of interplay between the two over time: dispositions that are

> both shaped by past events and structures, and that shape current practices and structures and also, importantly, that condition our very perceptions of these.
>
> *(Bourdieu, 1977: 170)*

Thus teacher disposition, shaped by cultural expectations of the role, carries with it a predisposition or tendency to hold certain perceptions about the power relationship between school and home. Critics of the usefulness of the concept of disposition (Nash, 1990; Jenkins, 1992) argue that at times it seems to imply conscious action and at other times, unconscious action. However, this fluidity seems to be part of Bourdieu's use of the construct as a 'thinking tool' (and is perhaps also a feature of the protean nature of translation from one language to another). His view of social practices as a set of 'regulated improvisations' (Bourdieu, 1977: 78) is a useful way to conceive of the teacher/researcher dispositions experienced in the project, capable of shifting in relation to specific contexts and over time (Navarro, 2006). For the teacher researchers involved in *BC: RLL*, it was sometimes difficult to shed the expected social practices and dispositions of the teacher and adopt the somewhat different stance and perceptions of a researcher disposition. The interplay between the two meant that there was continuing overlapping, merging and separation of perceptions and positioning as they became co-partners in the research and took on the disposition of researchers.

Becoming co-partners in research

Teacher research foregrounds connections between reflection, inquiry and action; it has been linked to the work of several scholars, most notably Dewey (1933/1985), Freire (1972), Stenhouse (1975), Schön (1987) and Berthoff (1987). Widely recognised as a potentially rich form of professional learning (Lankshear and Knobel, 2006), it has been defined as 'systematic and intentional inquiry carried out by teachers' (Cochran-Smith and Lytle, 1993: 7) and is seen to include both empirical and conceptual work in the form, for example, of action research in the classroom, scholarly study, autobiographical accounts and inquiries to gather staff perspectives. Cochran-Smith and Lytle (2009), who interpret teacher research as 'emic' – grounded within teachers' insider experiences and intellectual frameworks, argue that it can generate both local knowledge and knowledge that is useful in wider public and policy contexts. While the goals and purposes of such research have been extensively debated, several scholars perceive it is primarily concerned with enhancing teachers' sense of their professional roles and identities (including awareness of the historical dimension), or contributing to their understanding of teaching and learning in the classroom (Hopkins, 1983; Fishman and McCarthy, 2000). Additionally, there is a long-standing association between practitioner research, emancipatory education and social justice (Carr and Kemmis, 1986; Elliott, 2005). Nonetheless, there are relatively few published accounts of teachers leaving the security of their own classrooms and undertaking data collection with a literacy focus beyond the boundaries of school.

Many of the studies which have encouraged teachers to consider children's homes and communities as fruitful contexts for literacy research have been collaborative school–university partnerships based upon Moll et al.'s (1992) work. In one of the original studies, teachers, positioned as participant observers undertook visits to children's homes accompanied by university anthropologists; the teachers were able to rely upon the observational and analytic expertise of these experienced ethnographic researchers (González et al., 2005) Two subsequent funds of knowledge studies in Australia also positioned teachers as co-participants and invited them to engage in data collection in children's homes (Comber and Kamler, 2005; Hill, 2010). In the former, in order to shift the educational outcomes for children from marginalised and low socio-economic groups, some of the ten cross-generational pairs of teachers visited the home of an 'at risk' learner, most of these were to the homes of the youngest children (Comber and Kamler, 2005; Kamler and Comber, 2008). In the latter, 25 teachers accompanied by university researchers, made home visits to document 4–8-year-olds' funds of knowledge, which in this research were the information and communication technologies used in homes and familiar to the children, later the practitioners reshaped the early years curriculum in response (Hill, 2010).

Becoming disposed to ethnography

The teachers and the LA co-ordinators were largely unfamiliar with the term 'ethnography' and its methods and principles. The research team were conscious of the need to introduce ethnographic approaches and methods in ways that would challenge the teachers but would not alienate them. The national meetings and local authority group sessions throughout the year provided opportunities to explain some fundamental principles, purposes and approaches and to give examples from previous ethnographic studies (see Chapter 3). Two members of the team had employed ethnography for their doctoral studies and offered first-hand examples of what this involved, why they had selected it and some of the findings that had emerged. The teachers were also given papers to read that might help them to gain an insight into ethnography as a principle and as research practice, including for example Mottram and Hall (2009), Marsh (2003) and chapters from González et al. (2005). For some, these readings, when accompanied by extended discussion, afforded what one teacher described as a 'light bulb moment', another commented it 'rang a bell, a big bell, in my head'. An LA co-ordinator described how the readings demanded emotional as well as intellectual engagement and that they 'came alive' when returning to them after supporting the teachers in dialogue around the visits. In keeping with the funds of knowledge approach and in a deliberate move away from the more traditional action research models for teacher engagement in enquiry, the project foregrounded the importance of positioning the teachers as learners.

Ethnography is a process perhaps best learnt by engagement and as González et al. (2005) note, it 'is difficult to reduce ... to formulaic terms because anything called ethnography is always in jeopardy of reductionist misuse' (9). Nevertheless, their threefold recommendation was adopted to provide the support and challenge that might enable teachers to begin to develop researcher (ethnographer) dispositions. These were: reading ethnographic literature; using role-play and discussion (supplemented by facilitated reflection) to help teachers evolve non-judgemental approaches to their fieldwork and analysis; and providing opportunities to think about, practise and reflect on observation and attention to details in the field. In addition, a sense of 'radical looking' (Clough and Nutbrown, 2012) was explicitly encouraged, with the emphasis on 'looking *for* as well as looking *at* ... seeking *meanings* as well as *evidence*' (53) and 'radical listening as opposed to merely hearing' (67) (original emphasis). This combination of activities over time in the local and national professional development sessions and data analysis meetings afforded open spaces where all involved could voice their views without fear of judgement, where challenge and debate were the norm and where collegiality was evidenced. These were some of the hallmarks noted by the external evaluator of the 'accessible and supportive community' which was built (Durrant, 2011: 6).

Unlike Moll and colleagues, the *BC: RLL* project team did not avoid the use of the term household 'culture' and replace it with household 'practices'. Instead, the teachers were encouraged to consider the possibility of many and varied forms and conceptualisations of culture(s), including what Holliday (1999) described as 'small cultures'. Within this paradigm, wherever there is cohesive behaviour, social groupings may be identified and these groupings may be sites for ethnographic research enquiries. This was a particularly helpful concept for the teachers who worked in schools where there was very little ethnic or noticeable linguistic diversity, as represented by 'large culture' paradigms in Holliday's (1999) terms, and who initially perceived that their enquiries would be 'bland', 'boring' or 'predictable' compared with their peers making Learner Visits in 'multicultural' areas. Coupled with the idea of radical looking and listening, the teachers were encouraged to explore beneath the obvious, delving 'to the roots of a situation: this is exploration which makes the familiar strange' (Clough and Nutbrown, 2004: 44). It was an early step in encouraging the teachers to expose their preconceptions and assumptions through progressive 'distancing and focusing' (Brenden, 2005: 207), enabled through reading, reflection and discussion.

Challenges and tensions

There were three main areas where the teachers' confidence faltered, each of which the project challenged: entering unfamiliar territory; coping with the openness and knowing what to look for and developing different kinds of relationships with parents (including sharing of themselves).

The difficulties of the combination of these concerns should not be underestimated. Teachers shared their unease with making themselves vulnerable and sharing of themselves with families outside their own domain of the classroom. When entering families' environments, teachers were out of their locus of control and knowledge, but still realised that they had responsibility for saying and doing the 'right things' while on unfamiliar ground. Some described journeys to children's homes in detail, charting their keenly felt emotions and concerns as they went and openly sharing these with each other and the linked researcher in data analysis meetings back at school. Relationships with families were sometimes difficult initially, making teachers feel awkward and intrusive; a few parents manoeuvred situations so that both of them could attend, or sought the support of a translator who would be a trusted ally. In a few cases, parents' organised the whole family to be present, time off work was organised and substantial family gatherings were instituted for the visit of their child's teacher. This was additionally demanding for the teacher-researchers, who regardless of the numbers of family members they expected to meet were generally nervous, as one typically noted: 'I was worried about what the parents would think of me ... in the beginning it was scary.' Nonetheless the parents were usually warm and respectful once trust had been won on both sides and were willing to reflect upon their family history, and share stories and confidences. One teacher was 'fit to burst' as sisters performed Indian dance for her and invited her to stay for a meal; another noted 'even after five minutes I felt at home, they were SO generous and delighted I'd come'. Teachers who felt they had achieved 'acceptance' learnt that this could be triggered by revealing something about themselves. Professional distance and maintenance of school–home power hierarchies did not work in this context; once trust was built it led, as later chapters will reveal, to parents approaching schools more willingly and seeking the teachers out.

Linked to this was the teachers' lack of confidence as researchers in terms of knowing what to record from the visits and interviews, not having time to listen and make notes at the same time, and worrying about what to do with all the rich information collected which was narrative and observational in nature; in particular, they worried that it might not seem to have obvious structure or validity in a scientific sense. The teachers took their responsibilities as researchers seriously and were supported by the linked university-based researchers, but the openness created insecurities and the visits often triggered emotions for which they felt unprepared. In the data analysis meetings, they tended to be enthusiastic in discussion but lacked confidence in writing, and in committing to paper their insights, many voiced concerns about 'getting it right'. One LA co-ordinator for example, described a teacher's concern that: 'the notes she was making weren't the correct ones . . . or that she was getting enough information', though others, perhaps more confident wrote copious notes, 'thinking out-loud really – stream of consciousness stuff' as one called it. Initially, however, recording the data in unstructured narrative was unsettling for many, especially set within a professional climate that valued quantitative analysis, tracking and progression towards clear outcomes externally specified. As one teacher put it:

> I think our questions were our security that we needed to go with; they formed the basis for why we were going and if we did run out of conversation we knew we had got those questions and actually those questions were a starter to conversation weren't they? (Interview)

However, writing down a series of questions to ask parents was sometimes found to limit the potential of the visits. By the second visit, the teachers seemed to settle into a more observational approach and some noted that they found it liberating to be asked to look, listen and learn as opposed to instruct, judge and be judged. They seemed to carry this back into their schools, offering observations about changes in children's attitude, behaviour and body language after a home visit, where previously they recognised they would have made judgemental statements that might have been based on assumptions and labels. They realised that the research, in particular the visiting, was revealing their own prejudices and stereo-typical views and questioning their well-established ways of working, sometimes leaving them raw and vulnerable with hosts of questions left to answer.

Additionally, many teachers felt vulnerable at the thought of sharing their own literacy lives with children and parents and some were not sure of the value of this, feeling that it strayed too far from their previously understood professional stance (see Chapter 7). In the Learner Visits personal and professional boundaries blurred which was uncomfortable for some, and felt strange on return to school. Critical reflexivity on the part of both the teachers and the research team members helped maintain an awareness of the frequently overlapping boundaries of the teacher/researcher roles and identities. However, teachers were carried through this challenging process by interest, enthusiasm and hard work in wishing to make these explorations and learn from them. Many were genuinely surprised by what they encountered, the experiences with families were overwhelmingly positive and they were learning much about themselves as well as their students, including through work in the classroom and detailed study of the selected children.

The core team recognised the tensions for teachers in positioning themselves between the urgent high profile 'what works' agenda and the new, patient more ethnographic research in which they became engrossed. Interpretive (including ethnographic) research relies heavily on reflexivity to hold a mirror to one's values, judgements, assumptions and biases and the influence of one's role, status, habits and preferences on the research processes and environment. Although the research team did not stipulate to the teachers a model to constitute the key ingredients of a 'researcher disposition', it was made clear in the national meetings that the project would involve *new actions* (making and reflecting on Learner Visits); *new perceptions* (seeking to understand assumptions, judgements and bias); and *new appreciations* (valuing funds of knowledge) that might influence ways of working – their practice – in their classrooms.

New actions

Many of the teachers were preoccupied with the act of making a Learner Visit, meeting families outside of school. They worried about what this would be like and what they would do and say when they got there. This seemed to apply equally to the few teachers who had prior experience of venturing into family homes and those who had not. Despite knowing the families on a fairly superficial level, the anxiety surrounding the initial visits concerned forming deeper relationships, sharing something of themselves (in relation to their literacy lives), 'doing' research (and 'doing it right') and meeting parents outside the familiar environment of the school. One teacher had previously been involved in interviewing parents as part of work for a research company; this teacher was the exception to the rule as she had experience of such research before, but again, positioned as a teacher and a researcher she found the dual role created challenges:

> *The daunting bit is that when I've done it* [interviewed families] *before, I've never known anything about the family . . . whereas now you're a bit closer to home with it all so it might be different . . . and you can't walk away because you're there* [a teacher in school] *all the time with the children.* (Interview)

After the second national meeting which focused upon supporting a researcher stance, there was evidence that some of the teachers were gaining confidence, for example Carol commented in a local meeting: 'Now we have a much better understanding of the project and the expectations of a researcher' suggesting she was becoming more in tune with the aims of the project. Her confidence was also boosted as she told other teachers about her thoughts and these 'were received in a very positive way'.

As time went by and the teachers reflected on their initial visits, some regretted that they had relied initially on structured interview questions (which they devised independently), but recognised that at the time these had been a source of comfort and support for an otherwise daunting prospect:

> *Both interviews flowed but I did feel that it was a little bit too much interview based and I'd have preferred it to be more observational with me taking a back seat and although I tried not to give leading questions it was me leading the discussion most of the time.* (Interview)

Some of the teachers expressed concerns about the research processes and the validity of their methods and their evidence:

> *I wish I could have gone without that prearranged time to get more of a feel of their everyday environment . . . I felt very much with both of the children we had this interview process going on, I didn't feel it was very natural in terms of I'd like to just come and meet you.* (Analysis meeting)

One teacher's reflection on her visit revealed her observations of the dynamics of the encounter, her concerns and her thoughts about how she might do things differently. Another teacher's experience showed a different dynamic she had noticed during the visit, in which she had felt that the encounter was controlled by the child's mother:

> *Jennie's Mum said, 'Are you alright to sit at the table?', which I was but I felt she had controlled it all, it was so very controlled again . . . Jessica sat beautifully and let*

> *mum do the talking quite a lot of the time . . . because I think possibly I had aimed*
> *all my questions at her.* (Analysis meeting)

Yet another noted the difficulty of perceived 'intrusion':

> *I just felt – Well is this fair? I know they'd agreed but did they really want me asking*
> *questions? I wouldn't like it if it were my daughter's teacher – I'd refuse.* (Interview)

As Watts (2006: 385) cautions: 'the line between empathy and exploitation is, in reality, a fine one . . . researcher integrity is complex and dynamic; it functions along a continuum of practical constraint that involves mutuality, negotiation and re-negotiation of boundaries with participants.' The shifts in position from teacher to researcher entering the homes of pupils raised issues of ethics which were constantly considered and revisited during the course of the project – a matter which again was unusual for the teachers whose ethical stance had previously been coloured by the physical context of the school. Moving the research into the pupils' homes meant that the project team as a whole had to be sensitive to the new position of the teacher researchers as they were being offered access to families' lives in a way unusual in education.

New perceptions

Once they had made their visits and were asked to record their immediate feelings as well as reflect on their transcripts, some of the teachers felt unsure about what they were meant to do or write. One LA co-ordinator noted: 'Mary was worried that the analytical process involved making judgements about the children and their families.' Others initially felt it was difficult to elicit anything meaningful from their field notes and transcripts of their conversations. The teachers' insecurity about analysis or about having anything worthwhile to offer is poignantly raised in the following interview extract:

> *Drawing out threads* [was difficult]. *We found it easier to do it by talking to each*
> *other. And Candace* [LA co-ordinator] *has helped us too. She has made connections,*
> *we said something and she made comments too. It was just a jumble in our head and*
> *we talked it out. When you* [linked researcher] *send us an e-mail or Candace sends*
> *us an e-mail saying, 'Oh that was really useful and you said some really good things*
> *and I have jotted them down' and that has made us think, because we genuinely didn't*
> *think that we were saying anything of any use.* (Final interview)

The opportunities for the teachers to work collaboratively in different local and national groupings with various members of the project team helped them to begin to trust the process, to reflect, to make sense of what they had observed or heard and to develop new perceptions. In this process they learnt from each other and from the tentative and probing dialogue that took place. There were opportunities for this in the informal conversations between teachers in the same school, in LA group sessions and national meetings as well as in the analysis meetings with linked researchers in schools. As colleagues in these contexts, the teachers were 'mutually engaged in refining methodology, interpretation and practice' (González *et al.*, 2005: 93). Through sharing and analysing their field notes, re-listening to the tapes with accompanying transcripts and conferring together about what they had seen and heard, what had surprised them and what had not, the teachers began to develop new perceptions based upon their classroom activities and the Learner Visits. There were multiple discussions and extended email debates within the team too about creating responsive classroom practice and many occasions when the readings which had been debated were drawn upon. As novice researchers visiting homes, the teachers were not only supported by the methodological guidance they had been given, they were also supported by their understanding of the key concepts under-pinning the work. The time set aside to debate theoretical perspectives, expressed in journal articles and chapters, and to explore their understanding of culture, of funds of knowledge, and multimodal literacies in theory and in practice was critical in this regard. This helped many to begin to theorise the practices they observed. It also positioned the teachers not as consumers of knowledge generated by external researchers, but as co-constructors of new knowledge, knowledge that was highly relevant to their roles as teachers. As González *et al.* note:

> It is important to emphasise that we do not create these new attitudes, or the vocabulary, about the families, simply by visiting them, but through theoretically inspired text analyses and reflections.
>
> *(González* et al., *2005: 22)*

In the analysis meetings held in school following the Learner Visits, the linked university-based researchers sought to mediate the teachers' learning, to help them develop their understanding of the children's lives and literacy practices. Through listening to the transcripts with the teachers, they played a role as co-analysts, though critically they were positioned as outsiders who wanted to know and understand the context. In this position they were able to help the practitioner-researchers articulate what their observations and conversations might mean and knowledge was jointly constructed.

In contrast to the field work described by Moll and colleagues in González *et al.* (2005) the majority of the teachers were unaccompanied during their Learner Visits. But there were some exceptions, for example when two project teachers chose to visit together, and on one occasion a trio of staff from a school visited. In a few cases too partners from other agencies participated in their visits to families' homes. Lisa recounted how she appreciated having a partner from the Minority Achievement Communities Service (MCAS) accompany her:

> *She's got a very good manner for a start. Very, very nice way of asking things and I felt that she really helped a lot. It's very good to have another professional to go with you on these visits.* (Final interview)

Her presence clearly afforded comfort, though interestingly on the second and third visits, Lisa was not always accompanied by her MCAS colleague; she had become more comfortable with the process. Another perspective was offered by Sofia, a Portuguese outreach worker, who accompanied Lyn on her Learner Visits:

> *I think the problem is that schools are quite focused on what they ask of them to achieve. I'm in a special position because . . . I come from a different perspective, give them a different view of what was happening with families that they work with.* (Final interview)

Sofia highlights the importance of understanding different perspectives in adopting an ethnographic approach. The role she undertook as a mediator of families' and children's learning, culturally and linguistically, informed the research process and provided an alternative interpretation of the children's literacy lives (see Chapter 9 for a related case study).

New appreciations

The process of making Learner Visits and then reflecting and discussing their experiences, insights and questions which arose, gave rise to teachers commenting that they felt they were differently positioned. This referred both to their developing confidence as practitioners of research and to their increased expertise as researchers recognising their own assumptions and influences. While it had always been the core team's intention to re-position the teachers as researchers, the Learner Visits proved pivotal in this. In contrast to Moll *et al.*'s (1992) research, in the UK project the teachers were more explicitly invited to share something in and of themselves and to make personal connections. This appeared to make a marked difference to the dynamics of the visits and accentuated the biographical, social and situated aspects of an ethnographic perspective.

As a consequence perhaps, reflecting upon the visits, some of the teachers came to recognise their own beliefs; one noted for example she had a 'rather judgemental standpoint I suppose', while another commented 'I had to ask myself – where does this come from? Why did I assume they'd [the parents] not be interested?' Kagan (1992) defines teacher beliefs as 'tacit, often unconsciously held assumptions about students, classrooms and academic material to be taught' (65), many of the BC: RLL teachers also held assumptions about parents and families from across the social and economic spectrum. These unconscious assumptions surfaced in part through adopting researcher dispositions since, as a pre-condition for undertaking the Learner Visits, the teachers were invited to adopt a reflexive stance and consider their pre-conceptions and expectations about the children and the families they were about to visit. Such introspection, which Finlay (2002) perceives is a key variant of researcher reflexivity, was introduced to help the teachers offer honest and ethically sound accounts of their visits. In addition to pre-visit reflections, they engaged in introspection through keeping journals, making notes in their portfolios, responding to prompt sheets at national meetings and through discussion in the data analysis meetings. These reflective opportunities acted as springboards for insights about their own perspectives and in many cases revealed new perceptions. Through undertaking visits as learners and as researchers, most of the teachers were surprised by what they found. They were prompted to challenge their perceptions of individual children, about whom, some later came to appreciate, they had developed somewhat fixed views. For example, Kara talked of a 7-year-old whose home she had visited and noted:

> *If I hadn't like seen him do that* [play on the computer for a full hour with his younger sister] *with my own eyes, I would never have believed he was capable of concentrating that long or sharing like that. In school he never sits still.* (Analysis meeting)

Many more such insights about the teachers' new perceptions were voiced across the project and are documented in the forthcoming chapters. They indicate that most, though not all, of the teachers became more sensitive to the value judgements they made about children and the tacit assumptions and perspectives they held about parents and families. As Lortie (1975) argues, influenced by a long 'apprenticeship of observation' teachers commonly rely on the familiar, what they have observed over their years in school. Such observations and experiences contribute to their tacit beliefs about what they should do, what they should value and what others, such as parents, should contribute. The Learner Visits provided opportunities for the teachers to begin to make visible these beliefs, and linked to the opportunities to surface their own literacy practices and share something of themselves, they began to re-consider their beliefs in the light of the newly available evidence.

For Katy and Charlotte, developing researcher dispositions offered new possibilities to tackle fundamental questions:

> Katy: *I'm not going in as a teacher, 'cos we're learning about their lives really, so we're more like other humans, other people but not teachers.*
> Charlotte: *Not teaching that's the exciting part really, you don't know what you are going to find out . . .*
> Katy: *And you can be more yourself . . .*
> Charlotte: *. . . and listen and think what else don't I know? What's important here?*
> (Analysis meeting)

For others too the opportunity to step back and revisit values and beliefs was important:

> *This project has given us a window on the world really – given us the chance to pause and consider what it is we believe in.* (Analysis meeting)

The teachers developed new knowledge of the children, shifted their views of literacy, their assurance in sharing something of themselves and many built new relationships with parents and children. The process also gave the teachers a greater appreciation of the hybrid role of 'teacher researcher' itself in which they laid bare the gaps in their knowledge, the assumptions used to fill those gaps, the framework in which their relationships were boundaried and the consequences for relationships in teaching and learning. In reflecting on their involvement in the project, two teachers voiced their new appreciations garnered through this work:

> *I think the biggest* [challenge] *was the cultural one . . . we should be proud of our heritage, of our family, of our home, of what we do, and we should try and find ways of sharing that more with each other.*

> *I think it is very easy as a teacher to lose sight of the child outside of the school environment and only think of the child as a person in your class between 9 am and 3.15 pm. And what* [the research] *reaffirms to me − I know deep down that it is so easy to lose along the way, with the busy-ness of school and the targets and the expectations and everything that drives school and academic prowess, and it is very easy to lose sight of actually there is an awful lot more learning that goes on outside of school and that it is so important to tap into children's interests and their other skills and abilities not just their academic abilities and to celebrate all that.*
> (Final interviews)

The teacher researchers recognised the value in making and reflecting on the Learner Visits as a source of knowledge from which to begin to construct different kinds of knowledge and understanding, new learning experiences and relationships. As documented in Chapters 6 and 7, some began to explore new ways of working in the classroom, though this was not without challenge, and some came to appreciate the possibilities involved in developing new relationships with both children and parents. A few, working in strong school communities, came collectively to consider their school's stance in relation to children's funds of knowledge and home–school relationships (see Chapter 8).

Freda visits Molly's home: A case study

This case study of Freda provides an example of the process of developing assurance as a researcher and adopting a researcher's disposition and skills over time. It reveals how through capitalising upon walking children home, as well as visiting homes, and through journal writing as well as discussing new insights in analysis meetings, Freda came to appreciate more about the emergent and reflexive process of being a researcher.

Freda worked in a small primary school; she taught Reception children (aged 4–5 years old) though she had been teaching older learners for some years. She was the school's literacy co-ordinator. Prior to making any Learner Visits, Freda xpressed concern about entering families' homes, noting:

It feels like a bit of cheek really, a kind of intrusion, I'm not sure I'd like it if my son's teacher wanted to come to us. I bet they'll be wondering what I'm really coming to say, even though we've said it's not like that. (Journal)

In discussion with Sophie, the other project teacher from her school, she created a set of interview questions, observing that she needed these and would not consider visiting without them. She voiced concern that not only had she never visited one of her pupils' homes before, she was used to 'doing the telling if you know what I mean – like being the teacher and letting them (the parents) know how their children are doing'. Positioned as a researcher, Freda was entering a more open uncertain space and clearly felt she needed the question sheet to support her; she was not visiting with knowledge to share, but in order to find out new knowledge. The very first visit she undertook was to Molly's home. She noted in her pre-visit notes that she hoped to 'find out about Molly and her life at home, she doesn't talk much in school yet so it's hard to get to know her'. She also recorded that she expected the house to be 'very tidy as Molly always comes to school very neatly dressed' and that 'I don't know much about her mum, but she's very prim I think, she doesn't ever seem relaxed out on the playground'.

For the first visit it was arranged Freda would walk Molly home, she made little comment about the journey in her field notes, only noting: 'she showed me the way and we chatted, but I was so worried about what was to come, I can't remember much of what we talked about though she pointed out a "M" in the road name.' The visit in Molly's home lasted around 20 minutes and to Freda's surprise Molly's mother, Karen, who as she observed afterwards did not 'look terribly comfortable; neither of us were' and did not drink her tea, did agree to their meeting being taped. Molly herself went straight into another room off the kitchen with a friend of the family and did not reappear. Freda used the prepared questions, few of which she developed or added to in any way and Karen's answers were, in Freda's words, 'fairly brief and focused. I hope she didn't think I was asking too much'. While Freda made one connection to an incident involving Molly at school, the remainder of the time she listened and then asked another question until the list ended. Karen pointed out her daughter's easel in the kitchen and Freda noticed children's books on the counter. Freda felt Molly's mother was keen to help her and 'say the right thing' as when the tape recorder was switched off she enquired if the 'results' were what was wanted. At the analysis meeting Freda noted:

Listening back to it, it's embarrassing, it sounds very stilted somehow though it didn't really feel like that at the time, I kept asking questions and didn't join in much or leave many spaces. . . . Maybe I need to probe a bit perhaps? (Analysis meeting)

The tape afforded an opportunity to listen to the dialogue again, to discern the atmosphere and the polite but somewhat overformal interchange between Freda and Karen. Pondering upon this Freda suggested that she might have positioned Molly's mother too 'officially' as an 'interviewee' and, that as Karen wanted to help her daughter's teacher, she may have tried to 'give the right answers – or what she thought these were' and may not have felt able to offer examples or give details. Reviewing her own words and questions on the tape in dialogue with her linked researcher helped Freda to understand how she had framed and shaped the conversation and closed down some spaces for Karen to contribute. She also considered how she might have felt or been positioned if her own son's teacher had visited her and identified a number of possible follow-up questions and prompts for a subsequent visit, several of which related to digital literacy practices of which she had seen no evidence and to which no reference had been made. The importance of developing dialogue and reciprocity between researcher and research participants (both Molly and her mother), was evident in this interchange and was a useful focus of discussion. The challenge of balancing interviewing at the same time as building rapport was not easy.

Prior to the next visit Freda again expressed concern about being 'seen to intrude'; she was concerned that ethically families might feel 'obliged' to accept her as a visitor and that Karen might not want her to return. But this was not the case. Nonetheless she remained sensitive to the families' rights not to have the meeting taped or to stop at any time and she reiterated this on each occasion.

After the second Learner Visit to Molly's home, Freda, again reflecting upon walking her home, observed in her fairly extensive field notes on this occasion that 'listening to her as she skipped along was quite a revelation'. At one point, prompted by roadside poppies, Molly asked why they were worn in November and was then silent for some moments, after which she explained that her Grandpa and his dog were up in heaven like the soldiers, and that when she misses them she hugs her toy dog, Max. Freda, who had met Max as he had been brought to school and was offered him on their arrival at her home, felt that Molly was alluding to the recent death of Freda's own father, noting:

> All the children know I've been off and why and she was reaching out I think, she didn't want to offend but she wanted to help. It was really remarkable. (Learner Visit notes)

The walk home offered both Molly and Freda a chance to talk on new territory, to share and make connections, not predominantly as teacher and pupil, nor as researcher and researched, but as individuals both of whom had experienced loss. The second visit lasted just under an hour. The atmosphere on the tape indicates this was a more informal and relaxed occasion; there was laughter and animation in the adult voices and Karen took more time to expand upon Molly's literacy practices and teased her daughter's teacher at one point. Freda made frequent connections to her own children and asked more spontaneous questions 'as they came to me'. Four-year-old Molly, present throughout, joined in with enthusiasm, often taking the discussion in other directions and intermittently running off to fetch things to share with her teacher. She took her mother's mobile out of her handbag and explained she could text her uncle and take photos, played and sang along to two of

her favourite songs on a CD, talked knowledgably about her favourite TV programmes and her hero Diego from the Nick Junior website and, while the adults
were talking, 'read' a book to her baby sister. Afterwards, Freda noted the difference
Molly's presence made as she was able to observe her in a boisterous playful mode
which was not part of her behaviour in school and she saw her interacting with her
mum and her sister, as well as the wealth of multimodal texts with which she
engaged with ease. On this occasion Freda perceived she was able to 'uncover more
and get beneath the surface' and noted:

> *I guess I was also calmer this time round and shared more of my own views and that
> we'd got past that breaking the ice bit of being in her home.* (Analysis meeting)

In the analysis meeting, Freda chose to discuss the moment when Molly took her
mother's mobile, noting that initially Karen had seemed uncomfortable and had
repeatedly asked Molly to put it away, 'almost as if she didn't think that's what
I wanted to know about or somehow didn't think I'd approve'. Freda considered
whether Karen, who was a young mother, was concerned to be seen as 'a good
mum' in her daughter's teacher's eyes and may have been worried about being
judged in some way in relation to the presence and use of digital texts in her home.
She thought it probable that Karen saw these as separate from, and potentially less
valuable than, more recognisable versions of school literacy. Karen was perhaps also
influenced by her own perceptions of the research, and may have 'performed' in
this interview context, albeit she was more relaxed than on the first occasion. She
may have said the kinds of things she perceived would place both Molly and herself
in a good light in relation to the school's literacy agenda. In highlighting the
juxtaposition between conceptualisations of interviews as research instruments,
with perceptions of research interviews as social practice, Talmy (2011) recognises
that while both orientations are interested in data gathering for analysis and answering research questions, when interviews are conceptualised as social practice,
they are treated 'not as sites for the excavation of information held by respondents,
but as participation in social practices' (Talmy, 2011: 28). This was discussed
with Freda who recognised her role in this fundamentally social context. She
also chose to discuss an extract in which she had shared her own sons' favourite
websites, perceiving that this had made her feel 'more at ease' and that it had
influenced the flow of conversation. She wondered whether at this point Molly's
mother had seen her:

> *As a mum as well as her daughter's teacher?* . . . *It made all the difference that* [talking
> about her own life], *me being me, rather than me being the teacher if you know
> what I mean.* (Analysis meeting)

Reflecting on the two visits afterwards, Freda appeared aware of her positional shifts
and the boundary crossing involved in enacting her identities as Molly's teacher,
as a researcher and as a mother. She found this interplay complex and interesting,

noting: 'When you leave and go back to school, the role of the teacher drags you back and that's difficult ... but you know them better and you keep thinking.' Following her new actions as a researcher making Learner Visits to Molly's and other children's homes, and through ongoing reflections and discussion with her linked researcher and in-school colleague from the project, Freda gained in confidence as a researcher. She commented upon the value of her field notes, of listening to the tapes and engaging in reflective writing:

> *When we started this I wasn't sure what to write and wasn't sure it would be of any significance, but now I trust myself more. I try to describe what I saw and what happened – not to judge ... I re-read them* [her reflections] *and think 'Am I doing that or are my values and assumptions creeping in round the edges?'* (Analysis meeting)

She recognised that her own somewhat tentative stance and list of questions had framed and constrained the first interview and came to challenge her initial perceptions about Molly and her mum. In order to build on her new appreciation of the children's home literacy practices, she was concerned to take action to develop her classroom practice, and in particular to 'connect to their digital skills and make literacy more meaningful in school' as well as stay connected to the parents. Examples of the way in which she mediated between homes and school are described in later chapters, suffice to note here that during the project Freda was also mediating the roles of teacher and researcher and seeking to hold them both in view. As Tenery (2005: 128) notes: 'Ethnographic research conducted by teachers represents a voice that lies somewhere between self and other, teacher and learner, insider and outsider.'

Conclusion

As a consequence of being positioned as researchers, new actions, new perceptions and new appreciations were generated. The tensions, challenges and uncertainties remained to a greater or lesser extent throughout the year's project as the teachers strove to accommodate to new experiences of being researchers of their own assumptions and practices, as well as finding out more about their pupils' literacy lives. Becoming learners themselves may have jolted some preconceptions and made previously 'safe ground' unstable, and indeed raised some questions about identity, but the shift in role opened up new areas of understanding and offered promise of 'a totally different way of working' as one teacher described the process of research.

Ethnography has been conversely described as 'making the strange familiar' or 'rendering the familiar strange' (Erikson, 1984). The teachers' activities drew simultaneously on these dichotomous descriptions: the act of repositioning them as learners through ethnography threw them into unfamiliar territory, unsettling their identities and challenging their assumptions about themselves, their roles, their relationships and their perceptions of the children and their families. Naturally there was a certain amount of personal and professional disquiet when the usual dis-courses of targets and content were set aside in order to pursue a more open agenda. There was even sometimes guilt when teachers were asked to digress from school-centred views of what 'literacy' means and implies for practice, into their own and their pupils' literacy lives. As learners and researchers, they were invited to engage in introspection, consider their assumptions share their own experiences and insights from the Learner Visits and concentrate on relationships, rather than levels of attainment.

The nature of the research, where expected positions shifted and transformed, allowed new understandings to emerge. Though it seems likely that the develop-ment of the teachers' researcher dispositions was at least partly influenced by their own professional biographies and narrative journeys, nonetheless as Kemmis and McTaggart point out:

> Practitioner research and action research have the capacity to open com-municative spaces in which 'the way things are' is open to question and exploration. It can imagine and explore how things might be. It can learn from the consequences – social, cultural, material – economic, personal – of how things are and other ways of doing things that we deliberately set out to test. It aims both to understand reality in order to transform it, and to transform reality in order to understand it.
>
> *(Kemmis and McTaggart, 2005: 565)*

From a position of being expected to 'know things' as teachers, the *BC: RLL* teach-ers were invited to develop a disposition of 'not knowing' in order to make their own familiar assumptions 'strange' to them. In this way they were able to reflect on their newly gathered knowledge about their pupils' and their families' literacy funds of knowledge. The Learner Visits were key to the process of being open to unknow-ingness. Although the teacher researchers undertook the visits without university researchers, the collegial nature of the research meant that the data gathered were discussed and analysed through the data analysis meetings and with colleagues from other schools, local authorities and the core team. The building of support networks, particularly strengthened by the local and national meetings, meant that all involved in the project could share anxieties and find reassurance in the posi-tion of teacher-researcher – 'this difficult boundary crossing, with its associated uncertainties about process and outcome – was a necessary part of the process' (Durrant, 2011: 29).

5

DEVELOPING KNOWLEDGE ABOUT THE CHILDREN

Fiona M. Collins and Rose Drury

In the *BC: RLL* project, teachers were supported as they became both learners and researchers, seeking to develop new knowledge about the children in their classes. Both in the classroom and by undertaking Learner Visits to children's homes, they sought to find out more about them as individuals and in particular to learn about their literacy lives. As Chapter 2 argues, children's home literacy experiences and practices, including the use of digital technologies, familiarity with different forms of popular culture, sport, hobbies, and home language experience all enrich them as learners (Gregory and Williams, 2000; Peterson and Heywood, 2007; Ren and Hu, 2011). Such funds of knowledge have the potential to contribute significantly to their school learning and understanding. The exclusion of this knowledge from the curriculum can have a detrimental effect on children's potential for learning, their self-esteem and sense of identity as learners (Comber and Kamler, 2004; Lingard and Keddie, 2013). Ignoring cultural difference – and inequality – can exacerbate educational disadvantage, side-lining children's cultural capital (Bourdieu, 2008). To counter this, teachers need to have knowledge of, and engage with, the out-of- school interests and experiences of the children they teach and arguably need to become what Luke (2010) describes as 'cosmopolitan' teachers. Such teachers take it upon themselves to find out about the children they teach and the current trends they are interested in both global and local, which relate to their pupils' personal knowledge and interests. As one of the project teachers noted:

> *In the end, though I know it's not rocket science to know your children and to know your families, I actually think it's terribly important and it does have an impact on their learning.* (Final interview)

However, the role of the teacher entering children's homes is by no means unproblematic. Most of the teachers expressed surprise about the literacy and learning environments which they witnessed on Learner Visits. They often took with them the baggage of assumptions they had made about the children's community practices or about their class or socioeconomic position (Andrews and Yee, 2010; Gregory and Ruby, 2011). Such assumptions were challenged, either by the teachers' own reflections on the visits or through a process of dialogue with project colleagues. This chapter offers an overview of the teachers' initial knowledge about the children's lives at the start of the work and then gives examples of the ways in which they sought to widen their knowledge and experience. This overview is followed by a case study describing the process of one teacher coming to understand and appreciate more about one child's cultural knowledge and home literacy experience.

The start of the journey

At the start of the school year the teachers were interviewed and were invited to share their knowledge about the three children that they had each chosen to focus upon (see Chapter 3 for details of the project organisation). They were invited to talk about each child's likes, dislikes, literacy practices and about their families. The interviews revealed very limited knowledge about the children's lives beyond school and almost no awareness of their wider interests and passions. Only two of the 18 teachers lived within walking distance of the school or within its immediate catchment and this may have had consequences in relation to their knowledge of the locality, but the marked lack of knowledge of children's personal interests and cultural experiences represented cause for concern. The interviews were undertaken in October–November so the teachers had been working with these focus pupils for some time. Undoubtedly the teachers cared for their children, but pressured by the need to ensure curriculum coverage and by the accountability regime, they perceived there was insufficient time to get to know the learners personally. They did demonstrate considerable knowledge about the children's literacy levels and agreed targets as measured by in-school assessments. But were not, at least in relation to their three focus children, knowledgeable about their cultural, linguistic, historical or personal situations – their funds of knowledge.

The teachers were also asked about the opportunities they currently had for finding out about children's lives and learning beyond school. The majority of responses focused on the traditional home–school links such as reading contact books or homework diaries. Other strategies, such as seeing parents in the playground and inviting parents into classrooms were mentioned by a few teachers but when probed it appeared that these conversations tended to focus on school-based activities and issues. In relation to the children's families, again knowledge was limited and patchy, with the teachers in the foundation stage knowing rather more in terms of the children's home circumstances than those in the later years. What was known often related to siblings in the school, to the children's mothers and the degree of support or otherwise that they were perceived to offer specifically in relation to reading. Teachers tended to present a somewhat detached and sometimes deficit view of the children and their homes. For example:

> *It's not very language rich and the language is not very diverse or wide ranging and some parents have common grammatical errors in their speech and the contact books.* (Initial interview)

In their descriptions of the children and their families it was evident that many teachers associated the children's levels of achievement with perceived levels of parental involvement, for example: 'he's a bright underachiever, not well supported by parents and she's extremely able, obviously immersed in a rich culture at home.' Several appeared to have chosen particular children to focus on in the project because they were struggling: 'He doesn't seem to be making progress (with literacy) … he's not turned onto reading'; 'He's a really clever boy but has very poor visual memory, problems with reading'. But in relation to their out-of-school literacy practices almost no knowledge was voiced, and teachers' responses almost invariably focused upon reading. Some in their comments again revealed their own assumptions about the home and the child's literacy ability; for example:

> *I don't know very much about his literacy outside of school. He does read fairly regularly … but whether he reads to his younger sister or does other things around reading I don't know, I doubt it.* (Initial interview)

Several teachers chose to focus on children who had recently arrived in school or were learning English as an additional language although some were unsure of the language(s) their focus children spoke, did not know what language was spoken at home. As one noted, 'It might be Urdu. I'll find out. He does go to Mosque I know that. But does he read in another language? I don't know', while another commented, 'I've never asked the children what languages they speak.' Teachers who were working with EAL nursery and reception children seemed to have more detailed knowledge of their children's language experiences, but those working with older primary children were again less knowledgeable about whether, for example, the children were literate in their home language; overall there was scant knowledge voiced about the children's cultural backgrounds. While the teachers recognised this was not ideal, they were unsure how to find out more:

> *I know I should know more about the children and the community round here but there's never time and in any case how do you get to know such stuff? I don't live round here, I live miles away.* (Initial interview)

This challenge of distance for the local community was commonly voiced, but it was not physical only, a strong professional distance also appeared to be operating. While Bernstein (1990) argued that 'if the culture of the teacher is to become part of the consciousness of the child, then the culture of the child must first be in the consciousness of the teacher' (46), it seemed at the start of the project this was not possible, since there was a limited knowledge about the children linguistically, culturally and socially. Notwithstanding this starting point, the teachers were hopeful that the project would help them find out more, as they observed: 'I want to try and look at what she brings with different eyes and find out about what she reads ... do we have high enough expectations?'; 'I'm hoping to find out how they learn at home;' and 'We hope to find out more about children in terms of what they enjoy outside school, what sort of literacy experiences they have and what we can build on.'

Children's lives beyond the school gate

Through classroom activities and in particular through conversation and observation in the Learner Visits, the teachers began to develop an awareness of 'funds of knowledge of the child's world outside the context of the classroom' (Moll *et al.*, 1992: 134). The German poet Morgenstern (1918) is credited with writing nearly a century ago, that 'home is not where you live, but where you are understood', and following the visits and through subsequent classroom-based work, the teachers perceived their understanding of the children markedly developed; they came to know more about them as rounded individuals, as family members and as learners beyond the bounded world of academic literacy. Both the teachers and the LA co-ordinators expressed surprise at the range of interests and competencies revealed by the children. In particular, the teachers noticed that when children were engaged at home in activities which motivated them and about which they had some a detailed understanding, they demonstrated increased assurance, knowledge and confidence. Many of their interests focused on popular cultural texts available to them in a range of media. The teachers were also surprised by the capacity of early years and primary aged learners to handle a wider than expected range of digital technologies. There was also evidence of bilingual children accessing a range of media and popular cultural texts in their own languages (Kenner, 2000).

In particular, the teachers developed a more coherent picture of the children as individuals and as family members, shaped by social and cultural factors beyond the school. For example, some teachers found out for the first time that various members of their classes attended Saturday school classes at the Mosque, one also attended the local Mosque daily from 5–8 pm and two attended Church of England Sunday school classes. As Gregory and Kenner's (2003) work indicates, such classes often 'not only teach a language, literacy or religion, but a whole way of life' (82) something that the teachers came to appreciate. The teachers also established a great deal of information about the various cultural heritages and diverse practices of the families whom they visited, and learnt about the languages children spoke and in several cases read and wrote in the home. Charlotte, for example, found that 7-year-old Dane from Slovakia had only been in the country for two years and had not, in his parents' view, settled as well as his older brother who was arguably more successful in terms of schooling. Charlotte had not known prior to the visit that he was a relatively recent arrival (nor that he had an older brother), and came to recognise that for Dane the change in circumstance, the separation from his previous friends and wider family and the marked reduction in outdoor space (he enjoyed sport), represented a challenge. In this way his struggles with written English were contextualised and his teacher expressed increased empathy and understanding of his situation.

Initially the teachers' expectations of particular children and their families framed their understanding of the children's home practices. Reflecting on the literacy heritage described by parents on one Learner Visit, Evelyn believed this explained the child's behaviours and limited competencies in school. Her reflections, aligned with own existing constructs of the child, focused on school processes and school literacy priorities. She seemed to struggle with or resisted opening up to the possibilities of new experiences and knowledge about this child and his home, and tended to use her own childhood as a yardstick for evaluating others and let her conception of school literacy dominate. It appeared that the process of repositioning herself outside the familiar (and safe) vantage point she had constructed for herself as a teacher, created a barrier to seeing through a different lens. Consequently, her analysis of her visits relied on her prior assumptions rather than peeling those away and starting afresh. Gradually, however, Evelyn, as with most of other project teachers, began to show that she was beginning to reflect on what she had learned about the children and herself as a teacher and the assumptions that she felt influenced her attitudes and practice.

> We need to be listening to parents too. We get too bogged down with sharing predictions of results and the academic side of things. We don't know about the other lovely things they do. Jennie had learnt to read music and play the recorder and that is nothing to do with me. (Interview)

There were multiple examples of teachers documenting the children learning in and through shared activities in the home: shared reading, play and interaction often with their siblings, parents and grandparents and other members of the extended family. The variety of these contexts and the involvement of siblings in each others' learning appeared to surprise many of the teachers (Kennedy and Bearne, 2009). This is understandable perhaps since in working with only one member of a family in school, the teachers were often unaware of the wealth of any child's interactions in the extended family units in the home. Recognising the role of siblings and others helped the teachers in various ways. For example, Freda found that due in part to the pressure of his parents' work, 5-year-old Lucca was regularly read to by his older sister. His parents, perceiving this to be their role, signed the contact book on her behalf, but expressed a degree of anxiety about this practice. Freda, who met his sister on the second visit, was able to communicate with her more openly as his reading partner and Lucca's parents seemed comfortable with this.

The teachers also began to develop increased awareness of the highly social nature of the children's learning in the home, alongside a renewed recognition of the rich and diverse opportunities for learning, for example through playful engagement in new media with their siblings, through involvement in the religious practices of their families, and through supporting family members in various ways. They came to see that world of schooled literacy, which travelled into the home from school via reading books and homework for example, represented only one small part (albeit often a highly valued part) of the range of literacy and learning practices in the home. This new knowledge of the children's lives and everyday literacy practices enabled deeper relationships to be developed in school; the teachers were able to make connections and came to appreciate more about the children as active and capable learners; they came to see them as multidimensional young people with diverse identities.

Significantly too, the teachers came to recognise that the children's wealth of interests, their depth of knowledge and the wide range of activities which they took part in with their peers and their families, contributed significantly to their literacy and learning. For example, several of the focus children were learning to play a musical instrument at home or could read music: Vincente, a 6-year-old was teaching himself the guitar and Jennie's father was teaching her the recorder, although neither of their teachers knew they played these instruments. Seeing children learning effectively in their homes was revelatory. Teachers observed the young people 'on task' for long periods on computer games and projects they were passionate about, 'bouncing off the furniture' with ideas within role play and engaging in study independent of school, such as attending Mosque School every evening or researching a non-school related topic of interest with Mum. Religious activity was significant and social for some, involving reading, speaking and singing in different languages while others were taking part in different community activities and sports groups for instance. Additionally, teachers found out that unknown to them at the start of the project, their focus children were variously and individually fascinated with: dinosaurs, princesses, animals in general, dogs in particular (because one child's family had previously had kept numerous dogs on their ranch in Albania), football, tropical fish, trucks, cooking, drawing, street dancing, ballet, tap dancing, music of all kinds (including pop, Latin Jazz, classical, samba), model making, gymnastics, hunting, nature and camping. Their personal interests powered the children's independent reading, both on the internet and in traditional print-based information. Previously the teachers' understanding of the children's 'prior knowledge and experience' had been framed almost exclusively by the literacy curriculum, in relation for example to their decoding skills or ability to write in a particular genre, it did not include an understanding of their strengths, interests and resources derived from home learning and literacy practices. The teachers' new knowledge related to individual children as rounded individuals, children with personal passions and related practices, children who were part of wider social worlds beyond the school gate.

Children's interest in and expertise with digital technology

From the classroom activities focused on their literacy lives and the Learner Visits it appeared that virtually all the children were confident and at ease with using a very diverse range of technologies such as the Wii, PlayStation, X-box, computer games, websites and mobile devices of different sorts. Irrespective of socio-economic factors and geographic locations, most children had regular access to computers, though sometimes this was at their grandparents' homes. Additionally, they were eager to learn how to use new devices or expand their digital repertoires, and as multiple other studies have shown, were often highly skilled digitally literate young-sters (Larson and Marsh, 2005; Hill, 2010; Alper, 2013). Through visiting homes in particular, the teachers were able to observe first-hand what children could do with new literacies at home, though as discussed further in the following chapter, some teachers showed a degree of 'digital blindness' when first visiting children's homes. Nonetheless, as Jenkins (2006) argues, experience with digital technologies makes a rich contribution to many social and personal aspects of learning: 'In terms of personal development, identity, expression and their social consequences – participation, social capital, civic culture – these are the activities that serve to network today's younger generation' (Jenkins, 2006: 5). Many of the teachers came to recognise these assets and their potential value to children's learning in the classroom.

In addition, the visits showed that the majority of the children were active participants in the world of popular culture and were both motivated and knowl-edgeable in this regard. Many of their literacy practices were influenced by popular cultural texts. For example, children were able to demonstrate detailed information about contemporary TV series as well as popular characters in the virtual world online. This involvement in popular culture and particularly digital popular culture is neither new nor surprising (Marsh, 2000; 2004; Marsh et al., 2005; Grugeon, 2005) but what was surprising was the teachers' relative lack of awareness of the children's extensive involvement with and depth of knowledge in this area. The teachers discovered the children's passion for popular cultural texts available to them in a range of media (Willett, Robinson and Marsh, 2008), for example, children enjoying the same narrative in different modes, noting: 'It's a multimodal thing – not just watching the film but buying the book, buying the game – the whole package.' Rachel found that Oliver, a 6-year-old with special educational needs, was both energised and informed about Batman and Spider Man, his favourite TV superheroes. In school, he showed no particular confidence in lessons, was unmotivated and rarely volunteered his views, yet at home his mother told his teacher that Oliver was:

> . . . like a drama queen. He does like to act out bits while it's playing in the back. You'll have Oliver being Batman or Spiderman. He's got dress-up stuff so he likes to dress up. Whatever he's watching he'll put on that outfit and he'll be spinning webs and stuff; jumping from furniture to furniture. I think he does go into his own little world. (Transcription from home visit)

Rachel encouraged him to bring his outfit to school where he was able to share his skills and knowledge and be successful in his own and his classmates' eyes; he stunned them with detailed knowledge of his superhero and his exploits, showing his understanding of narrative and characterisation (Robinson and Turnbull, 2005). Rachel recognised the significance of this discovery:

> *This was a completely different side I hadn't seen before. His speech is not good and this was going on in his head. I didn't know about his imagination; he is a creator. His language was hidden away.* (Interview)

This example highlights the importance of teachers recognising the relationship between home and school learning (Alper, 2013) and of increased awareness of children's 'longing and belonging' in relation to popular cultural experience (Pugh, 2009). As part of her growing understanding she saw a different aspect of Oliver's language when she spoke to him about his digital interests:

> *I think as well his technical language . . . if you were to talk to Oliver in a normal kind of capacity and then listen to him talk about a computer game, the technological language that he is using is very, very different.* (Final interview)

Oliver was not the only child to engage at home in complex and well-informed play narratives. Several of the other early years practitioners noted (through observations in class and on Learner Visits) that the children created playful story worlds built upon their popular cultural knowledge. One teacher, Ludmilla, realising her early years children's delight in and depth of knowledge of popular cultural texts, began to watch some of their favourite children's programmes herself. She came to understand their enthusiasm and join in (though she was concerned not to interfere or be directive) the world in which the children were engaged:

> *Now I know more about their own individual interests we've got a much closer relationship as I have become more knowledgeable of Go-goes, Ben 10, Gormities, Space and so on. . . . previously I was only their teacher, now I have become more of a partner during their play.* (Presentation)

Such playful engagement chimes with Jenkins' (2006) view on how the participatory culture of play contributes to learning. In tune with the work of Marsh (2003a), Ludmilla and Rachel, and the majority of the other teachers in the project, found that when children were able to make connections to the knowledge they had gained through watching and playing with particular story worlds on the TV and computer, they were not only more motivated to talk, to read, to write, to share and to play imaginatively (building on their detailed knowledge bases), they also remained focused for much longer than usual.

Until their involvement in this project, the teachers had not fully appreciated the genuine depth of knowledge which the children possessed in relation to popular cultural figures and the related literacy practices in which the children of their own volition engaged. Nor had these practitioners appreciated the full potential of popular culture and media texts in the classroom. They had, by their own admission, tended to dismiss or sideline popular culture in their classrooms, focusing on more traditionally conceived texts framed within notions of school literacy (Levy, 2009). Perhaps they were concerned that the children's highly interactive media-related play and talk was not appropriate within the boundaries of the school day (Lambirth, 2003; Marsh, 2003b). Perhaps too the curriculum and assessment structure in England, which pays limited attention to non-traditional literacy practices, had devalued these in the eyes of the teachers, prompting them to be seen as 'unofficial' and by implication less relevant or valuable for learning. Nevertheless, as they began to appreciate the impact, influence and passion associated with these texts, the teachers sought ways to remain open to them, to offer spaces for playful engagement and sharing and sought to build on the children's specialist knowledge in this area.

Recognising these funds of knowledge as assets for learning

For the majority of the teachers, the Learner Visits in particular opened their eyes to new understanding about children's capacities, desires and interests in the world beyond school and the complexities inherent in this. The teachers came to see that, in all the families visited, literacy surrounded the children's activities and despite its diversity and contextual variety it was part of the fabric of family life. Some saw, that in line with McNaughton's (1995) categories, there were at least three different ways in which families supported literacy learning: through joint activity, through personal activity in which children practised particular forms of literacy of their own, and through ambient activities, those that occurred in the daily routines of family life. The children revealed themselves to be highly knowledgeable about specific areas of interest and demonstrated marked degrees of expertise, not noticed or known about by their teachers prior to the project work. They were also seen to capitalise on the wealth of opportunities for pleasure and/or self-expression through literacy available in their homes and communities. In these contexts they experienced literacy as multiple and culturally embedded and used it to carry out a number of social functions. In addition, extending McNaughton's (1995) categories, it was observed that the children engaged in independent literacy/learning activities without intervention on the part of parents or other family members, indicating the children's agency. The teachers noticed that the children frequently demonstrated considerable assurance and ease as they handled a wide range of digital technologies for their own purposes in the home, indicating a high degree of volition and decision making, which they were not, their teachers commonly perceived, able to exercise in school.

The children's interests and commitments, their everyday literacy and learning practices and their many roles in the home altered their teachers' perceptions of the competencies these learners could bring to school and as a consequence the variations across individuals and families were gradually seen to be a resource rather than a fixed influence upon children's 'schooled' literacy success. However, Andrews and Yee (2010) warn against analysing findings in a way which 'essentialises the lives and experiences of children and their families' (438). Through their reflective journals, discussions and data analysis meetings, the teachers came to appreciate the uniqueness of the children's and families' funds of knowledge, unpicking previously held assumptions. They frequently used words such as 'astounded', 'amazed', 'surprised', 'taken aback' and regularly voiced the view that their previous knowledge of the children had been much more limited than they had appreciated. As one typically noted:

> *I didn't know anything about them really – I thought I did – because you are with them all day you assume you do I guess, I did know something of their personalities, but apart from that it was all based on assessments and targets.* (Interview)

At one national meeting the teachers recorded new knowledge about each of their focus children on hexagons; these were joined to make a massive 'asset blanket' of the diverse competencies, interests and literacy practices of the young learners (Figure 5.1).

While recognising the uniqueness of each child's home literacy practices reflected in their hexagon, common themes could also be noted. These included that when at home, the focus children frequently:

- read, wrote, talked and learned about subjects and issues that passionately interested them;
- employed a wide range of digital texts for their own purposes and for pleasure;
- took the time/space they needed/desired unrestricted by tight time frames;

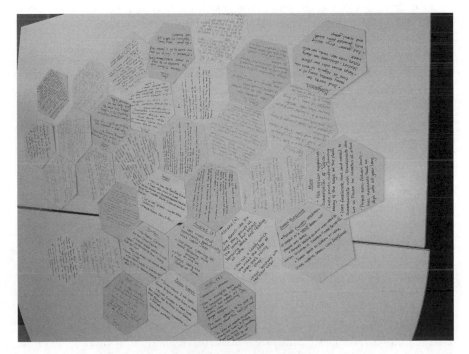

FIGURE 5.1 The emerging asset blanket of new knowledge

- learned in social, interactive and collaborative contexts in the company of their siblings and parents;
- exercised choice over their activities;
- demonstrated independence as learners who made their own decisions.

The teachers' new knowledge about the children as actively engaged literacy and language users in the home began to shift their perceptions and expectations of them in school; it also challenged the teachers to consider whether they catered appropriately for these young learners. While the teachers overall felt their new knowledge was located in the particular children, whose homes and families they had visited, many noted increased sensitivity to all the children, and perceived that they were more attentive to classroom conversations in which aspects of home lives and real world practices were revealed. As a consequence the teachers sought to make use of the children's learning assets and in so doing placed value upon them. This motivated the young people and enabled them, and in some cases their parents, to begin to recognise these as strengths. More broadly, the teachers also sought to re-design their approaches to teaching and learning based on their new knowledge and understanding (see Chapter 6).

Carol learns about Cole: a case study

This case study gives an example of how the knowledge gained from Learner Visits enabled Carol, one of the project teachers, not only to understand more about one child's interests and learning assets, but to reflect upon and as a consequence alter, the opportunities she afforded him in school to use these.

Carol taught 5–6-year-olds in an outer London borough school for children aged 3–7 years. An assistant head, she had worked in Station Road Infant School for 11 years: 'I have been here quite a long time in the school and I've taught siblings. Parents still come to me if they have a problem.' She also grew up in the local area which was not the norm for most of the project teachers. The school has a four form entry with 299 children in Key Stage 1 plus 78 part-time nursery children. It is 1930s low rise red brick, in the middle of a large housing estate which was built between the 1920s and 1930s by the London County Council in order to re-house people from poor housing of the east end of London. At its completion it was the largest social housing scheme in Europe. It was also part of the 'Homes for Heroes' post-WW1 project. In 1931 the Ford Motor Car assembly plant opened nearby and was the main employer in the area until relatively recently.

The headteacher had been at the school for many years. She described the school population as being 'very mixed'. It had changed over the last five years from mainly white working class to 50 per cent of the children coming from Minority Ethnic families. At the time of the project the school had a number of West African families (16 per cent), who are the largest percentage, and a growing number of eastern European families (Lithuanian, Albanian and Polish). The head noted of the Eastern European families that they are: 'quite inspirational, they are very supportive but they work very long hours'. Carol commented that literacy levels were low in school due to parents struggling with literacy themselves and felt even where English was spoken some parents might not feel sufficiently confident to help. The school makes links with the local Church of England and the Mosque and tries to bring the local community into school.

At the beginning of the project year Carol showed enthusiasm for learning about her children's out-of-school literacy lives and about the Learner Visits, even though she was a nervous about making the visits. Carol observed that she learned about the children's home literacy from the home–school reading diaries, though acknowledged they did not offer much information. In the first term of the project she talked to the children about their lives outside school and occasionally shared her own reading with them. To give status to the children's home interests their contributions were written on cards in the shape of apples and hung on a tree and children also shared their interests through, for example, demonstrating street dancing and other skills in Show and Tell sessions.

Visiting Cole at home

Cole was one of Carol's three focus children for the project. A White British 5-year-old Carol described him as articulate but noted that his literacy levels did not reflect his spoken language: 'He knows all the sounds but can't it put down on paper, he can't write a whole story.' Carol perceived Cole's mother Amy was very supportive and so chose him in order to 'try to unpick why he is struggling' and why he was often disengaged in literacy activities. Cole's older sisters had previously attended the school so that Carol felt she 'knew' the family, though she found out a great deal more about Cole during the Learner Visit. Carol and the project teacher who accompanied her, both commented how open Amy was with them. The family lived in a house on the local estate and the first thing that Carol noticed was the range of reading material on nature and the countryside scattered around the house. On the coffee table Carol noted *Countryman's Weekly* magazine and a bird spotting book. In the garden there were bird feeders and in the kitchen binoculars lay on the table. Amy told them that he 'goes fishing, ferreting, and hunting with his father. They go on land which they have to write permission for and Cole reads these letters'. Cole's interest in nature and country pursuits was reflected in the texts he chose to read at home. Carol learnt the family had bought Cole his own bird books because he started reading adult ones that he could not understand. She knew he preferred non-fiction books but had not been aware of his interest in nature and wildlife. She also learnt that Cole 'has worm books and ferret books, and he will sit and try and copy things out . . . you can see that he's written three or four words out of the book'. Amy told Carol that she heard him read regularly, he also looked at his books in bed and that the siblings played together:

> *Upstairs they play schools – some of the things he brings down and he tries to sound them out to us . . . the other day he was trying to sound out 'thank you for all my*

presents' but he'd written it down in one word, but every letter, you could see where he was coming from, and when he sounded it out, we was looking at it and he was laughing 'it's not right is it?' and I was going 'no, but you've done really well boy, to just do that'. (Transcription from home visit)

Amy also explained that Cole had his own desk in his bedroom:

He does sit there and work; he'll go up there and he's got his pot of pens. His father's always coming home with boxes of paper, new pads, new pens, highlighter pens, Tippex pens . . . on his desk area – Sellotape and hole punchers. (Transcription from home visit)

Carol realised that at home Cole was engaged in multiple literacy practices of his own volition and that there was 'evidence of literacy everywhere'. The visit allowed her to compare Cole's home literacy, where he was willing to read and write, with his attitude in school where he showed himself to be a reluctant reader and writer even though he was articulate and willing to talk.

Carol also found out about Cole's digital interest, as Amy told her 'He's well into Indiana Jones and Star Wars and I don't know how to set it up' but Cole did, reflecting the children's technical knowledge drawn from home experience evidenced across the project. Cole's play was also influenced by this interest: 'He'll make up new characters; even with the laptop . . . if he wants to change the letters, the size of the letters, I wouldn't know how to do it.' She also told Carol that he knew how to use a button entitled back-up launch: 'He would never be able to read back-up launch but he knows that is the button and he knows the word says back-up launch.' Another aspect of Cole's out-of-school interests was sport. Carol learnt that he enjoyed football, gym and trampolining, his interest in football once again influenced his story choices: 'He likes stories about football and pirates.' Within the family Carol felt there was an emphasis on the outdoors and the children's physical involvement.

Through the Learner Visit and the follow-up data analysis conversations, Carol came to understand much more about Cole as a learner. Cole's interest in nature was developed from his father, echoing Clark's finding that:

In most of the homes both parents played a crucial role in their children's intellectual development and . . . a number of boys particularly were modelling their speech and interest on those of their father.

(Clark, 1975: 97)

Cole was seen by the school as struggling with literacy and was viewed as disinterested and somewhat unwilling to engage, whereas Clark's study was of children who were highly successful readers. The Learner Visit, which enlightened Carol about Cole's knowledge of 'outdoorsy stuff' and his experience of digital technology, changed her perception of his potential as a learner. She could see the family valued education and learning, and that his home practices were very diverse. Yet she knew at school Cole found it hard to engage. Amy told her that Cole did not enjoy school and that she had to bribe him to attend regularly. As she said: 'Can't mess around though; you've got to go to school and learn because he doesn't like going to school. It's a nag to get him over there.' This knowledge itself was enlightening and productive.

A shifting frame of reference

From the early Learner Visits Carol's perceptions of the children's out-of-school literacy lives began to change. Through reflecting upon and discussing the children's practices she came to recognize that she was developing a fuller view of what literacy might encompass:

> *My own concept of literacy was quite limited until I did the project and it has made me realise there is more to literacy.* (Interview)

Over time Carol became more thoughtful in her practice as she began to understand the impact that out-of-school interests had on the children's learning. Lingard and Keddie (2013) note the potentially narrowing effect of teachers being 'unconnected with students' lives and communities', referring to 'pedagogies of indifference' (437). While this seems a somewhat harsh term to apply to well-intentioned teachers, these scholars, in tune with Moll *et al.* (1992) argue that teachers need to know about and use the diversity of home literacy learning in order to develop children's learning.

After the Learner Visit to Cole's home, Carol asked him to bring in his fishing rod and net and talk to the class about it. Previously he had been reluctant to write in school but as Carol's view of him as a learner changed, so she noted did Cole's attitude to school:

> [Cole] *has completely changed his attitude towards writing, from very negative 'I can't do it' to a much more positive view. This only began after encouraging him to write about his out-of-school experiences and showing him that this was okay to do so.* (Journal)

One significant event indicates the increased awareness which Carol was developing and reflects the possible effects of disconnections between school and home. During a writing session Cole wrote a story about a hunter:

> *One day the hunter woke up. He wanted to go hunting. He found a rabbit house. The hunter shot the rabbit. He took the rabbit home.*

Carol asked what happened to the rabbit when it was taken home. When Cole replied that it was skinned, gutted and cooked for supper, Carol suggested he write that down, to which he immediately replied: 'Can I?' Reflecting on this incident later with her linked researcher, Carol realised the significance of Cole's question; it reflected what he felt was appropriate to write about in school. Even at the age of five, he recognised that was deemed legitimate in school and at home was different, and that boundaries existed between them. According to Kress: 'One of the major problems for young people in schools [is] the gap between the expectations that they bring from their world and the expectations that exist in school from a former world' (Kress, 2005: 294).

Since Carol knew more about Cole, his previously invisible experiences – his social and cultural capital – was able to be recognised and validated in the classroom. Carol came to realise that without meaning to do so, she was constantly signalling what was considered acceptable in school and was framing what counted as literacy in her classroom. She wondered if she had not come to understand Cole better if she would have expressed 'offense' or displeasure at the rabbit's demise. Cole's robust knowledge that rabbits can be killed, skinned, cooked and eaten ran counter to the kind of 'rabbit lore' which Carol perceived she had probably promoted previously: with rabbits seen as fluffy, cute and sometimes mischievous characters in storybooks. Carol perceived that once Cole became aware that he was 'allowed' to bring his own experience into the classroom, he began to feel more assured. As she noted:

> *His attitude has changed completely. Now he does everything we ask him to do. His body language is different where before it was very negative. Now he seems more alert.* (Journal)

Just as important as Cole's more engaged behaviour, Carol's practice as a teacher had undergone a shift. Later in the project, through sustaining her work on Interest Trees and shaping Show and Tell time in innovative ways, as well as through sharing more of herself as a reader and a learner, she perceived that the children were 'more engaged and motivated'. Though she recognised this was not easy:

> *I think teachers have got bogged down with 'You have got to teach this' and 'You have got to teach that' and it's thinking 'When do we get the time to do it?' We all know that when you talk to children you find out about them and [. . .] you do get hung up on the everyday stuff like 'oh it's Assessment week', so got to get that out of the way, and it is about making time within that curriculum – that is part of your curriculum – and you make that time to speak to the children and find out about them.* (Final interview)

Conclusion

While all teachers care for their pupils, this is not enough, arguably as this work has shown they need to take the next step and show they care enough to make the time to learn, to understand, and to know their students' social, historical and personal situations – their funds of knowledge. Furthermore, the following step too is crucial and that is enabling the children to use their assets for learning in school. In *BC: RLL*, exploring the children's interests, passions and literacy practices through classroom work and Learner Visits to their homes, expanded the teachers' initially very limited knowledge of their learners and challenged many of their assumptions. Over time, they became much more aware of the diverse social, cultural and linguistic practices in the children's homes. One major element of this understanding lay in the evidence of the presence and use of digital media in the homes (Hill, 2010). As the project progressed the teachers came to recognise the children's individual passions; their extensive knowledge of popular cultural texts and of a range of digital technologies as well as the active, independent ways that children learn outside school and their unique learning identities. Though, as discussed further in Chapter 6, some of the teachers initially shared a degree of 'digital blindness' and did not immediately notice the diversity of digital technology in children's homes. Alongside their own lack of assurance with digital technology, this may have constrained their efforts to challenge the dominant discourse of print-based texts and widen their pedagogic practice affording opportunities for the consumption as well as production of digital texts in school (see Chapter 6).

One of the significant challenges – and eventual strengths – of the project was to question over-generalised assumptions about homes, families and communities and their contributions to the children's literacy and learning. In particular, the teachers came to grasp more fully that 'learning doesn't just happen at school', and that in the words of the often quoted English Bullock Report from nearly 40 years ago:

> No child should be expected to cast off the language and culture of the home as he crosses the school threshold, nor to live and act as though school and home represent two totally separate and different cultures which have to be kept firmly apart.
>
> *(DfES, 1976: 286)*

While progress has been slow since this assertion, at least in England, multiple initiatives to connect home and school and recognise children's home learning have developed. The project *BC: RLL* represents another such attempt. In this the Learner Visits afforded an opportunity for teachers to develop an understanding of the uniqueness of families and children, regardless of their ethnicity or cultural background. Some of the teachers came to appreciate the socially and historically mediated nature of literacy and that, importantly, the children's funds of knowledge drawn from home, rest on a bedrock of them understanding what is expected because the 'learning' – informal as it may be – happens in a known context of familiar activity (Rosemberg *et al.*, 2013). Such perceptions allowed the teachers to consider ways in which they might connect to or 'recover' (ibid.: 69) funds of knowledge in the school and classroom setting, an issue discussed in the following chapter.

6

CHANGING VIEWS OF LITERACY AND PEDAGOGIC PRACTICE

Marilyn Mottram and Fiona M. Collins

Through work in their classrooms, finding out about the children's literacy lives and through research in homes, the *BC: RLL* project teachers were enabled to develop new knowledge and understanding about the children's everyday literacy lives and practices. They were also involved in reflecting upon their own literacy practices and in reading related academic texts. As Edwards (2010) notes, there are often contradictory beliefs within the profession; some educators 'see a family's lack of school-like literacy as a barrier to learning' while others see the 'home literacy practices that are already present – however different from school based literacy – as a bridge to new learning' (189). The project explicitly adopted the latter belief and sought to help teachers explore and extend their own stances and build on the children's home literacy practices that they observed and documented. As the Chief Ofsted Inspector for English, a member of the project's Steering Committee observed: 'What's really important here is what the teachers do with their new knowledge and understanding – what difference it makes' (Jarrett, 2010).

This chapter offers an overview of the shifts in teachers' conceptions of literacy and their pedagogy and practice. Many of the teachers came to recognise the limitations of conceiving of literacy as a fixed unit, a set of skills that can be taught and tested, and began to adopt a social practice approach to literacy. Rather than starting from the more conventional approach of the given school curriculum, the teachers took account of the children's funds of knowledge and sought to integrate these within the curriculum, making subtle pedagogic shifts in the process. A case study explores Viv and Razia's journeys as they learned more about Idris and came to re-shape the one-to-one curriculum provision for him with positive consequences. While embedding this approach more systematically into the wider curriculum represented a challenge, more flexible and responsive classroom approaches were adopted, characterised by greater choice and independence, more space for digital literacy, and more attention to the children's lives and interests.

Changing views of literacy: the start of the journey

From initial interviews it was evident the majority of the teachers held a view of literacy centred on the original, arguably limited, conceptualisations of reading and writing in the UK government's first National Literacy Strategy (DfEE, 1998) which aimed to raise standards of literacy. While the later Primary National Strategy (DfES, 2006) adopted a broader conception of literacy, included oracy and recognised reading and writing on screen as well as on paper, the need to remain focused on 'the basics' continued to dominate the educational agenda in both political and media forums, as indeed it does today (DfE, 2013). An 'autonomous' model of literacy (Street, 1984) continues to underpin policy in England. Framing literacy as a set of self-contained transferrable skills, it recognises neither difference nor diversity in relation to children's everyday literacy practices in different social cultural contexts. Thus the project teachers were oriented towards instructional targets related to the standards agenda; officially they were not expected to pay attention to children's literacy practices beyond those measured by the assessment system.

This orientation was demonstrated through Erica's experience; in her journal at the beginning of the project she explained how she tried to build on one child's interest in fishing to stimulate his reading but that this was difficult because of perceived 'problems':

> Erica: *There are a lot of children with problems here. Also I try to connect you know to individuals, for example Charlie is keen on fishing – we were just talking in class last year and suddenly he was off – all about bait and that and I thought hang on a minute here – so I tried to get some reading books for him he might be interested in.*
> Researcher: *Does that sort of thing happen a lot?*
> Erica: *No not really I guess – rarely in fact and with the SENCO info – well it's a certain sort of info – if you know what I mean – behaviour problems and special needs and that – as well as social problems at home.* (Initial interview)

This position was echoed in other teacher commentaries at the start of the project. For example, teachers referred to 'a lack of support for reading at home', and observed for example that 'it's not the kind of home where literacy counts for much'. These commentaries, which were not atypical, indicate, as Comber and Kamler (2004) point out, that even with the most well-intentioned teachers, pervasive deficit discourses continue to exist in classrooms and are also reflected in records of pupil progress and assessment processes. These can significantly lower teachers' expectations and hinder children's success. Such discourses were not merely employed by the project teachers in relation to children from 'those kinds of homes – if you know what I mean' as one noted, but to children from homes across the socioeconomic spectrum. Initially when teachers voiced their perceptions about their focus children's literacy, where difficulties existed these were often connected to the support they were perceived to receive at home. For example, 'he struggles but then he gets no support for his reading, his parents just don't seem to be interested – they never sign his book' and 'They both work full time so he gets free rein and his homework's never done, but what can you expect?' The strong impression here was that some of the children's homes were deficient in the values and specific literacy practices that schools want to promote.

Additionally, at the start of the project, the teachers, as custodians of literacy in their own classrooms, tended to refer to reading and writing in ways that related to print texts and that focused on the genres expected to be studied. It seems that the work of the New Literacy Studies (Cope and Kalantzis, 2000) has failed to permeate many primary classrooms and that initially few of the teachers involved in the project saw literacy as plural, multiple and an evolving set of practices, rather they tended to perceive it as a singular and definable set of skills and abilities, framed by the assessment system. Additionally few were aware of the deep significance of digital literacy in the lives of their pupils and in the same manner, some of the teachers, as others have also noted (Volk, 2004; Gregory and Williams, 2000) did not fully value the linguistic and cultural advantages that their multilingual learners brought to school. While demonstrating confidence in relation to their knowledge of school-focused curriculum requirements for teaching literacy, it was clear that few of the teachers had given serious thought to the richness of the literacy practices of their pupils beyond school. The research team realised that this was a challenge not only because of the size of task, the timescale and the historical context, but also because the majority of the teachers had not been involved in the earlier project (Cremin et al., 2014), and had not therefore been party to developing new understandings about children's contemporary out-of-school reading practices or identities.

To different degrees, during the course of the project the teachers all expanded their conceptions of literacy according to their experience, the different positions held during their careers, the contexts in which they worked and the case study children upon whom they focused. Three strands of the work in particular encouraged the teachers to widen their conceptualisations of literacy in the twenty-first century, to re-view literacy as social practice and to explore the relationship between literacy and learning. They were involved in:

- Exploring and sharing their own literacy practices. This included, for example, teachers creating their own literacy histories and sharing some of their own involvement in literacy and learning in school. (See Chapter 7.)
- Developing a range of classroom activities designed to involve the children in capturing and communicating their everyday literacy practices.
- Undertaking Learner Visits in order to learn more about the children's literacy and learning practices in the home.

Learning about children's out-of-school literacy practices though classroom activity

In an effort to find out about the children's out-of-school literacy practices the project teachers explored a range of strategies which initially focused upon children's personal reading practices at home. Most teachers invited children to bring in favourite texts to share. When two teachers, Sharon and Jocelyn working in the same school, organised weekly paired reading between their classes and a reading group after school, they found that many of the books which the children brought along linked to popular culture and digital media. As Gregory and Williams (2000) established over a decade ago, many children choose such arguably 'unofficial' (Luke, 1988) texts to read at home. Yet in these teachers' classrooms, books linked to television series or films, and comics and magazines were not regularly available for reading. However, through allowing the children to share their favourites, Sharon and Jocelyn began to recognise and significantly validate a wider than usual range of texts in their classrooms. In this way, they demonstrated both to themselves and to the children that textual diversity was both normal and acceptable. In so doing they were arguably broadening their own conceptions of literacy, and recognising themselves as key agents in maintaining or contesting more limited schooled notions of literacy.

Most of the teachers came to recognise this textual and reader diversity and widened their understanding of the significance of texts that resonate with the lives and interests of the learners. This move to explore the material that children read, wrote or designed privately was enlightening; children led their teachers into new textual territories which prompted the practitioners to broaden the range of material that was welcomed in school. Over time this variously encompassed magazines and comics, graphic novels and catalogues, books, fiction and non-fiction, poetry, newspapers – both local and national, sports reports, junk mail and reading online. For example, after developing Literacy Rivers with their classes (collages of their reading and writing over a weekend), Katy and Charlotte were astonished by the diversity reflected in them. Both were completely unaware that particular children had access to and enjoyed Polish comics and magazines, and were surprised by the number of websites, drawing and computer work depicted. They were also encouraged by the enthusiasm that the children showed when talking about their everyday practices which were more diverse, more demanding and more complex than either of the teachers had appreciated. Charlotte noted: 'I had no idea of all of this, it's just amazing – so much more than I imagined', while Katy observed:

> *I hadn't really thought about it before and I guess if I am honest I didn't think many of them really read or wrote much at home, there is never anything much in their contact books. But there is masses in their rivers, so many examples, so many different kinds of literacy, hidden literacy really. I'm not sure I'd have seen all this as literacy before. It's certainly different from school literacy.* (Journal)

Through making space to discover the children's home literacy experiences and preferences, the teachers gave public credence, space and time to profile a wider conceptualisation of literacy and came to recognise and affirm the children's interests and the ways in which these texts linked to their identities. Significantly, many also began to question the weight afforded school literacy.

In one local authority, the project teachers all sent disposable cameras home with their case-study pupils. Drawing on the work of Pahl (2002) and Yamada Rice (2010), the children were invited to take photos of their literacy lives and from the subsequent teacher pupil and whole class discussions about the images depicted, the teachers were able to ascertain a much richer understanding of the children's perspectives of their home literacy lives. Teachers too took photos of their own literacy lives beyond the school and shared these. A key factor in this was that the children had chosen the images they took so that their own preoccupations and interests were at the forefront. It became clear that reading material was linked to television viewing and to toys (Carrington, 2007) and that family members, grand-parents, siblings as well as parents, and even pets, were important companions in literacy (Gregory, 2007). In the classes' photographs, screens were in evidence and children mentioned television programmes, and many screen-based games and computer activities as well as writing on paper and screen and text messaging. Most striking was the diversity in types of literacy that the children captured in photographs or mentioned when talking about their literacy practices. This surprised the teachers – while cognisant of technological changes they were less aware of the deep commitment, knowledge and expertise which the young people demonstrated in the resultant conversations about their home-based digital practices.

Learning about children's literacy practices through Learner Visits

Through the Learner Visits the teachers were able to observe the children in their home environments and learn from their parents about their daily routines, personal passions and practices; these helped them learn about the children's literacy lives. However, in the data analysis (post visit) sessions with their linked university-based researchers, many of the teachers had to be prompted to recall whether there were computers, Wii, PlayStations and other forms of digital technology visible in the home. It appeared that the presence of digital texts either did not seem obvious enough for some of them to note, that such technology was 'taken for granted' or was perhaps not yet recognised as an integral part of the children's literacy lives. While several teachers commented upon the size of the televisions observed and the fact that these were often playing unwatched in the background during the visits, (potentially affirming a sense of otherness as part of a deficit discourse), others appeared to demonstrate a degree of 'digital blindness' to the presence of technologies in the homes. Several only began to uncover the layers of media and digital literacy on their second or third visit. In addition, in a couple of instances it appeared that the parents themselves may also have viewed literacy as more conventionally book/print bound, and only opened up and shared examples of the children's digital practices when these were explicitly mentioned by the teachers. It is possible that parents may 'not have wanted to own up' to (as one teacher put it) to other forms of literacy, in case these might be considered inferior by their child's teacher. Mollie's mother, for example, pointed out an easel in her kitchen on the first visit and referred to the fun her daughter had copying words and drawing on it. Children's books were also in evidence. On the second visit, through the presence of Mollie and gentle probing, it became evident that a wider range of non-print based texts were also shared and used by Mollie in her home. Her teacher Freda felt that Mollie's mum wanted to be seen as a 'good mum':

> [placing] *what she perceived to be markers of this for literacy there so I'd notice them. It wasn't that she was hiding the digital and other popular texts, but I don't think she saw them in the same way, or thought I wouldn't want to see them perhaps?* (Journal)

Was Mollie's mother concerned about being judged in relation to such texts? This raises the important point about the possible relationship between how parents view texts and how teachers, through sending home particular school literacy work, may frame, define and validate a narrow perception of what counts as valuable literacy.

It is perhaps likely that the teachers were looking for, or were more alert to, more conventional forms of literacy, such as books or newspapers. Framed by notions of school literacy exemplified in policy documentation and the assessment system, perhaps they did not perceive computers and televisions as textual sources or as the focus of a range of literacy practices. With prompting and through discussion and documentation however, the project teachers identified a rich and diverse range of texts that were in everyday use by the children in their homes and communities. These included, for example Wiis, PlayStations, television, CDs, and mobile phones, their own or their parents' and the computer. The computer was also a rich source of literacy activities including playing computer games, searching for cheats, Skyping, emailing, searching for information about subjects of interest in addition to home-work, game playing on internet sites, as well as watching programmes on BBC iPlayer. Observing the children's pleasurable engagement with these multimodal texts in the home, discussing this and the significance of it in children's lives had a significant impact on the teachers' conceptions of literacy. As Andrews and Yee (2006) point out, 'children's own perspectives need to be respected and acknow-ledged so that stereotyped understandings of their lives out of school are not devel-oped' (14). In addition, however, they draw attention to the fact that in terms of investigating funds of knowledge, 'knowledge is not a static entity and new learning and new interests emerge and develop over time' (ibid.) so that pedagogic practices need to be alert to children's changing literacy experiences in order to accord them validity and build upon them; this is particularly the case in an age when new technologies and multimodal texts are flourishing.

The centrality of talk and the influence of the oral tradition such as storying – dialogue and narrative – in some children's families and cultures were also noted by the teachers. They appeared to be particularly visible in multi-ethnic, multilingual communities and where families were in transition; this was expressed emphatically by some parents in such phrases as 'I want her to know where she comes from'.

Children's roots, values and cultures as well as experiences and aspirations were seen to be part of their literacy lives and shared through sustained family narratives, such as that of the grandmother who told stories of her childhood in India to her grand-children in England on Skype from New York. Interestingly, the verbal research medium of interviews and conversations was mirrored in the oral narrative medium of literacy lives explored, moving the teachers' focus away from books and tradi-tional text-based notions of literacy to a broader conceptual frame. In one local authority this was particularly highlighted as teachers noted that 'speaking and lis-tening' in the English curriculum tended to derive from reading and writing, creat-ing a disjunction with the everyday storytelling and dialogue that they heard and saw as a habitual, natural part of some families' lives and cultures. Children's lived experience of talk did not relate easily to speaking and listening 'exercises' or time-bound text-based talk activities which some of the teachers' described were part of their spoken language focus. This lack of alignment prompted conversations about the value of oral storytelling and talk as a tool for learning.

Interrelated shifts in curriculum, pedagogy and practice

As a consequence of undertaking classroom activities and Learner Visits, the project teachers were challenged to develop classroom approaches that built on the children's literacy lives and fostered positive literacy identities. Their reflections were gathered as an 'asset blanket' of the new knowledge they developed (see Figure 5.1). Con-siderable discussion ensued about the commonality demonstrated: the agency, autonomy and personal passion observed, the ways in which the children used digital texts with ease and the highly social and interactive nature of their literacy practices. As a consequence, the teachers were invited to:

- continue to consider the consequences of their new knowledge, and their possible re-positioning in relation to children, parents, communities and other teachers;
- be open to what the children shared of themselves and their learning, incidentally and through observation, reflect on what it might mean and seek to build upon it; and
- plan at least one unit of work which explicitly built on the new strands of knowledge identified and the key elements and consider the consequences for themselves and the children.

Drawing upon the research literature and readings discussed at national meetings (see Chapter 2), the project team and the teachers identified some key elements of classroom communities in which teachers built upon children's funds of knowledge and home learning. The features noted included common elements of good prac-tice, such as offering choice and fostering independence; child ownership of the curriculum; time and space for exploration; collaboration and achers' full involve-ment. It was also recognised that building upon children's twenty-first century literacy practices and connecting to their lives and interests meant quite substantially re-shaping the curriculum, not merely making token gestures. Creating relevant, responsive and co-authored curricula that use children's local community and cultural experience as a starting point for building learning is a complex and long-term task, as previous studies and development projects have shown (Thomson, 2002; Comber and Kamler, 2005; Comber *et al.*, 2007). Indeed, this aspect of the *BC: RLL* project was genuinely challenging to the teachers, who were, in the eyes of their LA co-ordinators, more comfortable drawing on the government's required literacy framework (DfES, 2006) and planning from set objectives rather than planning from principles which drew on identified knowledge about the children. As one LA co-ordinator noted, they are 'used to delivering a given curriculum, not planning a responsive curriculum built on the learners' practices; this makes it very demanding'. The teachers expressed concerns about generalising from the case study homes they had visited and needed considerable support from the LA co-ordinators and the university-based linked researchers to take the risk and make changes to their classroom approaches and curricula based on their observations and new understandings about the young people's literacy passions and practices. The focus on pedagogy and practice created new opportunities and challenges for the LA co-ordinators too, some of whom moved into a position of more active support for the teachers in their classrooms, as they sought to help them move out of their comfort zones and operate more adaptably, building work around children's home learning.

Nonetheless institutional and wider policy contexts constrained the potential pedagogic developments. As González *et al.* (1995: 107) also acknowledged, while curriculum units connected to households' funds of knowledge were created, the task of 'developing a tangible systemic link to classroom practice has been more elusive'. Rodriquez (2013), in reviewing the body of work connected to and originated in the funds of knowledge approach, questions the sustained transformational nature of pedagogical change, suggesting it focuses more on changing teachers than changing practice. She argues that although in the original work examples are offered of 'how practitioners, within the limits of their very real structural constraints, [can realistically] carry out emancipatory and liberatory pedagogies' (González *et al.*, 2005: 2) their efforts are always local and, she suggests that the approach 'never distances itself theoretically or in practice from the surrounding environments of neighbourhoods and society' (Rodriquez, 2013: 112).

Notwithstanding these concerns and the challenges relating to the *BC: RLL* teachers' inexperience at responsive curriculum planning, the practitioners did seek to build on what they had learned and over time some began to adopt more flexible and responsive classroom approaches. These were characterised by: greater choice and independence, more space for digital literacy, and more attention to the children's lives and interests, though such attention did not always follow through into sustained curriculum transformation. As they worked to 'turn around to the children' (Comber and Kamler, 2005: 7) they came to recognise the young people's knowledge, capacities and interests, and began to see these as potential assets for learning. In several cases teachers came to re-connect with young learners whom they had chosen to case study and developed more permeable curricula.

Offering more choice and fostering independence

In appreciating that in the home most of the children made their own choices about their after-school activities and demonstrated considerable independence and volition as learners, most of the project teachers worked to offer more choice and nurture the children's competence as decision makers and autonomous learners in school. In so doing they arguably shifted from enacting more highly performative pedagogies to offering more control to the learners as in competence pedagogies (Bernstein, 1996). These are not simple dualisms however; teachers may employ both a product-oriented pedagogy and one more focused upon the learner at different times, though tendencies can be seen. The data suggest that the project teachers, drawing on their experience of children's agency in the home sought to afford them more space for self-regulation in school, thus orienting more towards competence pedagogies. For example, Charlotte who taught 6–7-year-olds observed: 'For me now, it's more about creating opportunities for the children to get involved in their own learning, by asking them what they want to do and learn about.' This was a marked shift for Charlotte, who in her own words had for planning purposes 'always relied upon downloads before' and now was seeking to make the curriculum relevant offering more choice and 'opening it up to them and not always letting the learning objectives dominate'.

Another teacher, Sophie, the deputy head in her school, noticed that 10-year-old Jo, whom she saw as a 'behaviour problem' in school showed considerable organisational ability and independence at home, choosing, shaping and following through activities related to his own interests, as well as collaborating with family and friends in ways that were supportive of their needs. Sophie was conscious that in class, she offered relatively few opportunities for children to make their own choices and decisions or to take responsibility for their learning in collaboration with others. Working with the oldest children in the school for whom the assessment stakes were high, it may have been the case that Sophie tended towards enacting performance pedagogies, which Bernstein characterised by a focus 'upon a specific output of the acquirer [learner] upon a particular text the acquirer is expected to construct and upon the specialised skills necessary to the production of this specific output, text or product' (1996: 44). In this more 'visible' practice as he describes it, the sequence, pace and criteria for assessment of the products will be known to the pupils in advance. After the Learner Visits in Sophie's account of her practice she appeared to be enacting a more competence oriented pedagogy in which 'the hierarchical rules, the rules of organisation and criteria were implicit and so not known to the pupils'; what Bernstein (1996: 109) describes as invisible pedagogic practice. For example, Sophie planned some open-ended choice driven project work, and set aside quite extensive periods of curriculum time, for this, which was not led or directed 'in the way I usually do' as Sophie observed. Jo found the independent project work on the theme of Exploration highly engaging, and chose to focus on Christopher Columbus. Unusually for him he completed four pieces of homework in a row about this topic, though these pieces were not 'set' in the usual manner with clear expectations, but remained open as spaces for the children to pursue their project work in whatever way they wished. In this way her practice afforded greater agency to the children. Jo also produced detailed drawings for his project with considerable enthusiasm. He knew that his teacher, who had seen his artwork at home, would credit this expertise and perhaps perceived he had been given 'permission' and the independence to use this skill in school. In this way Sophie began to stand back and avoid over-intervention, making the curriculum more accessible, building on the children's expertise and increasing their volition. She commented: 'now I actually let the children run some things. It's a control thing, 'cos if I take away some of my control they're actually easier and more engaged.' In addition, she deliberately took some of the pressure off them, since through the Learner Visits she had come to realise that the parents' aspirations for their children were not focused entirely upon academic standards: 'it's not the be all and end all in their lives; it is in school because that is what we're measured against, but it's not their only concern.' As she loosened the reins of the curriculum, she offered more opportunities for individuality and child-led activities and perhaps also loosened up herself in the classroom. (See Chapter 7 for a case study of Sophie learning about Jo.) Furthermore, she sought to offer more collaborative work and commented on the consequences for the boys she had visited:

> *At home they both helped family members; in school they both tended to dominate, so I set up more group work with less competition and more collaboration. It hasn't all been plain sailing, but they have worked in teams . . . Jo was great helping Emma, just like he helped his sister. I told him so and he grinned.* (Journal)

Issues of control and ownership of the curriculum were also raised by several of the LA co-ordinators, one of whom also noted that their teachers had become 'less controlling of the learning and provision' and were showing an increased 'respect for what and how children want to learn'. This was marked across the project and built upon the self-directed literacy practices seen within the home. It reflected not only less emphasis on performance pedagogies and more orientation to competence pedagogies, but also a 'pedagogy of mutuality' where teachers recognise pupils' agency and build relationships to enhance learning so that 'the distribution of expertise in classrooms and schools shifts and pupils and teachers become self-regulating learners' (Murphy and Wolfenden, 2013: 271).

Including more digital literacy

Despite the wealth of research evidence demonstrating that children's literacy practices in the home are varied and frequently focused on digital media and popular cultural texts (e.g. Marsh, 2004; Grieshaber *et al.*, 2012) it appeared that few of the teachers in the project had previously recognised the breadth of these experiences or considered their place in children's literacy development. As they began to do so, and saw these practices embedded in social contexts in the home, some of the teachers challenged themselves to make more use of the pupils' digital expertise, so that learning in school was more closely rooted in children's life experiences and connected to their expertise.

On visiting the homes of Molly and Lucca (both 4-year-olds) Freda was 'amazed' as she observed each of them log onto the computer and connect to the internet. She found that their favourite sites included Ben 10, Club Penguin and C Beebies, that Molly's hero was Diego (a character from the Nick Junior website), that she regularly texted her uncle on her mother's phone, was devoted to her Mamma Mia DVD and knew many of the songs by heart. Also that Lucca, a young Italian child could access his favourite apps on the family iPad and was knowledgeable about them, often seeking out new ones in the App Store. Freda had not fully appreciated before that this was part of the competence of such young children and while she was somewhat nervous of using technology in school could see this had potential:

> *I would have shrunk away from it in class and might have said, 'that's for when they're a bit older', but because I know now that they're really into the computer at home I try to bring digital things into the classroom more, so the camcorders which I would have been terrified of, I could see that they're so comfortable with. The power of image as well because they do watch a lot of DVD's, and bringing that into the school is a good way forward.* (Final interview)

Offering the children increased chances to use the computer and the digi-blue cameras for the first time had several consequences in her classroom. Lucca was new to the area, had not attended a local nursery and had found it hard to settle in the school, but when he was given the chance to use and share his digital expertise, he developed increased assurance and standing in the classroom:

> *Watching Lucca now I mean he helps everybody in the class if they're going on the computer. He goes through all the different tabs to get to the website so he's using more when he's doing that, he'll shrink away from having to read a school book but he's accessing loads on screen.* (Final interview)

Freda also established a project with her reception children that involved visits from a number of the children's and other local grandmothers to share their skills and life experiences, passions and interests with the children. There were mini teach-ins on yoga, cake baking, philately and gardening for example, some of which were filmed by the children. Significantly, the visits also involved the children teaching their visitors about using digital technology, giving demonstrations, writing instructions and labelling pictures showing how to text, to access and use internet sites and download games for example.

Several teachers, however, did not build explicitly on the children's digital practices, and the discontinuities between their home and school literacies in relation to the use of new technologies remained. In the context of their homes the teachers documented that the young people were engaged in purposeful interactions with multimodal screen-based texts, and although they began to recognise this, they did not feel sufficiently well equipped to bridge the boundaries in school and were uncertain about the way forward. Whether this uncertainty emerged from the tensions around their own identities as literacy teachers in this new media age is not known. There are resonances, however, with McDougall's (2009) assertion of a professional identity crisis in the primary phase due to the changing face of literacy. Sophie, for example, while recognising: 'it's where we have to go, because that's what their future is' and 'it's a huge part of their skill set', perceived she lacked the expertise to plan a curriculum involving digital analysis and production: 'I'm not a digital phobic or anything but I am just not sure how to build on all this.' Sophie and several other teachers explained their limited use of new media for learning on the grounds that they did not feel that they had the assurance or skills to engage with digital texts meaningfully in class. Such a lack of confidence, McDougall (2009) suggests is characteristic of professionals in 'survival mode' and that this creates tension and a reluctance to move forward into curriculum action. It may be this also relates to the 'digital blindness' noted earlier, where some of the teachers appeared not to recognise the presence of digital texts in the home. Was this because unconsciously they were concerned about their capacity to facilitate such learning though their teaching? As Bearne (2009: 184), points out, teachers' awareness and use of 'the semiotic resources of different modes and media and a sense of their distinctive qualities', linked to 'deliberate teaching' are essential if children's contemporary communicative practices are to be given status in the classroom and curriculum. While Sophie might be described as in 'survival mode', like some of her colleagues, she may have been caught in competing discourses which on the one hand espouse new and more progressive views of 'literacy' as plural, while policy and institutional discourses reflect more traditional views. Such tensions, created by coming to terms with competing expectations, can leave teachers 'expressing emotions ranging from a steely determination to resist change, to feelings of confusion, guilt and frustration' (McDougall, 2009: 6). However, some of these tensions may have acted as catalysts to change. The opportunity to undertake Learner Visits and to see 'first-hand' the breadth of digital literacy practices in the home arguably helped many teachers move away from a traditional approach to literacy and in the process not only widened their understanding of new literacies, but opened up for them the relationship between literacy and learning and learning and literacy.

Where teachers felt able to respond to their newly acquired knowledge of children's multi-literacies experience, they noted shifts in pedagogy which altered some of the messages about ownership and control in their classrooms and prompted subtle changes in power relations. Some sought to use the children's evident expertise and knowledge about digital and multimodal texts as a scaffold for new learning, and built upon their prior experience and their enthusiasm. However, including digital and multimodal texts in classroom activities is not an automatic route to a more responsive curriculum. Developing multiliteracies pedagogy (New London Group, 2000; Unsworth, 2001) is not in itself sufficient; there is need, as Lankshear and Knobel (2006) argue, for a new mindset. As the project showed, teachers have to be in a position to recognise the funds of knowledge about texts children possess, to reflect critically on their own practice, *and* to be able to co-construct a pedagogy that can accommodate the shifts in power necessary for greater space to be afforded to children's expertise with and experience of contemporary multimodal and digital texts.

Becoming more flexible, attentive and open

Following the Learner Visits and the teachers' increased awareness of children's learning assets, many voiced the view that they perceived there was more openness and attentiveness in the classroom. One described this as: 'I open up and let the children in now', perhaps referring to her own sense of sharing as well as a more open attitude in the classroom. Moll *et al.* (1992) argue that listening to children, observing them and learning from them is critical and this was evident in the project, as one teacher noted: 'I've slowed down a lot, and take more time to listen to the children and not just say oh I haven't got time for that . . . I make the time.' As the project progressed there were various examples of the teachers being more open to what the young learners brought to school, whether this was in the form of physical artefacts, comments in informal conversations or was expressed in their written work, attitudes or responses. These were attended to more assiduously. As one teacher observed when a child in her class had commented her father had been telling her stories 'without books' she immediately wanted to know more. She found he was a professional storyteller and invited him in to school, noting 'in the past I reckon I would just have said "that's nice" and left it at that'. The teachers commonly sought to create spaces within the curriculum which enabled them as practitioners to connect to the children's personal interests, lives and passions. One found that when she turned her role play area into a building site, it was not only the case study child who revealed an in-depth vocabulary (as she had expected having done Learner Visits) but others too, based she perceived, on having fathers in the trade. Several tried to be less predetermined in planning work and allowed more time and space for children's funds of knowledge to both be drawn upon and help shape the unfolding unit of work or activity. Rachel, for example, teaching a class of 6 and 7-year-olds, began to make use of a new 'Show and Tell' time which she perceived became: 'an unexpected source of information regarding children's literacy practices and identities'. While unsure whether this activity might be seen by other staff as 'time-consuming or elitist', Rachel persisted with it and found the children valued the sustained time to talk to their friends about subjects and objects of their own choosing and recent activities. She believed that setting this time aside to 'actually listen properly' helped her to recognise the highly agentic role children took in their out-of-school lives, some of their multiple literacy practices, the influence and involvement of their siblings, and the potency of popular culture on their emerging identities. She also noted the children brought passion, enthusiasm and motivation and were keen to listen to others, enabling in her words a 'mini-community to be created'.

Later Rachel built on these insights through her Learner Visits; in one she visited 6-year-old Oliver's home where she found he was an ardent Batman fan. He liked dressing up as Batman while watching the film and often acted out the scenes as they were being shown and in role voiced lines from the text 'as if in his own world'. He also had a Batman game on his PlayStation. As Kinder (1991) argues, such transmedia intertextuality is frequently present in children's play as they take pleasure in engaging in the same narrative in a variety of forms, whether through digital texts, print-based media or in play. In talking to him about his Batman PlayStation game, Rachel found that the language Oliver used in this animated conversation was far more advanced than she had heard him use before. Although he was on the Special Educational Needs register at school, at home he used a specialised language and knowledge about the text and could read difficult vocabulary, including for example: 'driving level, gas mask and poisonous spray'. Additionally, and unprompted, he wrote with passion and more skill than usual about his hero while at home. Realising the significance of this for Oliver, Rachel invited him to bring in his costume into school, dress up and talk to the class about being Batman. They kept it a secret between them and he changed in the school office, later leaping into the classroom and taking up Batman poses and posture. In role he responded with assurance to questions about his daily schedule, his friend Robin, imaginary objects attached to his belt and so on. As she noted:

> It demonstrated a 'fund of knowledge' which I might not have tapped into had I not done the interview with mum and probed a bit more . . . It seems to reveal a wealth of interest, motivation and experience around the character, vocabulary specific to the character, plot and genre, and merchandising. (Journal)

Afterwards, in order to support his academic progress, Rachel sought to ensure the extra literacy help Oliver received was embedded in a strong narrative context, linked to Batman and other popular cultural heroes. His investment in this cult figure highlighted for Rachel, as the other teachers also noted, that children's knowledge, experience and home practices may remain invisible in school and their resources for learning may remain unused, unless teachers seek to establish the resources buried deep within their 'virtual schools bags' (Thomson, 2002). The teachers repeatedly voiced the view that they had come not only to see the children differently, but that they were learning to listen in new ways, to 'really hear' as one noted. Another commented: 'my ears are open now, both ears rather than just one of them'. As Charlotte commented:

> *It feels like I pay more attention to them as children now, I listen harder and think, what is he telling me, why is he saying this, rather than just nod and move on if you know what I mean? . . . I find I can make connections if I try, they may not be earth shattering, but it's personal and they know it.* (Interview)

These more attentive child-focused approaches indicate a disposition towards a more culturally responsive pedagogy (Conrad, 2012) which recognises culture as a lens 'through which human beings experience the world and is an integral part of their students' identities, worldviews, etc' (31). However, as Conrad warns, such a disposition has to be deeply embedded if it is to contribute to a culturally responsive frame: 'to engage in personalized pedagogy, what is being taught and how it is being taught, has to be meaningful to the teacher and cannot simply be something the teacher says or does' (2012: 32).

Those teachers who were able to 'open both ears' and had the confidence to take time with learning, not be driven by the perceived demands of curriculum delivery, found that their practices fundamentally shifted to accommodate to the newly acquired information about the children's diverse communicative practices, capacities, interests and cultural investments.

Planning for a more permeable literacy curriculum

The project teachers frequently commented upon the increased flexibility and assurance needed to shift to a more responsive curriculum, which also connected to the prescribed curriculum and its multiple objectives. They were very challenged by this strand of the work and some faltered, though many planned work which offered more choice and created more 'open' spaces in which teachers and children could explore together, taking an arguably more iterative journey across a day or in a unit of work, rather than a more prearranged route. In addition, the content of units did not always remain the exclusive domain of the teachers, nor was the plan rigidly adhered to; rather the teachers sought more explicitly to share some of the responsibility for the selection of content and areas of enquiry with the children. As Kara noted: 'For me what's been important has been making the curriculum flexible enough to allow time for children's interests to be addressed ... and I'm working on making learning relevant for the children, I want them to own it.' There were multiple examples of teachers making small shifts and being more open to what young learners bring, as well as sharing more of themselves with children and parents and helping to build new kinds of communities. Some of the teachers were supported in moving from the pervading school-centric culture and prescribed curricula by individual headteachers who, through meeting with their project teachers and learning about the insights gained from the Learner Visits, were more open to developing a curriculum more connected to the children's funds of knowledge. As one headteacher observed: 'how dare we have created and imposed a curriculum all these years that doesn't have anything to do with the children's lives?'

One of the pairs of project teachers, who sought to involve all members of staff in building on the new knowledge and understanding of children's home learning practices, described how their curriculum planning became more focused on children's needs and interests and less focused on set outcomes. They talked about tensions between two seemingly irreconcilable approaches: the need to keep high expectations of all children ensuring the highest possible outcomes related to the standards agenda and the need to plan more flexibly for learning that is more open-ended and responsive to what the learners bring:

> *I think what we tend to do is . . . over-scaffold the learning. We try to ensure the best work from all the children – and we really try to ensure their success really. But it just doesn't leave any space.* (Final interview)

The Learner Visits provided new insights about how rich and diverse the children's everyday interests and cultural practices were outside school and the teachers in this staff team were eager to find ways of organising learning in school to take account of this, nevertheless they found this very demanding:

> *But, how do we do this? How do we build on this so that we have a curriculum that is more child-led but still providing challenge and high quality learning opportunities for all the children?* (Journal)

As they planned literacy units of work, the staff team considered whether or not there were sufficient opportunities for children to have ownership and make choices about the learning and whether there was sufficient space for connections to be made to children's lives and interests. They were willing to be more flexible so that time could be well-matched to learning and not pre-planned. One pair started a unit of work by sharing a personal memory box with the class:

> *The idea of using memory boxes was a perfect starting point for our poetry work. So, for example, this class is very boy-heavy and we really didn't think that they would respond to the idea of sharing memory boxes – after we shared our own memory boxes we weren't certain whether they would engage, but actually they took it on wholesale. In fact they took over. It became theirs!* (Final interview)

The teachers were surprised and delighted at the change in attitude and motivation, but the breadth of learning took unexpected turns:

> *They came up with this list of protocols to support their individual presentations and some basic rules about how everyone was to be respectful . . . and they even made sure that there was a timetable for presentations* [to each other's class's] *each day and*

this time was secured. It was really really good. And so much writing came from it. (Final interview)

In this context it appeared the children were afforded more control and seized it; they exercised their individual and collective agency and the teachers took more of a facilitative role and perceived that this subtly shifted their relationships with the young learners, who were 'eager to lead and more committed than usual'. As a consequence of appreciating the rich multidimensional nature of the children and the families whose homes they visited, the project teachers came to recognise the need to flex their classroom approaches in order to enable increased choice and ownership, more links to the digital practices of their world and more openness on their own part. They began to see that the perceived boundaries between school and home learning were in fact less clearly defined than they might have supposed and that there was value in validating home literacy experiences and connecting to them in the classroom. In commenting upon the consequences of the Learner Visits in relation to developing the curriculum, one LA co-ordinator summarised her perception of this enhanced permeability by observing that in her group there had been:

- *A move from sometimes uninspiring and unquestioning following of a given curriculum towards a more innovative and confident approach which takes into account the unique nature and literacy practices of the individuals in the class.*
- *Less controlling of the learning and provision and respect for what and how children want to learn.*
- *Greater respect for the children and their families; less judgemental and assumptive attitudes.*
- *More openness in trying to understand what the learning needs are, based on genuine interest in their backgrounds, their personal and their family strengths.* (Report)

It appeared that teachers and LA co-ordinators were beginning, many for the first time to acknowledge the crucial significance of creating learning environments that allow agency and decision making to be experienced by all learners and to develop curricula which were more open, permeable and responsive to children's everyday literacy lives beyond school. There were also local links made in one school to a community theatre project which foregrounded the history of the local community and to which the project teachers, their classes and the children's families were specifically invited to contribute. This not only honoured the teachers' new knowledge but widened it still further, providing a connected curriculum focus which expanded well beyond the remit of the actual project year.

However, it should be acknowledged for many of the teachers, radically reshaping the curriculum around children's funds of knowledge was a step too far in the highly prescribed and controlling accountability culture in which they worked. Many of the younger practitioners expressed the view that they had not been expected to plan literacy curricula before and explained they were used to relying upon commercial plans or plans received from the school's literacy co-ordinator or age phase leader for example. Significant support was needed for these and other teachers and although as described above, there were forward moves, the tight timeframe of the project with only the summer term for such explicit development work (following the Learner Visits), constrained these developments still further. While there was some discomfort in attending to practices aimed to open the school to home knowledge and make the curriculum more permeable, there was also productive friction in taking risks in order to increase understanding. For some of the teachers in the project, the work meant coming to understand and acknowledge that they were in a position of power in defining for parents and children what counts as valid and valuable literacy. Greater cultural responsiveness led to asking themselves some hard questions about their own – and the school's – role in either creating or breaking down barriers to learning between home and school experience. What became clear, however, through observation and practice, was that when the teachers adopted a more open and responsive approach in the classroom, there was a marked difference in the children's motivation and engagement as learners. This can be seen in the following case study.

Viv and Razia learn about Idris: a case study

This case study shows how one teacher steadily developed a more open and flexible approach to teaching literacy and to learning as a result of developing her pedagogy to accommodate recognition of the children's funds of knowledge. Viv, the Deputy Head and Razia, who taught 10–11-year-olds both worked at St Mary's Primary School in a large city authority where all the children speak languages other than English at home and in the community. (See Chapter 8 for a fuller case study of the school as a whole.) Razia and Viv identified 3 children aged between 10 and 11 as their focus group for the project:

> *We selected three children from different ethnic groups, different home languages and different abilities. They were chosen for different reasons: hard-to-reach parents . . . the older children often came in alone or they were being tracked for literacy . . . reluctant writers.* (Interview)

One of these children was Idris. Viv recorded what she knew about him:

> *I am working with him for one-to-one tuition and find him fascinating. . . . He is a level 3a reader but he doesn't usually read much at home. He needs a lot of support with spelling and sentence structure.* (Journal)

She expressed concern for him as an unmotivated reader, who did not read much at home and was not a library member. Later that term, however, when the class were asked to draw images of a reader, Idris chose to draw an 'X Factor' contestant showing Jamie Archer as a reader (see Figure 6.1). In Viv's session with him she was able to talk to him about this and his other popular cultural and reading

FIGURE 6.1 Idris' *Draw a Reader*

preferences. She discovered that they shared a love of biographies and was thrilled to find they also shared a similar sense of humour. The nature of the one-to-one tuition sessions began to change as Viv was able to make connections with the things she now knew about Idris' interests and choices. As he enjoyed biographies they decided to write autobiographies and Idris planned his by plotting his timeline (see Figure 6.2), including:

- 1998 – The day I was born.
- 2001 – I went to Bangladesh for 2 months.
- 2002 – I had started nursery when I was four, my sister was born as well.
- 2003 – I went to my first cinema.
- 2004 – My little brother was born.
- 2005 – I went my first football match.
- 2007 – My baby brother was born, went Bangladesh again.
- 2009 – Won against a football team. I also got my 50m badge.
- 2009 – Started Year 6.

In noting events that marked important times in his life, Idris shared these with Viv and this opened up additional discussions. In this way she was able to develop new knowledge about him which she perceived began to have an impact on their relationship in the one-to-one sessions and beyond.

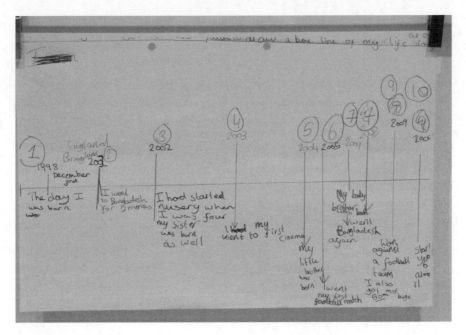

FIGURE 6.2 Idris' timeline

Visiting Idris at home

In undertaking Learner Visits to Idris' home, Razia and Viv who went together began to expand their knowledge and understanding of this young Bangladeshi boy. On their first visit they were accompanied by Anna, a support teacher. All three teachers walked to Idris' home after school one day. Idris led the way. Viv recorded her feelings:

> *The household visit really does begin long before you enter the home. We walked from school with Idris chatting away, telling us about the shops as we walked past: 'In God we Trust' written in Arabic over one of the shop doors. The road was very busy with lots of litter and fast food venues, food being sold on the pavement, chicken roasted on a spit, groups of men standing around – so very noisy. Razia said it was a 'buzz' and 'like Pakistan'.* (Journal)

The team all noted how proud Idris seemed as he 'marched ahead, leading the way'. When they arrived at the flats Idris pressed the buzzer and called upstairs. As they began to walk up the steps to the top floor flat, other children came out of the various flats and were peering over the balcony smiling and laughing:

> *There was such great excitement that we were visiting Idris' family. Samara had her head through the railings! There are six children in the family and it's a two bedroom flat!* (Learner Visit notes)

As the team entered the flat they all immediately noticed and recorded some salient things:

> *A nail was prominent on the door and the school book bags were hanging there. Idris immediately hung his book bag on the nail. Music was playing in one of the flats below, the toddler was singing and playing with a small pile of books, the Qu'ran was on the shelf, and there was a faint smell of curry cooking in the kitchen.* (Learner Visit notes)

Viv, Anna and Razia talked about being struck by the warmth of their welcome and by the way that the atmosphere lightened very quickly when Viv shared some of her own experiences living in the area as a child when her own family arrived from Ireland to settle in England. Sharing this experience opened the door for Idris' mother to talk about her life in Bangladesh. The team noted how proud his mother was of her children's successes. She spoke to them about her eldest son, Jugpal for example explaining that:

> *He started at St Mary's when he was aged five, he couldn't speak any English and I couldn't speak any English either . . . he couldn't do anything . . . and now he is nearly twenty and he is finishing college.* (Transcription from home visit)

She also talked about Idris' sister Samara who had started at the local secondary school. Idris showed them some books that Samara had brought home from the school library for him and it was clear there was a tiered support system between the siblings for reading, books and school work. Throughout the visit Idris' 2-year-old brother was playing at reading some picture books and he repeatedly took books to Viv to read to her. As the teachers commented afterwards the audio recording was constantly interrupted by the baby shouting, laughing and singing. When Idris' older brother, Jugpal arrived there was additional laughter and evident camaraderie, as he teased Idris' about his love of Michael Jackson and passed comments on Idris' skills at X–Box and football.

After the visit, Anna's reflective summary noted that for her the salient moments were:

- *The nail on the wall*
- *The tiered down effect of older siblings reading with young ones*
- *Samara bringing books home for Idris/Idris reading to his younger brother*
- *Mother reading books brought home by Samara*
- *The little board books that were on the floor for the baby*
- *The sharing on the computer with Jugpal and Idris.* (Journal)

A key consequence for all three teachers was the immediate impact the Learner Visit had on their relationship with Idris at school. Razia captured this when she commented, 'I saw him differently, I just saw him differently because I knew him as a whole person.'Viv also added that Idris' mum had seen her across the playground the next day, and came straight over to her and gave her a hug.

The initial notes about Idris (recorded in his teacher's portfolio) suggested that he did not read at home, that he was disaffected, unmotivated and that the family did not use local facilities such as the library. The Learner Visits revealed that Idris did read at home – both on and off screen. By adopting a more inclusive view of what counts as reading, the school team were able to see a greater breadth of reading experiences in Idris' life. He engaged with his X-Box and with computer games and digital texts daily with his older brother. He enjoyed biographies linked to popular celebrities, was a football fan keen to follow his team's results, and enjoyed watching popular TV shows like X Factor. Additionally they noted his sister brought books home for him from her school library and he even ordered some from her, requesting another in a series or books his friends had recommended. It was clear that the siblings supported each other's learning and the teachers also found that his mother reads their school books too – for her own learning. Idris' parents deeply value education: the nail on the wall and its incidental yet daily use was a potent sign of the importance given to school books in his home. The Learner Visits, in which the teachers were positioned as learners and enquirers, uncovered a complex web of learning processes and social interactions across a diverse range of situations and contexts in Idris' life. They raised questions about learning and pedagogy and the implications of a deeper understanding of Idris' and other learners' cultural and socio-historical situations.

The effect of recognising Idris' funds of knowledge

Viv's discoveries about Idris and her fuller understanding of his potential for learning are a reminder of the need for pedagogy that is informed by authentic knowledge of children's home learning and literacy experience, the 'informal' learning highlighted by Moll *et al.* (2013). There is a danger that if these funds of knowledge are not taken into account, children will lose confidence in their own literacy practices (Levy, 2009) or, worse, become alienated from an educational system that they feel they cannot or do not wish to 'buy into'. Views of situated learning have led to an understanding of communities of practice (Lave and Wenger, 1991) but this case study, and the project as a whole, suggests that there should be a closer focus on where the communities of practice of the school and the home intersect and overlap. If, as Wenger (1998) argues, communities of practice develop through 'the sustained pursuit of a shared enterprise' (45) then, as argued in Chapter 2, the classroom needs to become a site which fosters the mutual exchange of children's and adults' funds of knowledge and the basis for the development of a newly forged community of practice. When Viv learned about Idris' home literacy experience and interests, she found a new dimension of shared understanding which not only informed her classroom practice, but shifted her view of literacy learning and where it might be located. Lave (2008), in arguing against the generally held view that learning means moving away from the ordinary and everyday, sees such a view as creating divisions and polarisations, shown in this project as a separation between home and school knowledge. He posits: If learning isn't movement away from ordinary social existence, perhaps it is movement more deeply into and through social existence (Lave, 2008: 13).

An intersection between the community of practice in the classroom and that of the home offers the possibility of such a move into and through a newly forged social existence, where pedagogy and the curriculum become hospitable to the children's funds of knowledge.

Conclusion

Initially working with fairly narrow conceptions of literacy, defined by the education system and its attendant assessment framework, many of the teachers came to expand their understanding of literacy significantly and sought ways to reflect this enriched and more diverse conception of literacies in school. Although some lacked confidence about linking to and extending children's digital competencies, even the most digitally averse teachers came to see the importance of home digital and media experience. In taking a more culturally responsive stance, the teachers not only widened their professional horizons, but began to work to recognise and validate the everyday literacy lives and popular cultural interests of the children, creating more responsive and flexible curricula that sought to build on the children's funds of knowledge and learning practices observed in homes. Not only did many of the teachers reconceptualise literacy to encompass a social literacies perspective which acknowledged the multiplicity of children's communicative practices, in some cases these new understandings led them to question the dominant discourse and encompassed shifts in power relations in the classroom.

There were significant changes in teachers' self-perceptions and professional practice, though many found this mediational work between home and school difficult in relation to fully transforming the prescribed curriculum. There are many potential barriers to shifts in practice becoming embedded within and across schools, especially if the school discourse about literacy is tightly framed and if national policy is changing (this was happening at the end of the project). If the school itself is not a community of practice, then individual teacher action may be significantly hampered. In re-examining the significance of 'productive pedagogies', developed in order to create more equitable educational experiences for marginalised students, Lingard and Keddie, drawing on Giroux, note that:

> Maximising the potential of the productive pedagogies is supported by a particular kind of teacher – a public and oppositional intellectual who takes seriously 'the supposition that in order for social arrangements to be otherwise, they must be able to think and act 'against the grain.
>
> *(Giroux, 2003: 6, quoted in Lingard and Keddie, 2013: 444)*

In the *BC: RLL* project, some teachers found it hard to go against the grain, whilst others found the friction caused by doing this resulted in a more satisfying and reflexive pedagogy, one that built upon a conception of literacy as social practice – as contextualised and culturally embedded – recognised the significance of the children's actual uses of reading and writing in everyday life and sought to build bridges between home and school practices. However, opening the classroom (and, indeed, the eyes and ears of the teacher) to new forms of text or different kinds of knowledge is not without risk. Some teachers were able to run with complexity and uncertainty as they strove to assimilate their growing awareness of the children's and families' funds of knowledge. That others were not so able to do this, or maintain their initial impetus in making changes, does not suggest wrong headedness or recalcitrance; rather, it may indicate the persistent pressures and constraints of the politics of literacy and the curriculum. In accountability cultures which retain a highly stratified view of learning, space for the development of professional knowledge or the emergence of a newly forged professional mindset is limited. This makes the contribution of participatory research projects even more significant, as they afford opportunities to develop new knowledge and understanding, question and contest poorly conceptualised policies and explore possible ways forward theoretically and pedagogically.

7

SHIFTING POSITIONS AND BUILDING RELATIONSHIPS

Teresa Cremin and Marilyn Mottram

The *BC: RLL* project invited teachers to position themselves alongside the children as learners not only to find out about the children's worlds, but also to share something of their own. The practitioners were encouraged to consider their own literacy lives and diverse twenty-first century literacy practices and the embedded nature of literacy in different cultural contexts beyond school, in order to explore the complex relationship between literacy and learning. An underlying assumption of this aspect of the work was that in sharing their literacy lives, teachers would be sharing something in and of themselves and would take a more personal stance and position in the classroom. In addition, and significantly, it was expected that through sharing something of themselves and inviting the children to do likewise, this would prompt more open and potentially stronger and more equivalent relationships between teachers and children, built on increased knowledge of one another as individuals. This perception was based on findings from *Teachers as Readers: Building Communities of Readers*, in which the sharing of teachers' reading lives was seen to be pivotal in the development of a shared/third space between teachers and children and the growth of strong reader relationships (Cremin *et al.*, 2014). It was also assumed that the opportunities for interaction with parents through the Learner Visits, especially when several repeat visits were made, would foster the development of new parent–teacher relationships.

This chapter offers an overview of the teachers' initial understanding and practice with regard to sharing something of themselves as literate individuals and lifelong learners. It highlights the challenges involved and offers examples of the ways in which teachers sought to do this through classroom activity and how, in the context of the Learner Visits, they found themselves doing so spontaneously. This overview is followed by a case study of one teacher Sophie who, like her colleagues across the project, found that shifts in her positioning and being more open and sharing something of herself as an individual, not just as a teacher, opened up new positions to the children and prompted new relationships to develop with them and their families.

The start of the journey

At the start of the year it appeared that while many of the teachers shared with children their personal pleasure in pieces of children's literature, few referred to sharing anything of their literacy lives beyond school. As one typically noted, 'In story time I will say this is one of my favourite books. But I don't know whether I have ever shared . . . well what *I* read'. Their comments in the initial interviews suggest that they had not previously considered positioning themselves as readers or writers in class and had not shared their literacy lives in school. This was viewed as a novel idea. Several were initially reticent to talk about their literacy practices and preferences, and many questioned the value of it given the constant pressure of time. Some also expressed concern that the children would not understand, for example one noted: 'a lot of our children haven't got any English at all so it's difficult to have that kind of personal conversation.'

Others were unsure that sharing something of their own lives and literacy practices would be of interest or make an impact on their relationship with the younger learners. Freda and Ludmilla, for example, asserted from the outset that their children were too young to be interested, and it was only after considerable encouragement that they began to share something of their literacy worlds. Evelyn too initially felt that the age difference meant few children would find connections with her interests and that she did not know theirs:

> If I still had young children I would find it quite different because I would be much more on their wavelength. But I tend not to watch CBeebies very often. So I find this quite hard, it's the stage at teaching which I am at, and the age of my children. (Initial interview)

Several teachers encountered conceptual and practical difficulties in developing this arguably more personal, discursive and reciprocal stance towards teaching and learning literacy and did not fully explore the possibilities. These practitioners tended to equate it with simply modelling activities (such as reflecting on their reading across 24 hours and sharing this) in order to prompt the children to share their literacy lives. They appeared to view their examples instrumentally as models for classroom activity, not as opportunities to reflect upon the role and nature of literacy and learning in everyday life. It is possible that these teachers' frame of reference was teaching, not teaching and learning. They may have implicitly construed teaching as a performance, such that straying into new unrehearsed and undeveloped areas and activities challenged the ways in which they constructed their professional identities and roles. Several expressed the view that while interested themselves in considering how their literacy and life experiences impacted upon their identity positioning and classroom practice, this would be of limited value to the children. It was perceived as personally and intellectually interesting, but was not seen to be educationally relevant. They were also reticent to risk introducing a more personal dimension through sharing something of themselves. As Glazier (2005) posits: 'One of the most difficult notions ... for teachers to consider is the idea that who they are and what they have experienced necessarily impacts on both how and what they teach' (231).

A common concern was one of personal exposure, typified in the worry, as one expressed it, of 'exposing myself, my life and that'. It was clear that for some the concept created such a degree of discomfort that it challenged their perceptions of the professional role. Tensions around the private and public dimensions of being teachers were evident in the hesitancy expressed. This was also noted by Debbie, who initially tried to encourage colleagues in school to share their reading lives:

> *We did it as a staff – we asked on a teacher day – everyone to bring in their favourite book and to talk to other people about it. And there were so many staff that were SO reticent. They just didn't want to do it. So we've got some work to do to get the teachers talking to the children about their reading lives.* (Interview)

After 12 years of prescribed literacy practice in line with government expectations in England (DfEE, 1998; DfES, 2007), the project teachers, many of whom had been trained within this period, found the open-ended and innovative nature of this concept challenging. It is not part of the current literacy discourse and while some may have referred to their lives in the context of personal, social and health education, their practices in literacy teaching may have become more tightly framed by the specified literacy objectives (DfEE, 1998; DfES, 2007). It has been argued that these objectives emphasised the development of literacy skills at the relative expense of children's emotional, social and cognitive engagement as readers and writers (Dombey, 1998; Frater, 2000; Cremin, 2009). So perhaps these teachers, seeking to ensure curriculum coverage at the required pace (Burns and Myhill, 2004), had also become somewhat disengaged from the affective, experiential and creative nature of language and literacy. Perhaps they had begun to deliver the given curriculum in a potentially technicist manner. Perhaps too, their work to develop children's reading comprehension had been framed predominantly by reference to the text, with less reference to the readers and their personal responses. If so this would have reduced still further the likelihood that teachers or children share personal connections and make the life to text and text to life moves that scholars argue are key to full and affective engagement (Meek, 2001; Martin, 2003; Krashen, 2004). Additionally, with a policy emphasis on synthetic phonics in reading instruction and a focus on print-based materials, it is not surprising that the teachers found it challenging to afford open discursive spaces for conversations about the lived experience of literacy in the twenty-first century.

However, despite the challenge of adopting a more personal stance and sharing their literacy lives with the children, several of the teachers were aware that this might have potential in relation to the project's exploration of connections between teachers, children, and parents. At the outset most voiced the view that they intended to investigate this, for example:

> *I think I share my life unconsciously, but the project will hopefully make me do it more consciously, make links to their literacy lives and consider the benefits – if there are any.*
> (Initial interview)

Over time, a continuum of practice developed: some teachers actively grasped the concept and developed what they considered to be a more open personal stance in the classroom, one which encompassed sharing their literacy practices and themselves as learners, while others made occasional forays in this area and continued to perceive this as a bounded 'activity', not an act of subtle re-positioning. In Moll's (1992) research, while the teachers were supported as ethnographers, and shared their own narratives when visiting homes, their lived experience of literacy was not foregrounded, nor were they explicitly invited to consider sharing more of their personal lives or literacy practices in the context of classrooms. In this way the project *BC: RLL* sought to open up new opportunities for relationship building within and beyond schools.

Sharing literacy practices in school

The research data on Reading Teachers – teachers who read and readers who teach (Commeyras *et al.*, 2003) from the earlier project (Cremin *et al.*, 2009), were shared with the *BC: RLL* project teachers. They were interested to find out more about the reciprocal reader relationships that developed as a consequence of the reader to reader sharing which developed. In the new project teachers engaged in reading and writing histories and in particular discussed their memories of the texts, contexts, and role of significant others in their literacy histories. The activities undertaken had a marked impact on several of the practitioners and LA co-ordinators, many of whom expressed surprise about the intensely social nature of their early and ongoing experiences of literacy. For example, in reflecting upon their early memories of learning to read, several teachers noted the significance of their family's religious practices, or recalled swapping and sharing comics and magazines with friends. Over time many came to appreciate the situated nature of their contemporary literacy practices too, both as teachers in school and as individuals in their homes and communities. In their current lives, the teachers offered diverse examples such as: taking part in a local amateur dramatic production; making Christmas lists; handwriting letters and cards to particular friends; searching Friends Reunited; creating Facebook pages; discussing news items; and researching holiday venues on the web and in travel books and magazines, all of which they noted differed according to context and the presence and involvement of others.

While reflecting upon their literacy histories and identities served as a catalyst for their widening conceptualisations of literacy, at first the emphasis in the classroom focused on teachers explicitly talking about their reading practices and early reading memories with the children. Most were surprised that the children were interested in their reading practices. For example:

> We talked about the autobiographies that my TA [Teaching Assistant] and I were reading – and – we swapped these in front of the children and they realised that they knew the faces of these celebrity writers and really seemed excited that they knew something about us. They kept saying 'I know her' – 'she's in my mum's magazine' and so on. I was surprised because they're only four. (Interview)

Some also shared life experiences triggered by children's literature which was being shared in school. As one noted, 'I linked my personal experiences to the books we've been reading – Seal Surfer by Michael Foreman – I talked about my experience of surfing, the stinging cold and the wet and the roughness of the sea'. The project teachers early sharing focused on books; this confirmed other project data suggesting that the teachers began with a relatively narrow conception of reading. Although gradually, and with support, they began to share more of the textual diversity in which they engaged, including magazines, newspapers, catalogues and travel texts for instance: 'I share my literacy life with my children at every available opportunity now . . . on my journey to school I read the free papers every day and I show them these and sometimes we talk about news items.' Informal, spontaneous conversations emerged in classrooms about what teachers were reading about: for example current news issues, hobbies, families and holiday plans and these were discussed, albeit briefly and often in small group contexts. In these spaces the children began to find out more about their teachers – their interests, values and emotional responses to texts. For the teachers this was new territory; many commented that these incidental conversations created, as Katy described it, 'space just to talk and to hear their views too'. Some also began to reflect upon and share aspects of their writing practices beyond school, as Charlotte observed:

> I've been trying to weave into my teaching some aspects of my home literacy life, to take the focus away from whole books or composing something at length and have been sharing snippets of whatever I'm involved in. It really helped before we did the Writing Rivers, I think it helped them realise we all write for different reasons and use lots of different forms. (Interview)

In undertaking Writing Rivers, an idea developed from Cliff-Hodges' (2010) use of Reading Rivers, the teachers paid attention to their writing practices as adults and made large collages of the range of writing activities they participated in over the weekend – for example the lists and notes, cards, emails and texts, forms and work plans and other documents completed on-screen or on paper. For several teachers this prompted a wider recognition of their practices as writers and an increased awareness of audience.

> It was only when we discussed it that I began to recognise, well notice all the things I do write. I am a writer, it's just that I don't well write much extended fictional stuff,

but it all depends upon your view of writing I suppose, I am on email a lot and I've set up my own Facebook account. (Interview)

Again surprisingly in the teachers' eyes, the children appeared fascinated:

Obviously they see me writing, I'm constantly writing, but that has more to do with the curriculum, so I've been trying to share more of my real world — out of school writing. When we did Writing Rivers a group of children gathered round mine and kept asking questions and making comments, 'I didn't know you doodled, when was that?' 'Where are you going on holiday then?' 'Do you do Facebook Miss?' 'Don't you Tweet?' 'My mum doesn't like texting' and so on. I think they began to see me differently just from that one collage of a weekend's worth of writing! (Interview)

One teacher, Sharon, began to write alongside children in her class making her own choices in independent writing time and keeping her own writer's notebook. She came to view this practice as salient in influencing the children's views of her as a literacy learner. It also helped her see herself as 'sharing her literacy' and triggered conversations about her life beyond school. Another teacher Freda took in evidence of being challenged as a writer and shared the crumpled drafts of notes she had written to her son's teacher. She explained:

It took me three attempts because I didn't want it to have any spelling mistakes, and I was particular about it. I screwed up the first pieces and found myself thinking this is how the children must feel, so I took them in and told them about it and explained that I'd been nervous and wanted to get it right and I wasn't satisfied so I kept starting again. They were amazed! They are only four or five after all, they probably think adults never make mistakes and get it right first time! (Interview)

In sharing something of their literacy practices and using the self as a teaching resource, the teachers invited children to share in a not dissimilar manner. All the teachers were urged to extend the regularity and depth of their own sharing and to consider their own practices and lives as a resource. Many seized opportunities to share specific experiences and anecdotes, for example Rachel brought in her old exercise books from secondary school which prompted considerable conversation and shared an ongoing saga with her class about the pigeons nesting on her balcony. Another teacher Kara filmed an interview with her daughter and partner about their reading at home which her class found fascinating and Erica showed the children the form she had completed to join a local adult education keep fit class; this triggered an extended conversation about the absence of a local swimming pool and their teacher's desire to lose weight, and generated personal connections: 'loads of them were saying their mums' were on diets too and their older sisters, they knew a lot about calorie counting – that surprised me.'

There was little documented evidence of teachers sharing their digital practices or highlighting the multimodal nature of their engagement with texts as viewers and media users. Although diversity was inherent in the teachers' Reading and

Writing Rivers, in their interviews and reflective notes, few mentioned talking in class about the TV or films they watched, the music they listened to or the computer games they played. An implicit hierarchy appeared to exist, perhaps perceptions of the appropriacy of popular cultural interests in school held some teachers back as Lambirth's (2003) work has shown.

Exploring the consequences

Several of the teachers perceived there were indirect benefits from the reciprocal process of sharing aspects of their literacy practices and learning lives in classrooms. Many not only observed that in opening up more, new conversations and unexpected discussions were triggered, and also that this created new connections. Sally felt it prompted her to 'recognise the value of relationships' and noted 'I think probably this project has helped me to get back to my instincts more – it's easy to get bogged down in this job – and in Year 6 it's really difficult not to become obsessed with the SATS' (national assessment tests). For Erica there were other consequences related to subtle shifts in her positioning in the classroom:

> *I think they are beginning to see me as an actual person rather than someone who lives in the school. Maybe it's because I've been in some of their homes and well I do share more, just mundane things and thoughts as well as more focused stuff like when we were discussing holidays we all brought photos in and they were fascinated by mine, particularly my children.* (Interview)

Another teacher Carol noted that while she had talked to her class about her young son's exploits, she had never previously shared anything of her literacy life: 'What I don't do is talk to them about the books or other texts that I have read; I don't know that they would be very interested, because they're adult books.' Later she reported having taken *The Hobbit* into school; the 5 and 6-year-olds in her class were surprised by the size and length of the book and the absence of pictures. This encouraged Carol, who talked of a gradual change in their relationship as she opened up and shared other aspects of her reading life and found out more about theirs. In Kara's classroom, a week's work developed in response to a news article which she had mentioned in passing. Like their teacher, the children were incensed at the injustice and animal cruelty involved and they spontaneously decided to research the issue, focusing on animal protection and writing letters of complaint to the local newspaper about their coverage of the incident.

At the last national meeting, the project teachers were asked to identify the most significant elements of the work from their point of view; over half noted that personal sharing, whether in the context of the classroom or in the Learner Visits had been highly influential. This was confirmed in both their written reflections and the final interviews. Freda, for example, who had been teaching for eight years, felt this aspect of the work had introduced her to a 'kind of different way of being' in the classroom. She had mainly taught older learners and commented

'I'd like to think I've always been quite down to earth and approachable, but it's always been being a teacher, not me being me'. In her teacher training she did not believe it had ever been suggested that she might share anything of herself or make personal literacy based connections in the classroom:

> We were told not to smile before Christmas and that teaching was like acting, 'cos you have to give a certain appearance and everyday you have to go in and be the same kind of thing. I'm not sure I agree with that now. (Final interview)

Freda also revealed how the external inspection framework and her desire to do her best had probably prevented her developing a more overt personal engagement with the children; previously she had perceived this was inappropriate:

> When you become a teacher, you learn that you have to do things the correct way to help children learn . . . and when you are observed by Ofsted there are things you have to put in place and what you have to say and do. But now if there was an Ofsted inspector sitting there I would still share part of myself, whereas before I wouldn't have dared because I would have thought they'd think that was wrong . . . I think you have to bring your personality in, and that's what's so good because obviously everyone's different so they're bringing a new dimension into the classroom, a personal dimension. (Final interview)

The project, combined with the new challenge of teaching younger children, had, she believed, prompted her to reconsider her stance and identity as a teacher in the classroom, and as a consequence a new degree of openness and authenticity developed. In Freda's view this had a positive influence on her relationships with the children and the way they viewed her:

> You have to find ways of delving deeper, the sharing yourself bit I think that's become really significant, I need to be doing that all the time with the children, and they open up if you share a bit of you, they open up to you. It might not be immediately but might be a few days later, but they'll make reference to something you've said and you'll realise that they've been taking it all in and they see you differently. (Final interview)

Several headteachers also noted the significance of this strand of the work in which the teachers were not just finding out about the children, but about themselves as educators and the consequences of this:

> Those teachers had given something of themselves. That was a big part of the presentations I heard. It's not just about us finding out about the children. It's about the staff giving something of themselves to the children as well. We are really trying to build this message in school – we did that as part of our transition work – you know – we said to the staff – it's not just about you finding out about them you need to do this as well.

This project has really been about changing the way you see the children but also changing the way your see yourself – as the teacher.

They're different my two [BC: RLL teachers]*, they've opened up, you can see it in the way the children are with them – and it's two-way – it's made a real difference to their relationships with one another.* (Final Interviews)

In tune with Glazier (2005), some of the teachers, having reflected upon their own professional stances and personal engagement in the classroom came to question long-held assumptions and long-practiced norms of behaviour. They began to share more of themselves through talking about their hobbies, passions, and reading and writing practices beyond school and found positioning themselves differently prompted new conversations, new connections, and new relationships with the children. The teachers' were almost universally surprised that the children were interested in their lives. Perhaps as Thomson *et al.* (2012) suggest, there has been a worrying 'de-humanising trend' in education in which the sociality of schools has been eroded, such that they are in danger of becoming 'non-places' (Auge, 1995), locales 'in which people are institutionally stripped of their humanity' (ibid.). If, as these authors argue in their analysis of the 'signature pedagogies' of artists working in schools, teachers are predominantly focused upon tests and targets, they may come to see children and young people 'primarily as outcomes and levels'. Thus the curriculum, Thomson *et al.* (2012) posit, will be delivered in order to ensure success against these criteria and teacher–child relationships will also be framed by these externally imposed goals. Intriguingly, the artists whose pedagogical practices served to raise standards, ensure commitment and move learning forwards, were heard to speak openly and frequently about their personal lives in classrooms. Assuming that the students would be interested in their lives and identities as artists beyond school, they openly shared anecdotes, personal histories and other information. Thomson *et al.* (2012) claim, that this, as the *BC: RLL* data also indicate, contributed to the creation of more open environments and stronger relationships between children and artists/teachers respectively. Imbuing previously institutionally framed relationships with a real sense of the personal, appeared to make a marked difference to the teachers' relationships with the children, and as will be seen, the parents.

Making new relationships through the Learner Visits

In the informal conversational context of the Learner Visits many of the teachers shared something of themselves with the parents and children. As they heard about parents' lives and experiences of schooling as well as their aspirations for their children, the teachers commented they quite naturally responded as interested adults and voiced connections to their own lives and histories. Their reflections suggest that after any initial awkwardness, where this existed, they began to feel more relaxed and many found themselves opening up and talking about themselves as mothers, daughters and family members for example. This seemed particularly noticeable on the second and third visits as relationships were built. The teachers frequently commented upon the difference that sharing personal experiences, however brief, made to the flow of conversation and their sense of ease in this novel situation:

> *When I was more open, they were more open, it was like a key to unlocking the conversation.*

> *When she said that about being homesick, I ended up talking about leaving home for the first time and how lonely I was, that was when it all shifted, after that, it seemed easier somehow and we just chatted. I did go back to my questions but kind of wove them in and it didn't feel awkward anymore.*

> *It made all the difference that [personal sharing], me being me, rather than me being their son's teacher if you know what I mean.* (Interviews)

Through listening to the parents and empathising with them, as well as through sharing connections, teachers began to develop a new and more informed respect towards those they visited. As a consequence they began to form new relationships with both the children and their parents. For example, when Katy visited Rachita's home, the family shared some memories and photos of their life in India (they had moved to the UK some five years before) and Rachita's mother asked Katy if she had ever visited India. While she had not, a close friend of Katy's had just married and gone to live in Kerala, and as she noted afterwards, Katy found herself talking about her own hopes and plans, both as a child and now as an expectant mother. In commenting on this episode which Katy chose to revisit in a data analysis meeting, she noted, 'it was here where it just took off really, perhaps because I'd opened up too'. Later, the whole family and Katy listened to music, the girls performed some classical Indian dances in full costume and Katy was invited and agreed to stay to supper. By the time she left she had been with the family for well over two hours, 'I felt so at home and we just kept chatting, they're lovely, so generous, it wasn't awkward at all'. Their warmth and 'strong sense of family' struck her and the following day she sent a small thank you gift home with Rachita who proudly told her friends about her teacher having supper with her family. In the weeks that followed, Katy noted that this normally shy youngster 'seemed to come out of her shell with me a bit more', and agreed to perform an Indian dance in class. It appeared that having shared this informal, non-school focused time together, Katy, Rachita and her parents had positioned themselves differently in relation to one another. This had several consequences which were also influenced by Katy's new understanding of their values and aspirations and their perspectives on education. As the headteacher commented:

> *Immediately after Katy had been there, even the first time, well you could see a difference, we began to see mum on the playground, I guess she must've been there before*

but I'd not noticed her, she started seeking Katy out, there was another level of communication going on. And now just sometimes she'll [Rachita's mum] *stop to chat and I've noticed her talking to some of the other mothers too and that's a real change. It's made Katy more open and reflective I think, it's has taken her out of the four walls of the school and given her space to think and listen to others.* (Final interview)

As a consequence, reciprocal relations began to develop. Through moving beyond the boundaries of the classroom, Katy had begun, albeit tentatively, to build a social relationship with Rachita's parents and other parents too; she came to recognise that 'there's complete diversity – well they're all different – all unique but they all care passionately about their children', I don't know why I didn't know that before, maybe I never thought about it'. This realisation of parental commitment and the creation of new connections and increased openness as a result of the Learner Visits was evident across the project; a sense of trust was developing, and as interaction increased over time relationships developed further. The teachers frequently commented upon this in relation to both individual parents and parents as a whole:

My relationship with her parents deepened and it's a more meaningful partnership as I've a better understanding of their daughter and her needs now, and they know that.

Parents' evenings were easier this term as there's a higher level of trust – you can feel it. (Presentations)

It's just so different, I used to feel a bit nervous when parents were around, wondering if they were going to complain or something, now I go out there [the playground] *and I just join in and chat.* (Final interview)

There were also, as noted above and in the case studies, many examples of parents talking more frequently with the project teachers and seeking them out on the playground, on the school trip, after assembly, in the summer fair and in other contexts where they met informally. In one case a parent who had been visited attended a parents' meeting for the first time, and some others volunteered to help in various ways that they had not before. In several cases a rapport between home and school emerged and the parents came to know more about their children's teachers as individuals. For example, in commenting on her new relationship with Molly's mother, Freda observed, 'we just, well talk now and I feel I know her better, it's made a huge difference, if we see each other we chat and I find I often look out for her'. It was clear Molly's mum also valued this, as quite unprompted, she commented to Freda after her second visit, 'Thanks for coming, I feel I know you better now. It's not just snatched moments at the beginning and end of the day. That can only be good.' She also lamented the fact that in her view the next teacher 'won't know us as a family in quite the same way' and 'won't know what makes Molly tick like you do'. While such knowledge may be perceived by some as irrelevant to the standards agenda, the teachers found that knowing the children as learners and their parents as people made a difference to their ability to make connections and create more inclusive learning communities in school. It was also evident that the parents' views prompted some teachers to question school practices, as Kara noted for example, 'we concentrate on passing on National Curriculum levels, assessments, and samples of work. Are these the only important aspects of a child's year at school? This is not all parents are interested in and we shouldn't be either'.

It seemed as if the teachers grew in confidence in their relationships with parents, not only those they visited but parents as a group. While the parents' perspectives on receiving Learner Visits were not documented in this study, as it was thought to add a layer of intrusivity, it appeared to the teachers that parents valued the chance to talk and to have a teacher visit them, to listen and to show interest in their child. The teachers commonly perceived the parents who had been visited were more relaxed with them, 'they're more comfortable with me and me with them' as Erica described it. Myriad examples were offered by the teachers of stronger connections with parents; many parents sought out the teachers to thank them for visiting and contributed in new and affective ways, for example with an unexpected hug or a confidence shared, which challenged teachers' traditional notions of both 'professional distance' and 'research objectivity'. Understanding this in theoretical terms gave the project teachers' integrity and this conceptual work was critical to their ongoing analysis and dialogue about the gradual development of trust – confianza – trust in mutual trust (González et al., 2005) within these new teacher–parent relationships.

Sophie learns about Jo and his family: a case study

This case study highlights some of the ways in which Sophie came to share more of herself as a learner, an adult and a mother through the project. In the process Sophie began to subtly shift the ways she positioned herself in class and in her contact with parents. She adopted numerous identity positions as teacher, researcher, deputy head, and mother. Through her increased openness and awareness of her identity positioning she connected to her own experiences, built stronger relationships with both children and parents and came to question her previous stance as an educator.

Sophie was deputy head of a small village school and the maths co-ordinator. She had worked in three schools teaching older primary aged learners for nearly 15 years. A member of the previous project led by the *BC: RLL* team, Sophie had developed as a Reading Teacher and shared her reading life with the young people in her class (Cremin et al., 2014). During the new project she taught a class of 10–11-year-olds and visited two boys' homes, one twice, the other three times. In contrast to Moll's work (Moll and Greenberg, 1990; Moll 1992; Gonzalez et al., 2005) and more recent work by Rosemberg et al. (2013) this teacher, like several others in the project was working with 'mainstream homes', where arguably similarities exist between home and school practices and discourses (Gee, 1996). Nonetheless, as will be seen Sophie still held a number of implicit assumptions about the boys and their families, which influenced her expectations of them. Through the Learner Visits, she came to reappraise these perceptions and alter her beliefs with consequences for her relationships and positioning in the classroom.

At the outset Sophie expressed concern that her school might be seen as 'imposing ways of working on the parents and families'. Indeed she noted 'we tell them what they should do and then moan if they don't do it'. The sense of parents as 'other', as 'them', was partly recognised by Sophie who saw the school's way of working as one-sided, though she wasn't sure how to change this and expressed considerable discomfort and reluctance about visiting parents at home. Nonetheless at the autumn term parents' evening, Sophie spontaneously shared the possibility of visiting, noting:

> After the initial shock, and you could actually see the parents' shock, I said you can come to my house and see the playmobile all over the floor if you want to! Some were a bit, 'Yes . . . er okay'. . ., but then after talking to them, and explaining that I am a mum and yes I know where you are coming from and I know what it's like at the end of the day, when you are tired, to do all the right things and I think it broke down a barrier, because one mum said 'When are you coming over?' (Interview)

While the parents demonstrated a degree of surprise and perhaps disquiet at the suggestion of bring visited, Sophie's intuitive response to share something of her own experiences and difficulties as a parent of two primary-aged children, derived from her personal funds of knowledge, appeared to have been reassuring, at least for some.

Initial knowledge and perceptions

Sophie selected Jo as a case study child. She saw him as 'a behaviour problem', and noted 'he's all front, a bouncy, dominant child', 'has yet to finish a book or anything really', and observed 'it's excuse, excuse, excuse, his homework's almost never done'. She knew Jo played rugby (not because he had told her or written about it, but because her own sons played at the same club) and so perhaps also chose to focus on him as she felt some unconscious affinity or connection with him. She also noted 'he's not a high achiever and I want to know what makes him tick'. Sophie's knowledge of Jo was not based entirely on his academic ability, his behaviour appeared to dominate her view of him. Sophie recalled having seen him 'being ejected from a classroom last year – he always seemed to be in trouble'. Her view was arguably somewhat fixed, and not yet enriched by any first-hand knowledge of Jo from home. It thus seems possible that Sophie expected Jo to behave in certain ways, possibly creating a self-fulfilling prophecy. As she commented:

> I think he has the potential to be quite unruly . . . he a big 'I am' and 'I know, I know, I know' and he's quite, well he doesn't comply but complains all the time. He has to have the last word. (Initial interview)

Sophie acknowledged that due to the behaviour difficulties which Jo and his younger brother and sister presented at school, she had made the assumption that his home life would be 'quite chaotic as the children are quite chaotic in school'. Another member of staff had expressed a similarly 'judgemental' stance when she heard Sophie was due to visit the family, 'It'll be a free for all probably – I bet they do what they want at home'. Sophie knew Jo's dad was working in Nigeria and thought his mum was a housewife with time on her hands:

> *The perception is, she drops them off – this is not just mine but other teachers as well. Lady of leisure, always in her PE kit, track suit, sports kit, always going off running or to the gym, you know. She never comes to any of the children's assemblies and often doesn't seem to know what's going on because she doesn't read the newsletter. She drops them off and swans about and isn't interested in their education. It seems a bit harsh but that's how it seems.* (Initial interview)

Her view, influenced by other teachers' comments and her own observations reflects a somewhat 'deficit discourse', related in this instance to a middle class mother who was deemed uninterested and a son who was described as 'bullish', 'egocentric' and 'in your face all the time'. Arguably too she was invoking the common conception of parental 'involvement' or attendance at school functions as a measure of success (Frey, 2010) and in this regard did not perceive Jo's mum as successfully 'involved' in her son's education.

Challenging perceptions

The Learner Visits were to disprove many of these preconceptions. On the afternoon of the first visit, Sophie drove Jo and his siblings home after school; they lived in a nearby town. Sophie noted that Jo appeared surprised at the mess in her car which the children helped her 'muck out', but that he proudly sat in the front seat confidently giving directions, choosing the long way home and talking animatedly throughout the 15-minute journey: pointing out his Scout hut, the local Sainsbury's store, the Chinese takeaway and where he walked his dogs. He also asked her questions about her family. Unusually perhaps, Jo was in a position to lead this conversation with his teacher; she was reliant upon him for directions and did not know the way. She noted with surprise that he assiduously 'checked' on his siblings in the back seats and drew them into the conversation. Sophie, still insecure about the visit, felt the journey helped her relax, although 'when I got out of the car I suddenly felt very unsure again – I wondered what she (his mum) was expecting'. As she walked towards Jo's home she commented afterwards she was 'acutely aware I was going into his space, their home', Sophie was visiting to learn, not to inform his mum Nikki about her son's literacy attainment or behaviour. As Holland *et al.* (1998) state, positional identities relate to 'how one identifies one's position relative to others, mediated through the ways one feels comfortable or constrained'. At this point it was clear Sophie felt rather tense, her identity as a teacher was arguably shifting as she sought to adopt the identity position of a researcher.

However, she was warmly welcomed by Nikki and their energetic Labradors and could see Nikki had been working in the kitchen; she was surrounded by books and papers. Though she was expecting 'chaos, energy, manic-ness', Sophie found a sense of purpose and calm prevailed. The children settled quickly onto a Lego computer game, while Nikki explained she was training part-time to join the police force. This was a long-held ambition she had put off for years having previously worked as a medical secretary and administrator elsewhere. Nikki was committed to training on Wednesdays (the assembly day) and Saturdays and had an ongoing assessment every other Sunday. She found her studies very demanding on top of effectively being a single mother; her husband came home from Nigeria four or five times annually. Sophie became acutely aware of the demands upon this young woman, who had begged her husband to move the family, but was now living in a new area, though near family friends, and studying for a new career. The police training centre was over an hour away so she had to cope with travelling, arranging for the children to be looked after during her weekend training sessions, as well as taking her children to and from school and clubs, visiting her parents up north and running the household. Sophie observed in the data analysis meeting, 'she must be run ragged, I know I would be'.

This new knowledge about Jo's mum as a unique person with her own commitments and challenges, prompted considerable empathy and their conversation convinced Sophie that her own and other staff assumptions about this 'lady of leisure' were completely erroneous. She came to appreciate that the ability to attend school functions is mitigated by personal circumstance and that Nikki's lack of presence in assembles did not equate to a lack of interest. Sophie came to recognise Nikki enacted a number of identity positions during the visit, including 'single mother', parent, trainee police officer and wife. Two days after the visit, Nikki sought Sophie out at the end of the school day and thanked her for coming, commenting 'sometimes I come down in the mornings and think – oh nobody understands, so it's good to talk'. Sophie became determined to visit again. The visit also triggered a number of unusually frank notes from Nikki in Jo's reading record, which Sophie noted 'made me reply more personally – like a dialogue, rather than just a signature politely implying I'd read what had been written'. One entry from his mum simply said 'I'VE HAD IT with Jo! – he hasn't done his homework again and we had a huge row – I don't know what else to do'. Their written interchanges acted as another source of connection between them. Prior to the visit, Nikki had never initiated a conversation with her son's teacher and had made very few entries in his reading record (when she had these had been to denote the pages read or Jo's comments about the book), this step towards personal communication, possibly mother to mother represented a significant shift in the relationship between Nikki and Sophie.

At Nikki's request, the second visit was arranged in half term 'when there would be more time' and mobile numbers were exchanged. This time Sophie felt more comfortable, and mentioned to Nikki she had been nervous about visiting the first time. To Sophie's surprise Nikki declared:

> *I feel like that when I come up for parents evening, I get panicky before I come up thinking 'Oh I don't like doing this on my own, what are they going to say this time?'* (Transcription from home visit)

School spaces for parent dialogue and involvement may be perceived as both uncomfortable and alienating to mothers, as Dryness (2007) found in her study of Latina mothers. For Jo's mother also, attending alone and potentially expecting a difficult conversation about her son, parents' evenings had caused her concern. This was one of the critical moments that Sophie selected to discuss with her linked researcher; she perceived Nikki's comment suggested a subtle shift in their relationship, commenting 'we were both honest with one another I suppose, and I think I began to see where she was coming from'. A sense of increased understanding and respect for each other was evidenced in this second visit which lasted an hour and a half and was described by Sophie as 'more of a chat, person to person, much more relaxed'. In this context she found out more about Jo's literacy and learning practices and behaviour at home.

Making connections

In all three visits, Sophie observed Jo, who in school was quite 'dominant and noisy', offering sensitive support to his siblings and undertaking a range of household tasks, including walking the dogs and helping his sister and his mother with their homework. Also, as his mum lacked confidence digitally and relied upon him for help: he had sorted out her new mobile's screen and ringtone and shown her how to use it. It was also his job to establish how best to communicate with his dad abroad: he had set up Skype, installed a webcam for the family to use and took family photos which he then sent on. Personally he preferred to text his father. Sophie was surprised to realise Jo played such an active and responsible role in the household, and undertook these responsibilities without complaint. This prompted Sophie to consider the degree of autonomy and responsibility he was offered in school:

> *He does so much there as the eldest and some of it independently as well, in school he doesn't have the same space or opportunity I guess.* (Data analysis meeting)

Jo also talked enthusiastically about his PlayStation and computer games, naming Guitar Hero, Lego Star Wars, Rachet and Clank, Harry Potter, Revenge of the Sith and Phantom as favourites, alongside Little Big Planet which he played online with friends. However, Nikki refused to let Jo purchase 'gun games where all they do is shoot one another' and observed she never played on the Wii or computer games herself. Sophie agreed 'it's not part of my leisure time either, I mean I use the computer massively, but if I had three hours spare I wouldn't go and choose to spend it doing that! (playing games)'. 'Me neither', Nikki replied. Sophie's personal knowledge and experience of being a mother afforded her a degree of alignment with Nikki on this issue; they both shared a sense of distance from Jo's passion for computer games, which they discussed as a generational issue. This agreement and concord was not the only one the two mothers shared. Nikki also voiced concern about some homework which she felt only involved 'cut, paste and print' and they discussed the difficulties of this together, with Sophie sharing her concerns about her own children's computer use. Their conversation at this point in the discussion arguably reflected their positions as parents sharing mutual worries about new technologies, though listening to it afterwards, Sophie observed that in effect Nikki had been pointing out the limitations of the homework she had set, noting 'I didn't see it like a criticism at the time and in any case she's probably right'.

On the third visit in particular Sophie learnt that Jo drew a lot at home, mostly connected to his games or prompted by movies. His digital competence was used here too; he had found and used websites such as Dragonart. On this occasion, Jo proudly shared two sketchbooks with his teacher who was amazed at the level of detail and the evident time and concentration he must have expended on them. In playing computer games and through his drawing, Jo, who in school 'never finished anything', appeared to set his own goals, exercised agency and was unquestionably focused and a finisher. This took his teacher by surprise. Demonstrating her genuine interest in and appreciation of Jo's skill at drawing and extensive knowledge and experience of digital texts appeared in some way to validate these practices in his mother's eyes, Nikki commented: 'You know it's only talking to you like this that I realise that you see Jo in a different light.' When Sophie asked in what way, she replied that she was so used to her son doodling and being 'computer savvy' that she just took it for granted. Through the visits, in which a rapport between the two adults developed, both Jo's mother and his teacher came to a renewed appreciation of his strengths and resources.

Positional shifts and new relationships with children

Following her first visits to Jo and Max's homes Sophie noted that back in school the boys were almost immediately 'pushing the boundaries' and she saw this as a challenge: 'We've gone from kind of formal teacher pupil relationships to much more informal relationships and I don't find it easy. They're dead friendly now, and it's almost too much if you know what I mean.' It seemed that for the boys the relationship boundaries had blurred and at times they felt comfortable positioning themselves differently with their teacher. Initially, Sophie was less than comfortable with their resultant behaviour and seemed to feel they had stepped over the threshold of what was appropriate, yet instinctively she did not wish to reprimand them. In conversation with other project teachers, Sophie was prompted to see this as part of a strengthening of relationships; as one colleague commented, 'it sounds like they're easier with you now'. The relationship developed further through a residential trip which Sophie and her husband led. In this context, Jo again showed his 'calm, caring and sensible side', for example he woke her to ask for help as another child was ill. As she noted, 'among his peers he wants to be top dog, but it doesn't mean he doesn't care and there's this really gentle side to him which I didn't see before'. Here too Sophie was positioned differently at times; she described talking about her fear of abseiling with the children and the fact that they saw her with her husband too.

In the final interview Sophie pondered on this new affinity, she considered it had also been nurtured by a gradual and increased openness and less professional distance on her part. During the year Sophie had set up literacy logs, informally shared her own reading and writing from beyond the classroom and invited children to share theirs, in some writing activities both the children and their teacher had leant upon the texts of their lives (Fecho, 2011). Sophie had also discussed her difficulties setting up a Facebook account with the class, made connections to her own family and shared personal photographs of places where this was relevant to the curriculum. In reflecting upon this, she commented: 'I'm amazed how inter-ested children are in our (the project teachers) own lives actually.' In addition, in the summer term she undertook her own project on the theme of Exploration along-side the children; they were given free choice under the overall theme, but Sophie found it hard to choose a focus. The children offered her advice and shared infor-mation sources: 'we sort of swapped roles in a way'. She also shared her writer's block and thought that through her engagement in the class project and through writing alongside them, this:

> Shifted them as well I think because I think sometimes they wait to be told and I lead too much ... I think sometimes they assume that teachers know everything and actually we don't. We're on a learning journey too, and that's good to share. (Interview)

Sophie began to be aware that her openness was moving well beyond literacy to a position where she was sharing more of herself as a person and a learner, however this made her feel more exposed:

> Sophie: I think I've shared much more by being involved in this project. You know, whereas perhaps before I'd opened myself up a little bit, my readerly self, in this you know you are stripped bare really.
> Researcher: In what way, go on?
> Sophie: I think your values ... I don't know. You've seen the children in their home environments, you've shared a very privileged part of their lives with them and their family, and I've actually shared a lot more of me too, who I am and my family as well. (Data analysis meeting)

In her notes for her final presentation Sophie recorded as a prompt to self, the words: 'Different position – in class, in homes, in myself' and talked about the con-sequences of this new positioning. Personally, she perceived that learning about Jo and Max had helped her realise the value of knowing the children better and felt she was becoming more receptive and thoughtful about all the children's behaviour, their views and concerns not just the two boys, as she described this, 'my ears are open now, both ears are open, rather than just one of them'. She was also developing a more questioning stance about her values: 'I think I've shifted myself and made myself think about what's actually important for these children in their lives ... I know I want my two [her own children] to feel at home in school and be *known* as people if you know what I mean.' Reflecting back on her visits Sophie observed that she had seen her focus children differently in the context of their homes and communities.

> *I saw them as children and not Year Six pupils. Does that make sense? ... They are there* [in their homes and communities] *in their entirety, here we just get a snippet. I know we have them for a long time during the day but actually we don't know them at all really, in terms of who they are and what they're like and who they want to be. We think we know them but we kid ourselves, we just know their scores and if there are any problems and we label them.* (Final interview)

Despite being a mother of two primary aged children herself, Sophie had, it seemed, previously kept separate her role positions and identities as mother and teacher. Through visiting as a learner and a researcher, she found herself drawing on her own funds of knowledge as a mother and began to review her own and her school's constrained and arguably somewhat one-dimensional knowledge of the children in the prevailing accountability culture. Sophie's realisation that this was insufficient and that personalising institutional relationships could make a significant difference, represented an important step forwards.

Positional shifts and new relationships with parents

In the new territory of children's' homes, Sophie constructed her positional identity in interaction with others: the children, their mothers, fathers and siblings. On the second visit to Jo's home, Sophie perceived she was positioned differently by Nikki since a new relationship had begun to form. As they sat chatting over several cups of tea, both of them shared personal anecdotes as parents. In drawing upon her life experience beyond school, Sophie was not primarily positioned as the deputy head, Jo's teacher or as an educator in the wider sense, nor did she perceive she was positioned primarily as a researcher in this context. In discussing the transcripts of the visits with her linked researcher, Sophie noticed that there were occasions when she positioned herself or was positioned by Jo or by Nikki as the 'teacher figure', but also many others when she enacted and claimed identity positions as a mother and a confidante. The analytic process seemed to help bring to the surface the complexity with which Nikki's and Sophie's personal histories and identities interacted socially. Sophie often voiced views which derived from her funds of knowledge as a parent, a parent who at times was challenged, as Nikki also was by the role. It was on these occasions that she perceived Nikki (and Max's mum – her other case study child) opened up, 'when I shared something of myself it just seemed to open new doors somehow'. This was a common finding across the project.

Sophie was convinced the visits had made a difference to her relationships with both the boys' parents, but not just these families:

> *Relationships at all levels really, with parents, with pupils, it's much more reciprocal. There's been a shift of power, well power's the wrong word but there's been a blurring of the edges shall we say. As soon as we step out of here and children step in we're not different people, we are the same people, though we do actually have to shift a little bit because we're in a different role, but less of that I think. They're getting a much truer teacher, picture of me and I think I'm getting a much truer picture of them and their parents.* (Final interview)

The professional and the personal were merging; boundaries were blurring. Sophie also noticed that she had begun to spend more time out on the playground at the end of the day. While she had done so when teaching younger aged children, she perceived she had unconsciously assumed the older learners' parents did not want or need to talk to her. Arguably more comfortable with parents now, she noted:

> Sophie: *You wander out there and people start talking . . . it's just much more sort of person to person rather than teacher to parent, it's more relaxed. Perhaps I'm not standing on ceremony anymore.*
> Researcher: *And why's that then?*
> Sophie: *I think shifts only happen if somebody makes them happen, so perhaps because I've shifted, I've realised it's not a scary, unknown territory now is it − to get to know these people, . . . I've changed in my approach. Knowing more about the families and trying to understand the learning in the home has kind of humanised them for me − and me for them perhaps? Perhaps I'm more approachable now?* (Final interview)

At the outset of the project Sophie, perceived herself as accessible and friendly, but through experiencing the uncertainty of being a researcher and listening to the parents' perspectives, she began to question just how approachable she really was and whether her professional distance was appropriate. As she commented: 'I turned it round, I thought "Well how am I perceived?" "How do they see me?" "Am I hard to reach?".' Her resultant move to go onto the playground more regularly was not the only new action she adopted. Despite being a parent of primary-aged children herself, Sophie had become accustomed to certain ways of engaging with parents, both as the deputy-head and a class teacher. For example, she had accepted that as a teacher predominantly talked about children's 'test scores and targets' at parents' evenings. She had not only conformed to this as an educator, she had not challenged it as a parent. The status quo was thus maintained until her involvement in the project when she came to question this. She made the decision to talk about the whole child, not just their academic attainment:

> *It's made me realise that actually parents are desperate for you to get to know their children, so during this consultation* [the summer term one] *I talked to them about*

their children, not about what they'd achieved really. . . . it was much more about them rather than what they'd achieved. (Final interview)

These examples represent subtle, but potentially significant markers of a shifting frameset and exploration of new identity positions. It was clear Sophie intended to retain this more personal, less distanced stance in her future work as an educator. When meeting her new class for the first time at the end of the summer term, she determined to get to know them individually. On Meet Your Teacher Day she radically altered her customary practice (which she described as a one-sided exposition about the academic challenges of Year 6 and the school's expectations of them), and encouraged the children to talk about themselves. She invited them to write letters to her about their interests, passions and families and intended to write letters back, making connections and sharing something of herself with each child. In addition, she planned to reshape more of the curriculum to 'give children much more choice and freedom . . . and allow them to bring themselves to school'.

Seeking to develop increased reciprocity with parents too, Sophie transformed the termly parents' evening, which was no longer formally arranged with teachers positioned behind desks, but was re-organised into a more informal dialogic arrangement involving armchairs for all. The time allocated each family was expanded and meetings in the day and evening were offered in order to increase access. There was a bookshop and chairs for those waiting, loosely grouped in the centre of the room where parents could browse and talk. Sophie noted 'many parents seemed visibly more relaxed . . . we've tried to make it less of a "them and us" and more of a "we're all in it together" set up' and described it as 'quite a monumental shift really for our school'. Whether the parent–teacher discourse altered in any way due to this re-configuration is not known, though the strategy suggests that more collaborative and reciprocal interactions and relationships were being sought.

In sum, this case study offers a portrait of a teacher in transition. In school Sophie shared something of her literacy life with the children and sought to learn about theirs; she extended this by undertaking Learner Visits to two boys' homes in order to find out more about their everyday literacy lives. She found adopting a researcher disposition and the idea of doing Learner Visits demanding, but as she did so and developed new knowledge and respect for the boys and their parents, she found that she too opened up and shared her own views and experiences. This fostered the forging of new, more equal, relationships.

Conclusion

The project teachers took pleasure in reflecting on their own literacy histories and identities and were surprised at the intensely social nature of their early and ongoing experiences of literacy. Their literacy histories acted as an effective catalyst (among others discussed in Chapter 6) for widening their conceptions of literacy. However, several of the practitioners encountered conceptual and practical difficulties in sharing their literacy lives and practices in school and a continuum of practice developed in this regard. Many were challenged by long-held perceptions of teachers' roles, construed teaching as a performance, and appeared to find making personal connections without the safety net of literacy objectives driving the inter-change (at least in literacy lessons), challenged the ways they constructed their professional identities and roles. Tensions surfaced between the private and public dimensions of being a teacher. However, over time some did share their literacy practices often spontaneously and these triggered conversations with the younger learners, enabled connections to be made and prompted some teachers to take up new positions as readers and writers alongside the children. Few of the teachers shared their everyday digital literacy practices in school.

Reflecting upon the Learner Visits, the teachers found that making connections and openly sharing their life experiences helped to establish relationships; offering parents and children a stronger sense of the personal in the professional. By being positioned as researchers and learners and through sharing their literacy lives, some teachers were prompted to question their assumptions and limited institutional knowledge about the children, and recognised a need to reduce professional dis-tance and re-personalise education. In some cases too, it appeared parents' and chil-dren's perceptions of individual teachers subtly changed as a result of the teachers' greater openness and the new relationships which were built.

8

SHIFTING PERSPECTIVES ABOUT PARENTS AND CHILDREN

Marilyn Mottram and Sacha Powell

In exploring children's literacy lives beyond school, the teacher-researchers on the *BC:RLL* project were invited to develop more sophisticated understandings about what they recognised, regarded and valued as literacy and learning. This required a degree of decentring, and a willingness to take risks on the part of the teachers and their headteachers. Both headteachers and leadership teams were central to the project; they were deemed pivotal to supporting the teachers and developing new whole-school attitudes, policies and practices. Headteachers also played a significant role in supporting their teachers to challenge any pre-existing assumptions and as will be shown, some were also prompted to re-consider their own breadth of knowledge of families and communities and question their own suppositions and working hypotheses about the community in which their schools were situated.

This chapter begins with an overview of the teachers' and the headteachers' initial perceptions and assumptions about their local communities, parents and families, considers how their thinking and approaches shifted over the duration of the project and reflects upon the constraints of adopting a more open view of what families and communities have to offer literacy learning. By focusing on what actually happens in children's lives and homes, instead of what they thought should be or might be happening, the *BC:RLL* project teachers were able to uncover a wealth of funds of knowledge that in many cases promoted a new awareness of their previous assumptions:

> *I realised that the biggest thing that has changed me is that I will now always challenge what I hear about our families. I will tackle the way we talk about our children – alter the way we view them.* They are children of promise – not deficit. (Presentation)

The chapter also includes a case study of one school, St Mary's Primary, and the ways in which the staff team in the institution began to shift their view about children and families, and came to adopt a less school-centric perspective. They recognised the long-term commitment involved in developing a view of learning that is appreciative of children's strengths and funds of knowledge found in their homes and communities and began to work towards this.

Initial knowledge of families and communities

At the beginning of the project teachers and headteachers were asked to identify what they knew about children's lives beyond school, how they made links with families and found out about children's interests, passions and literacy and learning in the home and community. When asked to describe their schools, each of the ten headteachers was able to provide statistical information such as the percentages of children with special educational needs (SEN), with English as an additional language, (EAL), in receipt of free school meals or in the care system. This was generally information that they were able to provide without reference to any documentation. They were also able to provide general information about the demographics of the communities from which their children were drawn, such as social class and ethnicity groupings. This was an unsurprising finding that reflects the dominant discourse and nature of the knowledge that headteachers are required to document and report upon annually. The following extract was typical of the information that headteachers were readily able to provide:

> HT: *We're a community school and we reflect our community so we have 78 per cent ethnic minorities, over 50 per cent EAL, 28 per cent SEN and we have quite a good reputation dealing with pupils with SEN, particularly with autistic children, so we have 11 statemented and quite a few pending, so we're quite popular with that. Boys and girls are equal mix; we have free school meals of over 40 per cent.*
> Researcher: *In terms of the EAL children, what are the main language groups?*
> HT: *We have a large Somalian community and also Turkish. Those are the two main languages, and then there is about 1–2 per cent that covers a huge range like Portuguese, French, Spanish.*
> Researcher: *So how many languages do you think are spoken in the school?*
> HT: *About 35 – a whole range.* (Initial interview)

Some had knowledge of existing local community and faith groups in the area and links existed with these. However, the majority of headteachers had fairly superficial knowledge of micro level information about individual families and the children's or their families' funds of knowledge and voiced perspectives in relation to their understandings of particular groups' perspectives:

> *There's a lot of unemployment, traditionally Ford employed many of the local population – 33,000 this has been cut to 5,000. Lots of single families – white UK – and their attitude is that [it's] the school's job to teach the children, not the parents.* (Initial interview)

The teachers' responses with regard to the local community suggested varying views of what 'community' might mean: reflecting a geographical understanding of community or definitions based on the social and economic status of parents and families or ethnic groupings. The definitions often included comments about how those factors influenced parental attitudes and dispositions, and also revealed some teachers' unconscious assumptions about particular groups.

> '*It's quite a deprived area and literacy levels are low*'.
> '*Lots of single mums working during the day so they can't help with literacy.*'
> '*Most families live in a home they own and most have somebody working.*'
> '*Mainly skilled workers around here rather than academic professionals.*'
> '*There are some from academic backgrounds and they strive for more and push their children on, but I think they are in the minority.*'
> '*There's quite a lot of ready cash to buy material things which they think are important and they like the children to be happy.*'
> '*We have a growing number of Arab children coming into the area and it seems to me they are generally low achievers.*'
> '*We get a lot of traveller children around here . . . I was going to choose a traveller but . . . I don't feel there's anything to build on.*'
> '*On the face of it, it looks fairly middle class but actually . . . it's diverse. We have children who come here without any breakfast – ranging to those who have been pulled out of private education due to the current climate, so a wide spectrum.*'
> '*This area has one of the highest deprivation indices in the country.*' (Initial interviews)

The headteachers and most of the teachers lived many miles away from the schools in which they worked, and only two of the 18 teachers lived within walking distance of the school or within its immediate catchment. The majority travelled some way to their place of work, often by car. This may have had consequences in relation to the teachers' knowledge of the locality and the children's community and cultural experiences. The teachers rarely used the possessive pronoun 'our' to describe the local community and there was a tendency for descriptions of communities to reflect an 'othered' frameset which was not necessarily negative but reflected a certain degree of distance; an 'us and them' scenario. However, while teacher knowledge was minimal, some of the teaching assistants who lived locally and were often school parents were found to possess considerable local community knowledge.

Links with parents and knowledge of literacy practices

At the start of the project the schools' links with parents reflected previous research suggesting the traffic is predominantly one-way (Feiler *et al.*, 2006). The teachers and headteachers reported activities designed to communicate with parents about curriculum issues and about their children. In essence, these were designed to inform them of and invite them to school events in order to learn more about the school's expectations and teaching approaches, and to discuss individual children's progress. Schools also described ways in which they sought to enlist parental support for fundraising events and supporting school-based activities such as reading. Specific ways to communicate with parents included: home–school contacts books, reading diaries, homework diaries, digital networking (Facebook for parents, online homework), weekend newsletters, seeing parents on the playground and inviting parents into classrooms.

Although parents' evenings and informal conversations at the school gate or on the playground were mentioned as ways of interacting with families, these too tended to include an emphasis on imparting information to families. There was a general sense that communication with parents, particularly those for whom English was not their first language, was an important professional requirement. However, this was often described as difficult to achieve. Nonetheless, headteachers presented themselves as visible and approachable to families, meeting them at parent–teacher consultations, greeting or chatting with families at the school gate or on the playground. Despite this reported approachability, and the fact that over half of the headteachers specifically described their schools as having an 'open door policy' for families, it seemed to be based on their own and teachers' availability and accessibility and was firmly on school property. The proverbial door did not, it appeared, swing both ways.

During the initial interviews, some of the headteachers described what they perceived to be the general features of families' literacies outside school. This pertained to knowledge of home languages (spoken), proficiency in spoken and written English and parents' support for children's school-directed literacy learning, for example:

> 'We have 90 per cent ethnic minorities with English as an additional language . . . they have difficulties with English.'
> 'Our parents generally have bad experiences of school themselves and this leads to difficult relationships now between us and them – they see education as our job – they're not part of it.'
> 'The school can take 708 pupils, at the moment we have 670. We have 30 per cent Free School Meals and 44 per cent are white UK [and these fare least well, some parents struggle with literacy].'
> 'They feel confident enough to say, "I'd like to help them read but I can't read myself". Lots of single Mums work during the day and therefore they can't do family literacy.'
> 'Polish is our largest community . . . they are often still keeping a day at the weekend for their Polish learning, not just their language but their curriculum with a view to eventually returning to Poland.'
> 'They might not have the same skills to express that care and that's a challenge because as professionals we have a professional speech and language and we need to be even more considerate in out communication with families who do not have that same level of understanding.'
> 'Most parents work with the children on their homework and the majority come to parents' evening and we're aware of those that don't and try to target them separately.

I'm absolutely clear that one of our growing issues is that children are making progress that in some instances far outstrips the knowledge and confidence of their families and so family learning has always been a key issue here.' (Initial interviews)

It was clear several schools worked hard to link with parents, to offer family learning opportunities, and some ran literacy and numeracy classes for parents. All were very well-intentioned, but nonetheless a sense of a deficit discourse remained and a strong sense of only seeking parental support for school-based literacy persisted. With regard to the teachers' knowledge of the children and of their home literacy practices, this was minimal (see Chapter 5). One headteacher described a lack of knowledge but felt unsure why the children and families seemed reticent in sharing personal information. She identified dialogue with parents as an important route to discovering more about children's literacy and home lives, but recognised this was not always successful:

We think we're knowledgeable about the families, but possibly there are things we're still finding out about these children. For example, we recently found out that a Year 2 girl is a really good gymnast and the whole family take it very seriously. And yet we've encouraged parents to let us know about outside activities so we can celebrate them . . . we're very aware of children with SEN and AEN and that's possibly because we have quite a lot of dialogue with those parents and we're also hot on child protection issues. But for other children, we've possibly got more work to do. (Initial interview)

This awareness of the need to do more was echoed in other headteachers' responses:

We are not learning from them [home visits for Reception children in contrast to the project Learner Visits]. *It's just an exchange of information, in effect we are saying 'This is what we are doing, this is the curriculum'. We are not actually taking anything on board from them I don't think.* (Initial interview)

In general, there appeared to be limited evidence that the headteachers or teachers knew much about children's wider interests, literacy practices, or experiences of life beyond school. While the university-based researchers were operating from a perspective that knowledge of family and home funds of knowledge would enhance understanding and so pedagogy and curriculum, the headteachers' and teachers' perspectives seemed to present a somewhat more deficit view of some homes, families and communities. Though they may have been reporting what they perceived the researchers wanted/expected to hear or may have been offering a professional 'shorthand' based on an assumption of shared knowledge of current political priorities. Schools in England are required to analyse the achievement and progress of particular groups of children (based on ethnicity, socio-economic status and gender) in terms of local and national expectations. They are obliged to operate within this paradigm. This meant a high level of challenge for schools involved in the project. The evidence suggests that they were trapped in a situation influenced by the accountability culture, in which learning and literacy is related only to the kinds of knowledge children are required to display in school, not linked to the literacy and learning drawn from home.

Shifting perspectives and assumptions

The project aimed to shift perceptions and assumptions from a deficit model to an asset model by providing the structures and support that enabled teachers to change their views through self-reflection and deeper understandings, though it was recognised this is a long-term process: teachers need time to internalise findings in order to shift their discourse (Gee, 2004; Finders, 2005). The classroom-based activities the teachers developed in the autumn term prompted the children (and their teachers) to share information about their lives beyond school and as a result new knowledge about children and families was ascertained, for example: 'we didn't know that he has family in New York and that they write letters from home' and 'there's a group of boys who collect the football cards that's interesting ... I didn't know'. In the spring term, when the teachers undertook Learner Visits they began to find out about children's literacy practices and interests as well as the broader contributions that parents and families make to children's lives.

As documented in earlier chapters, many of the teachers found their conceptions and expectations of the children's behaviour and cognitive abilities were challenged when they visited them at home. For example, Jo's teacher Sophie viewed him as 'quite a challenge behaviourally' and found his boisterous manner and the position he adopted in class of 'top dog' somewhat difficult to handle. However, the Learner Visits allowed Sophie to see Jo in a context where the 'rules' and expectations about children were different. In each of her three visits, she saw that he was much more responsive and sensitive to others than she had expected. He was in charge of walking the dogs, helped his sister with her homework, was observed supporting his brother in finding cheats for a computer game and regularly tested his mum in preparation for her weekly police tests. Seeing Jo as an aide for his mum's learning cast this 10-year-old in a new light for Sophie. Additionally, within the extended family, he helped look after his siblings on the weekends when mum was training and within the extended family he was known as 'the loveable rogue'. Sophie was able to think about Jo differently when she was removed – physically and metaphorically – from the boundaries of the school/classroom. She began to recognise different qualities in him, hearing descriptions of him snuggling up to his mum and nana while watching The One Show together or taking his siblings to the park. His dad worked abroad and moved from base to base, and it was clear Jo missed him; he told Sophie 'when he goes if we can't Skype I have to memorise his face'. In this and other comments Sophie was able to see a vulnerable side to Jo that she hadn't really acknowledged before and this gave her cause to consider the way she expected him to behave in class and the positions being made available to him (for a case study of Jo and Sophie, see Chapter 7).

Teachers often observed that through the Learner Visits in particular they came to 'see' the children differently, as Katy noted she 'saw the children in a different way – more as people'. For Katy, this altered perception of the children (and their parents) had an impact on her as an educator, reminding her perhaps of the difference between perceiving the learners as pupils with targets to achieve and as young people, each uniquely different and individual. Additionally, many of the teachers came to question their reliance on knowledge mainly relating to their pupils' academic achievements; they frequently expressed surprise and a sense of re-connection to wider values.

> *This just gives you a completely different perspective on the whole thing. This is what education is about.'* (Analysis meeting)

> *'It's reminded me of why I am came into education, but you get so caught up with the tests and targets and of course Ofsted that you just lose sight of them* [the children]. (Interview)

The *BC: RLL* project offered schools and teachers the chance to position themselves differently in relation to families and to communities, as learners who sought to find out more about the children's everyday literacy lives. New knowledge of children's lives changed attitudes and perceptions of the children and of the families. The use of the metaphor of a 'brick wall of the unconscious assumptions' held about the children and families visited, which the teachers discussed at one of the national meetings, placed alongside the 'asset blanket' (see Chapter 5) of children's cultural and linguistic resources which they literally made, helped to highlight the disparity. These metaphors were useful devices which in the view of the evaluator became 'part of the language of participants and their schools ... They are deceptively simple and very memorable hooks for reflection, dialogue and learning that are easily applied in different contexts and quickly take people to the heart of the issues that concern and challenge them' (Durrant, 2011: 9). Through coming to recognise their own taken-for-granted assumptions about children and families, some teachers made significant shifts in terms of moving from a deficit to an asset model in classrooms, though this varied across individual teachers and schools. In the final interviews, all the headteachers voiced the view that they and/or their project teachers had begun to challenge their thinking about the children and the families:

> *I think they* [the project teachers] *were challenging assumptions because although we are quite shy about talking about it now, to be honest we all have assumptions and we all have a first impression of people and I think sometimes it's good to, well the only way you can get past it is to really experience it and it was good for them to see that really.*

> *We had preconceived ideas* [such as] *"what can you expect of these children?" – for some focus children.*

Now we're putting relationships on a different level, meeting families on their ground and on their terms . . . what we need to do is meet families half way.

To me the . . . I think the most striking thing has been that we don't really know our children as well as we think we do. I think that was the biggest thing; I was gutted really. I've always thought I have known children and their parents really well but actually . . . we need to understand that what they do at home is just as important, if not more important than what they do here. (Final interviews)

The headteachers frequently observed that they thought they/their staff had known the children well enough, but now realised there was much more to learn. The insights gained in the pivotal Learner Visits served as catalysts for both headteachers and teachers appreciating that 'far too often' as one headteacher noted, assumptions and judgements based on limited information were made. At the close of the work, all felt they needed to make concerted efforts to learn more about the lived experience of children and their families. This recognition helped some school staff, working together, to perceive themselves as potential 'agents of change' (González *et al.*, 2005: 108), although the challenge of deeply ingrained school-centric perspectives persisted in some schools.

Recognising school-centricity

The headteachers' new knowledge of families often mirrored that of their teachers. Most teachers and some headteachers showed shifting perspectives about the children and their families which also applied to their wider local communities or macro-level 'social groupings' in some cases. But in other schools, the attitudes and approach towards families and the community seemed fundamentally to remain the same: some continued to see themselves in a school-to-home transmission mode and adopted a 'school-centric' (Tveit, 2009) orientation towards parents. Some comments at final interviews with headteachers and teachers suggest that their assumptions continued to be premised on a view that more school-like literacy tasks needed to be done at home. As one teacher noted:

I made the assumption that she [mum] *wasn't helping, and I don't think she was particularly. But I made the assumption that she couldn't be bothered . . . but she clearly can be bothered – or maybe it's because she knows now what she can do to help him. She has seen how, and that would never have happened without that meeting.'* (Final interview)

In this example, while there has been a shift in the teacher's perception of the parent and in the quality of their understanding and relationship, the position of power in terms of what counts as knowledge and learning is still unequal and clearly sits with the school. Perhaps this is the next stage of development for those schools wishing to develop a more equivalent approach to parents, homes and communities. The challenge at teacher level is considerable but embracing a whole school approach is far more demanding. For a funds of knowledge approach to flourish, schools need to consider how they position themselves in relation to parents and families and find ways of opening doors and engaging as learners in partnerships where respect and power are equal. Tveit's (2006) review of research and policy literature about parent–teacher relations in Norway emphasised the 'school-centric' nature of many home–school partnerships and the tendency for groups of parents – particularly from low-income, minority ethnic groups – to be seen as deficient.

In the *BC: RLL* project, all schools arguably began the work with a strongly school-centric perspective in relation to parents, tending to position themselves somewhat hierarchically as institutions. While they engaged in a wealth of activities to encourage parental involvement, the vast majority of these related to the school agenda and required parents and families to support their children's school literacy work. There was no evidence of two-way traffic between home and school, but a marked perception of needing to 'educate' the parents in what was required by the school, as well as evidence of deficit assumptions. However, through engaging in Learner Visits and working with children to discover more about their own and their families' funds of knowledge, some teachers and schools began to recognise their school-centric perspectives and orientations and took steps to develop more open, two-way perspectives that recognised, legitimated and built on the children's knowledges, experiences and dispositions from beyond the classroom. The positioning of schools remained complex and fluid, and can be conceptualised on a continuum of school-centricity as in Figure 8.1. (This is discussed further in Chapter 10 – see Figure 10.1.)

Increasingly cognisant of the fact that they are framed by an accountability culture, which measures attainment narrowly and focuses on school literacy, some of the schools began to adopt a less school-centric perspective and sought ways to tailor the National Curriculum in responsive ways that built on what the children brought to school. The complexity and fluidity of their positioning was reflected by the motives underlying the voices of headteachers; there was evidence of variability both within individual interview transcripts as well as between individuals. At times, some voiced views which were more school-centric in so far as they focused upon knowledge that would enhance the school's ability to improve parental engagement with existing set agendas; for example, as one headteacher noted:

> The idea of actually taking the curriculum into the community . . . we try and push towards not just looking at challenges of the child and not just themselves in their behaviour, but looking at the challenges of the child in terms of parenting and the

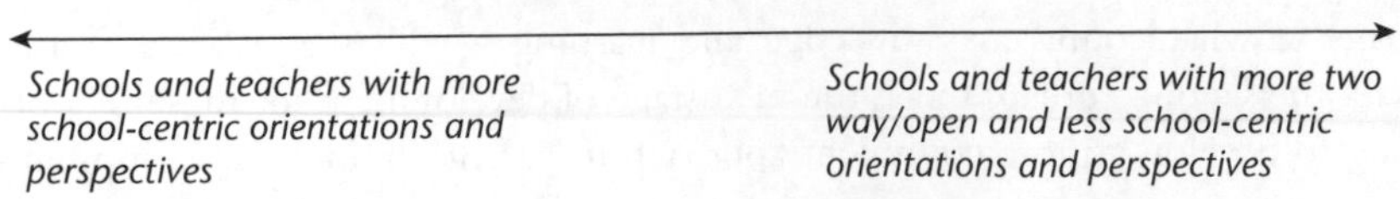

Schools and teachers with more school-centric orientations and perspectives

Schools and teachers with more two way/open and less school-centric orientations and perspectives

FIGURE 8.1 A continuum of school-centricity

family environment and then now beyond that trying to get to the teachers [to see that] *actually the child behaves that way because of their life experiences in the family.* (Initial interview)

This view suggests a strong sense of school-centricity and also perhaps a residual deficit view of families, whereas other headteachers and indeed sometimes the same headteacher at different points in the interview, adopted a less school-centric position and more positive view of families which recognised the assets children bring:

And it is achievements really, things that they might have done outside of school that we might not know about. We tend to have the same children bringing in their football trophies . . . there are talented children out there – for example one goes to Chinese school on a Saturday. That little lad . . . we could have done a lot more with him . . . he could have told us about Chinese New Year, Chinese writing and Chinese language, far more than we worked with him. (Initial interview)

There were times when headteachers described families according to deficit/ inadequacy views and others where the same person described parents as capable. The picture was complex and multi-layered and seemed to evidence some ambiguity on the part of headteachers. Such mixed views are suggestive of the complex nature of pedagogy and the teacher's professional role which involve relationships as well as structures and processes. Any movement towards change – in perspective and/or practice – is one of uneven evolution which demands an understanding of how the different partners in change may find ways of drawing on each other's knowledge and expertise.

The following case study illustrates how the project became a central part of one school's improvement process, evolving into a set of core principles and values to drive the school forward. As the leadership team worked in partnership with an Education Action Zone (EAZ) support teacher and a class teacher to find new ways of engaging with parents and families, a subtle and complex shift in attitudes and perceptions took place.

St Mary's School: a case study

St Mary's Primary School is part of an EAZ in a large city authority. This means that schools in the area work collaboratively on common developmental needs and priorities. They are supported by a zone director and a small team of support teachers who co-ordinate professional development programmes and provide a central point of contact for zone schools. The school lies just ten minutes outside the city centre, tucked away behind a busy road, lined with terraced houses, flats, bustling shops and small businesses. Historically, the area is one where families new to the country settle; it is identified as having one of the highest levels of unemployment in the country. There are approximately 240 children on the school roll and all children speak languages other than English at home and in the community.

At the beginning of the autumn term, the senior leadership teams from all zone schools met to discuss priorities for the coming year and the LA co-ordinator, Shania, met with the schools and talked to them about the previous Phase of the project in which she had been involved (Cremin *et al.*, 2014) St Mary's were keen to be part of a national project as the leadership team and several of the staff were new to the school or the profession. The school project team comprised: Laura, the headteacher; Viv, the deputy headteacher; Anna, the EAZ support teacher and Razia, the teacher of 10–11-year-olds; at the time Razia was in her third year of teaching.

Having a new, young staff and a new leadership team brings challenges but it also opens up new opportunities. Laura and Viv both had a commitment to working more closely with families and the community and to developing a more exciting and innovative curriculum that engaged with children's lives. They shared a vision for the school and a philosophy that included child-focused approaches and recognised that transformation of any kind requires different degrees of support as well as challenge, and that everyone needed to have ownership of the vision. As Viv noted:

> We need to develop staff confidence about what we might be able to do . . . we need to know more about the children's lives and experiences and . . . to work more closely with the parents on something together – but you know – staff are going to need support too. It's okay wanting to do it – but the how we do it and what difference it makes – that's the key. (Initial interview)

The school and the community

In the initial interview Laura, the headteacher described the characteristics of the school:

> The majority of children have EAL, mainly Muslim Pakistani families but some Bangladesh/Indian families and we have a growing Yemeni/Arabic population as well. We often find that this group are generally a lower achieving group, the Arabic speaking families, so we are having to put a lot of interventions in place to support those children. (Initial interview)

It is important to note that St Mary's, like many others, had (and still has) to be extremely mindful of the standards agenda. The priority to raise standards in literacy and numeracy in England has been paramount and various infrastructures have been used to maximise and track children's progress and monitor the impact of any intervention programmes and strategies. Schools are required to analyse data on the attainment and achievement of individual children, to monitor any underperformance of different groups of children and compare the performance of those groups with national performance data for similar groups. In St Mary's, children come from all over the world and a high number of families constantly move in and out of the area. This requires a fine balancing act between the standards agenda and an approach that calls for emphasis on the whole child and on the different sorts of knowledge and experience that may be found in homes and local communities.

As part of her deputy head role, Viv was responsible for leading literacy and curriculum development across the school. Supporting Razia, she also taught the oldest class of 10–11-year-olds, often working intensively with children who were not achieving national expectations in literacy and numeracy using intervention strategies of one-to-one tuition, booster groups and targeted group work to accelerate their progress. When asked about relationships between home and school at the beginning of the project, Laura and Viv were clearly working hard to strengthen the links. They described the parents as often 'lacking the confidence' to come into the school and talk informally but said that parent consultation evenings were well attended. They explained how they shared the children's literacy learning targets with parents and talked to parents about how they might help this school learning at home.

Tveit's (2009) review provides a useful analysis to understand how St Mary's was positioning itself at the beginning of the project. Tveit offers a set of oppositional pairings which describe the different ways in which parents might be perceived and parent/school relationships might be described. For example, up/down in relation to 'whether teachers and parents are described as equals or as up/down' (Tveit, 2009: 291), other pairings include: 'full' or 'empty' and link easily with notions of asset and deficit models. Parents seen as 'full' are perceived as having lots to offer; as empty they are seen to be lacking. Citing Lightfoot's (2004) findings, Tveit identifies the correlation found between such pairings and social, economic and cultural factors: 'well educated, upper middle-class parents' often fall into the category of 'full', described as 'overflowing containers whose involvement in school is to be valued' (294). Conversely, low-income, culturally, linguistically or racially diverse parents were seen to fall into the 'empty' category, 'containers which need to be filled by school before providing anything of value' (294). The yardstick used to measure the degree of involvement is often controlled and established by the school.

These tools can be used to consider the perspective and assumptions at play at St Mary's. Comments made at the beginning of the project from members of the leadership team reveal their position:

> We need to get [parent workshops] *started next week . . . we need to look at the outcomes . . . did we achieve what we wanted to achieve?*

> *One of the things we are trying to do with parents is to get them to use the local community facilities more.*

> *They're happy to support the things that we say and to support with behaviour etc – but they don't particularly see helping their children at home as part of their job.* (Initial interviews)

While the team was genuinely committed to deepening and broadening the school's relationship with parents and families, at the start of the project it seemed they viewed parents and families as 'empty containers' in Tveit's (2009) terms. The school saw itself as responsible for providing the parents with the tools necessary to support their children. Albeit unconsciously, this view reflected a relationship that is 'up/down' with school 'up' and parents 'down'; unequal.

Although the school wanted to build on the knowledge and experiences in homes and communities, they were unaware of how this might be conceptualised beyond the traditional parental involvement paradigm. They were making a number of assumptions about *how* relationships with parents and families could be strengthened and these placed the responsibility firmly on the school's shoulders: the parent workshops, the local community facilities, finding ways of getting the parents to understand the school's agenda more fully. When asked what the school knew about children's out of school social and cultural experiences, the headteacher Laura was clear:

> *This is something we are hoping to get from this project . . . we do it in a small way . . . when we meet for parent consultations.* (Initial interview)

When pressed by the researcher to talk about the nature of the conversations at parent consultations, it was clearly one-way traffic and focused on the standards agenda, for example as Laura explained:

> *We talk about what the children's targets are for their learning – how the parents can help with this at home. We share levels and progress made since the last parent consultation.* (Initial interview)

The critical point is that although the leadership team in the school had no real concept of the different funds of knowledge that might be found in households or what a new model of parent/school relationships might look like, they wanted to know what the children's interests were and hoped to use any new knowledge gained from the project to engage the children in more meaningful learning in school. The new knowledge they gained became the fulcrum for a complex change in attitudes and perspectives. Finding out about the routines, practices and events in children's homes and with their families positioned the leadership team differently, and resulted in a significant shift in perspective.

Early signs of change

During the autumn term, Viv and Anna chose three case study children for the project: Ayannah, Idris and Sharna:

> *We selected three children from different ethnic groups, different home languages and different abilities. They were chosen for different reasons: hard-to-reach parents . . . the older children often came in alone or they were being tracked for literacy . . . reluctant writers.* (Initial interview)

Viv and Anna began the project work in earnest, working with staff across the school but particularly working with the class of 10–11-year-olds. Anna taught this class every morning, while Razia and Viv worked with small groups of children, including the project focus children in small groups and in 1–1 activities. They introduced a variety of strategies and approaches from the *Building Communities of Readers* research (Cremin *et al.*, 2014). For example, children from every year group were asked to act as Reading Representatives across the school and as advocates for reading for pleasure. A wealth of professional development took place involving the whole school, staff and children. As children interviewed staff and each other and conducted surveys across the year groups, the Reading Representatives reported that the 7–8-year-olds wanted:

> *more cushions,*
> *more space to read in,*
> *more attractive decorations,*
> *an area to sit,*
> *more suspense books,*
> *more Horrid Henry books.* (Reading Representatives, notes in teacher's portfolio)

Viv and Anna began to transform the school approach to the reading curriculum with a more child-focused approach. The ways in which children were engaged in learning across the school began to show subtle signs of change as the team designed learning opportunities that not only offered space for children to bring something of themselves, but for teachers to bring something of themselves too. Teachers shared their own reading lives and practices, 'Reading Rivers' were undertaken and staff began to discern the depth and diversity of their own and the children's reading practices beyond school (for more examples of such activities, see Cremin *et al.*, 2014).

The Learner Visits

Anna organised the Learner Visits, working hard to negotiate translators where necessary and ensure that all the practicalities were in place. (See Chapter 6 for an account of the Learner Visit to Idris' home.) From visiting Sharna's home Anna, Viv and Razia discovered that her father runs a shop and spends time each day writing everyday maths problems for the children in their home 'exercise' books:

> *There was such a strong sense of routine and work ethic from mum . . . and dad must be the same because he sets out maths problems for children while he is at work in his shop – he writes down all sorts of maths puzzles and problems – writes them all out in the children's own exercise books – for them to do at home. There is a* tremendous *emphasis on learning.* (Journal)

After the three initial visits where the team were able to witness the strength of the home literacy and learning environments, Viv noted things that had surprised her:

- *I thought I knew about our families – how naïve!*
- *I had no real idea of what goes on in their homes – that's a challenge to my thinking.*
- *How education is seen as a key to success – but also escape.*
- *How nervous I was before I went and how much more comfortable I was after I shared something of myself and mum relaxed too.*
- *My whole perspective has changed – it's made me challenge the assumptions that lead us to believe that children's experiences at home fail to prepare them for success.*
- *The three year old* [In Idris' home] *kept wanting to read his books to me during the whole visit – code-switching in English and Bengali!* (Interview)

During the first data analysis meeting, the school team were eager to talk about the experience. Their enthusiasm was evident and is captured by the researcher's notes:

When I arrived the team were all seated in the headteacher's office around a table with the tape recorder and their Learner Reflections. They were excited. I was surprised to learn that Razia had been present at the Learner Visit as I had not heard her on the tape but I noted that all their Learner Reflection sheets were written on extensively. Although the headteacher was working on her computer she was listening and joining in and she had clearly already listened to the tape with the teachers and enjoyed a great deal of discussion. (Field notes)

At the close of the project, Viv talked about the Learner Visits and what she perceived they had revealed to her as an experienced practitioner and senior school leader:

What we have found out about the children has been absolutely fascinating – Idris was so interesting but the others too are absolutely incredible. I mean Sharna's experiences at school in Afghanistan – we knew nothing about it – and as we were walking with her she just started talking as she skipped along with Razia. We didn't even know that she and Marium had been to school together in Afghanistan and they told us all about their memories. If it wasn't for this project we just wouldn't have known – we still wouldn't know! (Final interview)

Shifting views about parents and families through professional learning

Many research studies have shown that families, while they may not appear to do what the school desires in relation to supporting school literacy, are nevertheless highly involved in their children's learning and do provide rich learning opportunities outside school (Jackson and Remillard, 2005). Deficit assumptions persist and particular families may not be seen by schools as supportive or helping their children.

However, the work at St Mary's and the project overall revealed that families have many different ways of supporting children's literacy learning and many different practices that engage children as learners as part of everyday routines and events. The funds of knowledge approach adopted by the project took an open and arguably positive stance. It sought to help teachers challenge any unconscious assumptions and avoid attaching value-laden terms to what it was perceived families had to offer judged by school terms. Rather, the project sought to help practitioners establish and describe individual family's assets in terms of what they have to offer to learning. In Tveit's (2009) terms, a funds of knowledge approach is premised on an assumption of each family 'having'; in such an approach there is no deficit position, no sense of 'lacking'.

The *BC:RLL* project, captured in microcosm in this case study, surfaced rich evidence to support this view. Until the Learner Visits, the team at St Mary's was operating with a school-centric approach: they perceived parents should contribute more to their children's learning and in particular school-focused ways. The yardstick by which parents and families were measured was set by the school and was framed, more or less, by the knowledge and skills required by the National Curriculum and assessment system. The whole focus was about how to engage parents and families with the pre-set school-focused agenda. Parents and families were viewed from a markedly school-centric perspective according to the knowledge and skills they could bring to this. There was a degree of unconsciousness about this on the part of the school involved, but by adopting this strongly school-centric perspective it was clear that parents and families were the ones who were expected to travel over the bridge. It was implied that parents must meet the schools' requirements. If parents and families were too far away and couldn't bridge this gap, they were seen as 'hard to reach'.

The notion of 'hard to reach' families is often tied in with assumptions about families in lower socio-economic categories being unable to support children's literacy learning (Harris and Goodall, 2007). However, as these researchers point out: 'parents who are viewed as "hard to reach" often see the school as "hard to reach"' (2007: 5) they also suggest 'schools that successfully engage parents in learning, consistently reinforce the fact that "parents matter"' (ibid.). It seems to be a matter not only of knowledge about what parents have to offer, but of value and the development of a two-way relationship based on mutual trust and respect. Such a relationship, Harris and Goodall (2007) argue, can lead to genuine partnership, resulting in pupils' improved achievement. However, they acknowledge that:

> Schools face certain barriers in engaging parents. These include practical issues such as lack of time, language barriers, child care issues and practical skills such as literacy issues and the ability to understand and negotiate the school system. Schools can offset these barriers by supporting parents to help their children learn; personalising provision for parents as learners; improving pastoral care; listening to parents and responding to real rather than perceived needs.
>
> *(Harris and Goodall, 2007: 520)*

It is noticeable though, that despite the positive views of parents, families and communities in their report, Harris and Goodall's research frame remains school-centric and fails to take into account home and community funds of knowledge. The need to take a more open view of family and community assets is emphasised by large-scale studies such as those carried out by Grieshaber *et al.* (2012). They note a deterministic relationship between assumptions about socio-economic status and children's home literacy environments and school achievements and question the deficit view that 'children from low income, minority and immigrant families are "literacy impoverished"' (Auerbach, 2001: 385, cited in Grieshaber *et al.*, 2012: 115). In the *BC: RLL* project, at least in some schools, awareness of the potential for family and community funds of knowledge to be seen differently developed, and parental participation came to be understood as 'an open ended and multifaceted activity' (Moll and Cammarota, 2010: 304). This carried possibilities for family members to be seen as 'co-participants in and contributors to the life project of educating students' (ibid.) and prompted teachers to widen their understanding of the significance and richness of children's home learning and everyday literacy practices.

By visiting homes, asking respectful questions and by learning to listen and look with a researcher's gaze – with a willingness and openness to learn more about others – the team at St Mary's not only uncovered a wealth of knowledge and learning experiences that existed there, but also became aware of the consequences of this. As a result they began to adopt a more two-way, open perspective that was at times markedly less school-centric and which fostered two-way traffic between home and school, as well as encompassing a broader view of literacy and the children's achievements and attitudes. The team came to realise how easy it is to view parents as a homogenous group when actually the families, as Anna noted:

> *may be the same ethnicity, the same socio-economic class or the same religion, but you know they are all so very very different.* (Final interview)

While indicators such as free school meals and ethnic groupings do have a role to play in characterising the community a school serves, there is a very real danger that these measures can predispose a view that is epistemologically unsound. The Learner Visits revealed the different sets of skills and routines that were part of different families' everyday practices which surprised the team at St Mary's and prompted them to recognise and validate increased diversity.

Implications

The school team involved in the project were committed to finding a way of challenging the prevailing school-centric agenda. They began this by undertaking Learner Visits and recognising the limitations of a school-oriented perspective. As they became aware that they needed to challenge their existing assumptions and establish a new philosophy right across the school, they acknowledged that it was going to be a long journey, underpinned by self-examination, the development of new knowledge and professional dialogue. In a final visit to the school Viv talked about the ways in which she felt the rest of the staff had noticed the changes that had taken place in her and in the headteacher:

> *We just respond differently now when we engage in conversations with our parents – it's different and it's beginning to have an effect on the staff. It isn't us up there and you know – them – well it isn't us and them anymore.* (Final interview)

But she also talked about how difficult it is to share the learning experience with others if they haven't 'lived through' it:

> *I've presented our work now to different people in different contexts across the city . . . but the problem is, it feels as though it's just a bit too much for everyone. To be honest I just don't know if they really get it . . . it can just come across as – you know – visits to the home and finding out more about children's lives. But for us, as a school, it's changed the way we think. It's changed the way we see our children and our families. And changing the way we see ourselves too. And you can't tell someone to change the way they think. They have to experience it.* (Final interview)

This suggests that reading, discussing and 'being informed' about diversity within one's school community is not an effective replacement for first-hand experience of children's everyday literacy lives and home and community contexts. After the research, the team at St Mary's continued to work with staff, children, and families to establish new ways of working together and sought to support more Learner Visits in different year groups across the school. They were (and still are) working with a network of like-minded schools to co-develop their curriculum in ways that open up space for children to make connections with their lives and learning beyond school. All the schools in the network are focusing on learning more about learning and creating opportunities for professional dialogue. Laura and Viv are working to build in time for staff to talk about and develop a view of learning that is appreciative of children's strengths as learners, assets sourced and developed in their homes and communities. As Viv noted, this is a serious long-term commitment, one which will require determination and perseverance:

> *I think we are going to need to do a lot of modelling and sharing about how and why Learner Visits can be so powerful – it's about a way of thinking – we're going to have to do a lot of talking and sharing – a lot of professional discussion needs to be mixed in with work that we do – but we are just determined to get there.* (Final interview)

Conclusion

By the end of the project, there was positive evidence of shifts in teachers' perspectives and assumptions about children and parents. Understanding more about the cultures and communities that the children came from made a marked and immediate impact on the teachers: where they began with deficit views or implicit assumptions about families, their opinions had changed noticeably by the end of the project although they were sometimes constrained by the dominant discourse that views parents as primarily supporters of school work. The picture is complex, however, as the perceptions and views of families' funds of knowledge held by teachers and headteachers was often mixed, at times ambiguous or even contradictory. Through the lens of greater or less school-centredness, most notably at the beginning of the project, some views expressed by the same headteacher or teacher could be seen as indicative of both a highly school-centric view and a more home-focused approach. The project work suggests that explicit recognition of these apparent contradictions may be necessary if change and development is to be secured.

Acknowledging complexity can be challenging, especially in an age where 'simple' views of literacy and reading prevail (Wyse and Styles, 2007). It is particularly difficult for teachers and headteachers who have the responsibility of answering to accountability measures. Nevertheless, the role of the headteacher and the senior leadership team is critical in developing a less school-centric approach, one which is more aware, open and values children's and families' funds of knowledge. However, if change is to happen, it will be through joint explorations and co-constructions with schools and families working together: a matter not just of awareness but of collaboration. Such collaboration makes demands on schools in terms of time, commitment, resources and support. It also requires a cultural shift that is only likely to develop through sustained professional development and the adoption by teachers of an ongoing research role.

9

PROFESSIONAL LEARNING JOURNEYS

Rose Drury and Sacha Powell

In *BC: RLL*, while the teachers actively mediated between homes and school (González *et al.*, 2005) the LA co-ordinators were also mediators. They mediated the learning between teachers, children, families, communities and the linked university-based researchers. This was an innovative aspect of this project, and one of its strengths; it added an additional 'layer' and new insights to the original funds of knowledge project (González *et al.*, 2005). In the original project, there was a core team of anthropological researchers and the teachers. In *BC:RLL* the organisation of the project facilitated five sub groups of LA co-ordinators and teachers, some of whom worked alongside partners from other agencies, such as the School's Library Service or specialists from the Minority Communities and Ethnic Achievement Service (MCAS), to develop the teachers' expectations and knowledge of children and their families' funds of knowledge. The work was fundamentally different from previous projects in which the LA co-ordinators had been involved which created tensions. They sought to support the teachers in considering their tacit assumptions and perceptions about children and their families and this too represented a challenge. The work caused several of the LA co-ordinators to shift their professional positions with regard to working with teachers, for example:

> *This has been different because we've not had an agenda coming from a national perspective; it's more open-ended and developmental . . . I had to do a lot more thinking on my feet, assessing things for the project. I've been working alongside the teachers more.* (Final interview)

In this chapter the challenges which the LA co-ordinators experienced are considered through their reports and reflective interviews, viewed through a sociocultural theoretical lens. These reveal that while they experienced common dilemmas, there was significant learning involved for the LA co-ordinators, both personally and professionally, in relation to the children's practices, their own perceptions of families and their understanding of professional development. This overview is followed by a case study, which offers a more detailed and coherent sense of the professional learning and mediation in one of the LA teams.

LA co-ordinators as mediators

Each of the LA professionals who took part in the project had been working in their LAs for over five years. One took a more overarching strategic role across the LA for learning and literacy, while the remainder were involved more directly in organising support for schools and planning, as well as working in schools on ways to raise literacy standards in the light of the Primary National Strategy (DfES, 2007). All but one was working to the remit of the Strategy, a government initiative that funded their posts as literacy consultants. The LA co-ordinators fulfilled a dual role within the project: as learners themselves and as facilitators in local discussions and enquiries, supporting the teachers as learners, as researchers and as curriculum developers in their schools. Additionally, they played a role in identifying appropriate schools and teachers in their LAs to be involved in the project and later meeting regularly with their linked teachers locally and attending each national meeting. The local meetings involved reading, reflection and discussion as well as sharing of the teachers' insights and concerns. Some co-ordinators also offered support through teaching alongside the practitioners and undertaking Learner Visits with teachers. They all sought to identify partnerships with other agencies and documented their own learning and the progress of the project through writing regular reports for the Steering Committee, keeping reflective logs and undertaking ongoing email dialogue with their linked researcher and the wider research team.

In adopting a socio-cultural approach, the project sought to develop a participatory perspective to researching children, families and communities. Central to this approach was the role of the LA co-ordinator as mediator in guiding and collaborating with the teachers in relation to their learning about children's home practices. Building on socio-cultural and socio-historical theories, the concept of 'guided participation' (Rogoff, 1990) provides a way of viewing shared endeavours as LA co-ordinators, teachers and families co-constructed understandings. In their exploration of professional development models Crafton and Kaiser (2011) draw on the work of Rogoff (1990) in relation to learning through participation as a 'form of cognitive apprenticeship' (108). Although Rogoff's work focuses on children's learning, the concept is applied here to LA co-ordinators who served as both guides and collaborators in the project. One of the basic processes of guided participation – 'mutual bridging of meanings' (Rogoff, 2003) – relates closely to the role of the LA co-ordinator, who, together with the teachers, sought to bridge different perspectives and help develop an understanding that people do not always attribute the same meanings to phenomena. This mutual involvement involves communication, co-ordination and adjustments and the growth of understanding. As she notes: 'Guided participation ... stresses the mutual involvement of individuals and their social partners, communicating and coordinating their involvement as they participate in socioculturally structured collective activity' (Rogoff, 2003: 62–63).

Challenges and tensions of mediation

The project work represented a genuine challenge for the LA colleagues and caused several of them to shift their professional positions with regard to working with teachers. They identified a number of dilemmas and difficulties including the differences in their project roles compared to their LA roles and particularly the openness involved in the new *BC: RLL* role. In their previous work for the government-funded Primary National Strategy, the role of the LA co-ordinator had been tied to an accountability agenda; their remit was to ensure higher standards of literacy and numeracy and although many forged harmonious working collaborations with teacher colleagues, nevertheless their shared history had been one of 'training' to raise standards. This meant that their relationships and conversations were, in the words of one LA co-ordinator 'often about targets, monitoring schedules, pupil progress meetings'. To move from these expected roles, both the co-ordinators and the teachers needed to undergo some shifts of consciousness about the shared enterprise of the project *BC: RLL*. Other challenges faced by the co-ordinators involved supporting teachers as researchers and working with partners from other agencies. These demands, and the ways in which co-ordinators mediated them, are illustrated in the case study later in this chapter.

The LA co-ordinators all commented on the marked contrast between this project and their normal LA roles and viewed the 'highly significant' differences as a potential, but not insurmountable, challenge. Four of them specifically mentioned that their LA role focused on raising standards and in contrast this project work was seen to be 'a complete side step.... a movement away from standards'; it was also described as 'deeper not just procedural, nor number crunching' and 'much more human'. The *BC: RLL* project was both a research and development project; this contrasted with their previous project experience. Although some had been involved in supporting teachers as action researchers, this had been more one-to-one or in small groups focused on concerns identified by the teachers related predominantly to raising literacy standards. As a general practice the LA co-ordinators were trained by the team of regional co-ordinators to deliver the next package of Primary National Strategy (DfES, 2007) training materials to the profession. They commented that the lack of a predetermined agenda in *BC: RLL* represented a new challenge for them in their professional work with teachers and that this raised questions about the nature of their 'normal' practice. For example:

> *This has been different because we've not had an agenda coming from a national perspective; it's more open-ended and developmental . . . I had to do a lot more thinking on my feet, assessing things for the project. I've been working alongside the teachers more.*

It's been less about coming up with ideas and more about encouraging the teachers to get stuck in and do the work for themselves. So, not about me having answers, which is traditionally the mode I slip into. . . . I feel a bit ashamed to think that my 'normal' work doesn't tend to be so developmental and responsive. (Final interviews)

The emergent nature of the project also appeared to create difficulties; the co-ordinators experienced a degree of uncertainty in working in this non-traditional manner and in a less directional role, as they were 'unsure what the teachers would find out', and were 'not clear about what we might do with the new knowledge when we had collected it'. This concern to 'get the right answer' was also a concern identified by the teachers (see Chapter 4) and reflects perhaps their lack of experience of research and enquiry work, or a sense of a lack of permission/opportunity to engage in exploratory research. In several of the LAs there was a strong tradition of evaluative research which focused on the debatable 'what works' agenda (Kincheloe, 2000), seeking answers to practical issues related to targets and tests and not aimed at understanding complex social and educational issues as this study did. As Kemmis (2006) observes, the focus of the standards agenda, framed and set by government, has constrained teacher action research. Another challenge for the co-ordinators was not leading the work, nor providing professional development input as framed by a traditional course. As one noted: 'I found leaving it to the teachers difficult on one level as I like to be in control and the nature of the project meant that I could cajole, suggest etc but had to leave it to them to make changes to their own practice.' This may also highlight the lack of professional autonomy afforded the profession in recent years. The LA co-ordinators were mainly literacy consultants working to a set government agenda which included high levels of curriculum prescription for teachers and, indeed, targets for them. Those whose remit had specifically been driven by the Primary National Strategy were used to the role of training teachers in a set scripted programme aimed at raising standards. This involved taking a necessarily directive stance. In reflecting on this, one of the LA co-ordinators commented: 'they're used to being told or expected to do things . . . there's always the priority of curriculum delivery'. The co-ordinators observed that their own practice as consultants may have inadvertently created for teachers a conception of 'training' or development which focused on 'conforming or playing safe'. This is in stark contrast to the project which sought to consider and question both teachers' and co-ordinators' thinking and beliefs as much as practice. In the context of the audit culture in education, focused on attainment scores as measured by national tests, this represented a not inconsiderable challenge and a shift in practice for the co-ordinators.

In this project the LA co-ordinators were invited to work as facilitators and mediators of professional learning, with support offered on the national meetings and LA group days, in the teachers' portfolio guidance, and on email. The project team sought to position everyone involved as learners, as equal but different. The co-ordinators were thus engaged in subtle positional shifts as they sought to work alongside the teachers to guide and not direct them, engaging in guided participation as mediators. This was clearly quite demanding for literacy consultants who were, in their LA work, positioned more hierarchically, as they observed:

> *It was a challenge. It's been like a different world. This has been a facilitating role. I enjoyed listening to you [researcher] talking to the teachers and the way you draw them out, because my role is more directing, yours is more like a kind of coaching.* (Final interview)

> *I think this research has been the most challenging work I have done in my LA role. They were in the lead not me. I was very open about this with the teachers and I think this honesty helped us all — it helped to level the field.*

> *Although it was not an easy journey, the tussle meant I learnt a lot about moving the quality of teaching through positioning myself as a learner too rather than making judgments about the quality of teaching.* (Final reports)

This generated a rich, enthusiastic discourse through which the wider project team were able to share concerns and discoveries, reinforce values, purposes and shared language, identify strategic opportunities, fathom developments and make meaning within the still developing, multi-layered conceptual framework. Communications were often 'streams of consciousness', but qualified and valued as such, while responses were constructed with care to maintain control of the project and move it forwards. The discussions led some to question their own long-held values and approaches. An LA co-ordinator wrote this at the end of a long email narrative in which she explored her 'light bulb moments', reflections and some of the ideas and possible developments for schools:

> *I've been challenged on this project to really examine where my inner beliefs are rooted about how I have approached teaching/training in the past. I think I did some of this unconsciously, but is that good enough when we know the power of doing it.* (Email)

The project arguably altered the power relationship between the LA co-ordinators and the teachers, and suggested that they would collaborate with the teachers in co-constructing knowledge within the community of practice created by the project. However, this was a significant departure from the historically created neo-liberal framework in which many of the co-ordinators had been operating. Their roles had been framed by the dominant Primary National Strategy discourse which tended to position teachers as passive recipients of knowledge requiring them to submit to authority outside of their own knowledge and experience (Belenky *et al.*, 1997) and equally positioned the 'deliverers' of such knowledge hierarchically in relation to the recipients. This included interpreting policy on behalf of the teachers, rather than participating in a collective discussion about developing policy and practice. This 'one size fits all' approach runs in sharp distinction to the reflective research-oriented ethos of *BC: RLL* so that the role of mediation taken on by the LA co-ordinators meant opening up spaces for dialogue and recognising that learning is an agentic and social experience.

Developing a 'shared conceptual space' (Kemmis and McTaggart, 2005) is no easy task as the role of the facilitator is not itself neutral and involves developing an 'informed critical perspective on social life among ordinary people' (570). For the LA co-ordinators, then, the role of mediation and facilitation was by no means straightforward. In order to make spaces for shared dialogue, they needed to take a few steps back from their accustomed role. In addition, the iterative nature of the research project was unsettling. They as well as the teachers were genuinely being invited to investigate ways of making the curriculum more responsive to the children's funds of knowledge. Not only were they not used to supporting teachers as researchers, they brought to the project their own conception of 'research' just as the teachers did. They had to handle the openness and ambiguity which ethnographic research encompasses and cope with not knowing what data would surface in terms of children's out-of-school lives and with what consequence. Their positioning as mediators, supporting the teachers in the project, meant that they had to face and accommodate to the 'complexities, contradictions, tensions and richness' (Gregory and Ruby, 2011: 164) involved in research which acknowledges 'disparities of power between teachers and families and families and researchers'. The contrast between supporting teachers as researchers and running professional literacy training was also highlighted:

> As researchers visiting homes they were positioned differently, they're used to me giving them formats for planning, delivering and evaluating and they didn't get that, so they needed re-assurance and kept wanting to know if they were doing it right. (Email)

One considered that in working as a 'researcher first' and 'literacy consultant second', their practice had been characterised by an 'unusual degree of authenticity and a close professional dialogue' which was in her view 'much more effective, if time consuming'. Such a stance was evidently new to this LA co-ordinator who, while in position since the onset of the National Strategy (DfEE, 1998) had perhaps positioned herself and had been differently positioned by the Strategy and her LA, although it should be acknowledged at this stage of the journey she still talked in the language of outcomes in relation to 'being effective'. Several of the co-ordinators also referred to the 'emotionally and intellectually' demanding nature of the theoretical readings which were set. As one noted, they had to do much more than read these; they had to think and work through their own emerging understandings about children's lives and literacies and face their own assumptions and stances towards working with teachers. Crafton and Kaiser (2011) argue that working towards change through a 'communities of practice' approach informed by sociocultural understandings including the processes of collaboration, inquiry and dialogue is more powerful than an 'expert'/'learner' perspective which can diminish the power and voice of teachers as agents for change. For the LA co-ordinators this process presented some uncomfortable, if ultimately creative, tensions.

Creating partnerships with a variety of agencies represented another area of difficulty for some of the LA co-ordinators; these were in all but one case newly established and their success varied considerably. Time to build these relationships was at a premium and historically, most local authorities did not have established links between education and training and other agencies and even where these existed, the co-ordinators perceived there was often a conflict of agendas. Some external partners from the Library Service and the Minority Communities and Ethnic Achievement Service for example, were keen to be involved and provided many offers of support, but these were not fully taken up, in part because both partners found it hard to align their different goals, and because the LA co-ordinators and the teachers were unused to and perhaps nervous of working with new partners. As one of the co-ordinators in this circumstance noted: 'I think the difficulty is one of bringing together different worlds that operate in different ways to work on a shared goal. Finding a common understanding proved difficult.'

This is a familiar challenge. As Atkinson *et al.* (2007) note in their review of the literature on multi-agency working, the establishment of effective working relationships between agencies often depends as much on opportunities to communicate as other structural features; they identify four key areas: clarifying roles and responsibilities; securing commitment at all levels; engendering trust and mutual respect; and fostering understanding between agencies (3). Attempts to align differently perceived goals can also have its challenges as historically developed 'agency cultures' (Atkinson *et al.*, 2002) can seem to be disrupted by multi-agency working (130). For some LA co-ordinators, the development of relationships with these potential partners may have created conceptual barriers which, as they lacked personal links with the individuals offering involvement, proved too demanding.

In other LAs, the partners from different agencies brought a considerable richness to the work as can be seen in a later case study in this chapter involving Sofia, a Portuguese Outreach worker. Not all the participating professionals from other agencies were as assured or experienced in working with teachers as Sofia, and the language barrier for the teachers with whom Sofia worked meant she was pivotally positioned to offer support. For example, while other colleagues from the Library Service enabled access to additional texts for the classes involved and joined the LA meetings to discuss the teachers' emerging insights into the children's and families funds of knowledge, they were not as well positioned to support the actual Learner Visits. The different perceptions of individual partners from other agencies and their own remits undoubtedly added to the challenge of the project for the LA co-ordinators.

Developing new understandings through mediation

Despite these many challenges and in part in response to them, it was documented that the co-ordinators came to widen their own knowledge and understanding of teachers' professional learning, of children's literacy lives beyond school and of themselves as learners and educators. They also developed new understandings about working with others and supporting teachers in curriculum construction: children's literacy and learning in the home; teachers' professional learning; professional learning communities and learning about supporting teachers in constructing culturally responsive curricula and the personal in the professional. These categories form the basis for the next sections of this chapter.

Learning about children's literacy and learning in the home

It was evident that all the co-ordinators felt their own knowledge of children's literacy and learning in the home widened through the project. Two strands in particular emerged as significant: the first was that, in tune with their teachers' shifting views, the LA co-ordinators developed a broader view of the social, cultural and context-specific nature of literacy. The second was that they all recognised and commented upon the range and depth of digital competencies that the children demonstrated in the home. As one observed:

> *I think that the biggest shift here for me was truly understanding literacy learning in the wider sense, both as a teacher and as a consultant I have been very focused upon the reading, writing and speaking element — whereas the children we researched were clearly developing in all these areas through their roles within the family, their commitment to religion, their relationships with extended family members, their interest in their own history . . . and the growth of values to live by. . . . Education is so much more than words on a page and children have so much more to bring to lessons than the ability to decipher letters and scribe them.* (Final report)

This senior LA consultant appeared to be recognising that her conception of literacy was an institutionalised one and that this arguably 'autonomous model of literacy' (Street, 1998) fails to notice the different ways in which literacy is viewed, supported and used as part of family cultural practices. Co-ordinators increased their awareness of diversity in literacy practices and the role of the social and cultural context; again this was a common theme across the dataset for both teachers and LA co-ordinators, as was the pervading influence of popular culture and digital technology:

> *Particularly interesting has been our exploration of 21st century technology and its move into popular culture as an integral aspect of children's literacy lives. . . . We often start with texts which are a long way from some of our children's experience.* (Interim report)

> *I am now more aware of the diversity of children and families literacy practices in the home. . . . .the importance of holy texts, particularly the Bible, in the lives of families . . . the way popular culture texts are related and read in a non-linear ways . . . and the fact that the majority of these are experienced as a family together.* (Final report)

They came to question their own previous positions on popular cultural texts and digital technology:

> *Having always banned the 'Disney version' in my practice in favour of 'quality texts' I now wonder if this, like the language of texting, computer games and popular music/TV, should be given a more careful scrutiny and exploited more at the point of planning.* (Final interview)

There was also evidence in many of the LA co-ordinators' reports and interviews of increased sensitivity and awareness of making assumptions about others, including parents. Again this was developed in parallel with the teachers, for example:

> *It's like I have been tuned into a new wavelength on the video; suddenly you listen to things that you wouldn't have noticed before. The things that people say about leadership, other consultants and advisors and teachers say about parents that I would have never have picked up before. I just didn't hear them.* (Final report)

> *I think I have probably learnt more and had more involvement with families in this short project than I did have in my whole teaching career.* (Final interview)

Personal connections to their own families, themselves as children and their roles as parents also prompted them to, as one expressed it: 'being open to viewing families differently'. One co-ordinator observed that the project had helped her reflect on her own son's literacy practices and made her wonder what assumptions the school might be making about their home life, and what field notes she would make as an observer in her own home. Another voiced the view that her own parents had never been able to or indeed been invited to share their views on education or their child's home learning. She was determined this should not remain the case for other parents:

> *This has tapped into where I'm coming from. It's made me think about my own family background, the way that my own parents were. And this whole thing about parents not being able to articulate the importance that they put on education – to the educators – and the fact that we need to look beyond that. We need to really open up a space for parents, regardless of their backgrounds, to really feel engaged in their children's learning. That they have got something to contribute. My parents couldn't articulate it and I don't think they ever did. I mean they always went to everything but it was always about them sitting back and listening and being told.* (Final interview)

Learning about teachers' professional learning

The opportunity to support teachers and prompt them to engage in professional dialogue and reflection, enabled the co-ordinators to gain new insights into the nature of professional learning which their previous work (one-to-one in struggling schools or in 'delivery and training') had not made available to them. Arguably, while undoubtedly interpreting their official work roles differently in each LA, all the co-ordinators had to some degree been obliged to 'accept' this way of working, as framed by the constant provision of training materials they were expected to use and 'deliver' to teachers. It is not known the extent to which the co-ordinators had either resisted this model or had re-constructed it within the Primary National Strategy remit, but what was clear is that they were more commonly involved in 'top down training'. Such training, Freedman (2004) argues, is a form of teacher control, and in effect it could be argued the official expectations of the LA co-ordinators, the requirement that they deliver pre-packaged materials to teachers was a means of controlling LA staff too. Used to such a top-down model, the co-ordinators found the *BC: RLL* project, with its more open, iterative and research-based agenda, both demanding and engaging. It was perhaps, that positioned as learners, they were able to appreciate the teachers' difficulties and development, for example:

> *I've learnt more about myself, my struggle as a learner, being in a place that's felt uncomfortable, to have to work hard at it.* (Interview)

In particular, several began to recognise some of the barriers to professional learning, including for example the discourse of performativity (Ball, 1998) and its tight framing of teachers' perceptions:

> *It really struck me how the 'standards agenda' can make it very difficult for teachers to see the bigger picture. Requirements for levels . . . movement within sub levels often remove us from the child at the heart of it.* (Interview)

They also observed that some teachers were constrained by the school context, the head teacher's views or values, and by a desire to 'get things right', while others needed more time. As one co-ordinator commented perceptively:

> *I think it's worked – the Learner Visits, with no agenda but a set of guidelines, it worked for the people who have got the right mindset. . . . I think the people who have got the most out of this have been those who have opened themselves out to the project.* (Final interview)

In pondering upon the construction of the teachers' professional thinking, several considered whether they had created an activity orientation in the profession; as one noted, the teachers 'were probably waiting for the gap tasks that we normally set at National Strategy training', which were often related to the accountability agenda. In addition, through email discussion, they explored further this recognition of their own roles in the construction of the teachers' thinking and two questioned whether they had developed 'a dependency culture' among teachers in their LAs by delivering what one described as a 'what works and how to do it' agenda, that positioned the teachers as 'doers' – technicists even, who arguably were not required to think but to 'implement' what they were told. An interesting parallel exists here between the ways in which the LA co-ordinators may have been expected to position teachers in the nationally constructed and locally delivered one size fits all Primary National Strategy (DfES, 2006) training over the years. Had the teachers been constructed as passive receivers? The LA co-ordinators began to question whether they had paid enough attention to the teachers' professional funds of knowledge and experience.

In contrast the *BC: RLL* project foregrounded teachers as thinkers and learners and involved the LA co-ordinators in supporting them in developing new insights with and through the children in class and through their Learner Visits. They were mediating the teachers' participation in the project and this involved considerable analysis and the identification of emergent issues as well as consideration of the ramifications in terms of relationships and the curriculum. In addition, in the wider community of practice, the project prompted reading, debate and reflection with colleagues from other LAs – another rare feature within the consultants' customary professional practice, as was the value of the readings for professional learning, for example:

> *I have also seen how the judicious use of relevant academic articles has been powerful in developing understanding and practice and will use these more frequently in the future.* (Interview)

It is certainly the case that busy professionals often lack time and access to academic or research reading unless they are engaged in further professional study. As Comber (2007) notes, sustaining reflective practice means helping professionals to 'get out more' (130): 'Breaking out of the intellectual confines of deficit or normativity may require. . . . theoretical journeys and dialogic enquiries.'

Establishing a theoretically informed 'community of enquiry' is a key feature of supporting practitioner research as Comber and Kamler (2004) explain: 'While some forms of teacher research de-emphasise the intellectual, analytic and theoretical resources needed to engage in research, stressing the adequacy of the practice wisdom teachers already have, we sought to establish a community of enquiry' (Comber and Kamler, 2004: 296).

In terms of this research, the introduction to key research literature and theoretically based professional materials supported co-ordinators' observations and continuing thinking. In these ways they learnt a great deal about professional learning, that teachers need to own their knowledge and experiences and to negotiate this with others. In tune with Hibbert *et al.* (2008), who outline some prerequisites for meaningful professional change and development, they perhaps appreciated more fully the need for teachers to build from their current knowledge and practices, and for them to question this for themselves and interrogate their assumptions.

Learning about professional learning communities

Another strand of the co-ordinators' learning related to the core concept of community, particularly the development of professional learning communities. The project adopted Williams' (1976) interpretation of community (see Chapter 2) which centres on notions of equality and the quality of human relationships, and the research team sought to build such a community within and across the colleagues involved, in part by positioning themselves as learners alongside the teachers and the LA co-ordinators. The emphasis was thus not upon project structures, although these existed, but on building trust and open relationships. The co-ordinators appeared to appreciate this, as one noted:

> The partnership with HE and UKLA has been more extensive and the close relationship between a group of LAs most welcome and edifying. (Final interview)

The national meetings were founded on an iterative and responsive approach which drew upon the teachers' contributions, their understanding and their ongoing learning. In this way the professional development opportunities, which sought to develop teachers as researchers and help them analyse and understand their new knowledge about the children's out-of-school literacy lives, broadly modelled and mirrored what the LA co-ordinators were encouraged to do locally with their teachers. This was to develop and share literacy histories, acknowledge family, community and cultural influences, consider their own values and positions regarding literacy and learning in the home, and examine and build on their new knowledge and understanding by developing responsive curricula in school. The local meetings also provided time and space for the teachers and co-ordinators to talk extensively and thereby to develop mutual trust and to agree plans for their local enquiries. In Rogoff's (1995) terms, as the LA co-ordinators came to understand their role as mediators more fully, what began as guided participa-tion became 'participatory appropriation' where the teachers, and indeed the LA co-ordinators, transformed their 'understanding of and responsibility for activities through their own participa-tion' (65). Kemmis and McTaggart note that 'not all theorists of action research place this emphasis on collaboration' (563) and argue that the reflective aspects of research are 'best undertaken collaboratively by co-participants' in the research (ibid.). The collaborative aspects of experience informed teachers' professional learning throughout and demonstrated for the LA co-ordinators the value of fostering a sustained community of learners through mediation.

In the professional spaces created by the project, there was evidence of the beginnings of strong relationships, open sharing of challenges and dilemmas, the exploration of values, misconceptions and assumptions and a growing awareness of the complexity of literacy and learning. Such conversations and debates are arguably essential to avoid teachers falling prey to the ideas that they alone are responsible for children's learning and that there is one 'right' way to 'teach' literacy (Hibbert et al., 2008: 306). In the diverse learning groups and communities which gradually developed there were at least two common features: a realisation of the significance of learning relationships and a recognition of the value of an open and personal stance in relation to this. As one co-ordinator observed about the teachers in her group:

> *I think they have re-found what teaching could be for them – forming positive personal and learning relationships with others and putting this first. . . . There is loads of potential for this to transform how we approach getting to know families and children.* (Email)

The co-ordinators all noticed that they became increasingly open both with one another and with their teachers, 'much more me than usual', as one explained. In the same way that the project was encouraging the teachers to be more open with children and the teachers were encouraging greater openness on the part of the children, the co-ordinators also appeared to be building more open and reciprocal relationships with their teachers. At a national meeting, two co-ordinators voiced the view they had sometimes made assumptions about teachers in the same way that teachers/schools make about families and that they felt 'guilty' about their value judgements, and knew they had not sought to understand the teachers' perspectives and positions. This marked degree of openness and shift in positioning meant that most LA co-ordinators were working alongside teachers more as equals than in their other work. This had consequences, with one observing: 'I've felt closer with these than any other teachers I've worked with' and another noting: 'It's been tough but we've really got to know one another in a deep way'. Others too recognised the value of authenticity and the need for strong relationships in these emerging professional communities of learners. For example:

> *I made a conscious decision to be honest about how I felt. I see myself in the group differently from how I normally see myself. I've enjoyed that, it feels more genuine in terms of relationships.* (Email)

> *How do we help teachers learn when we don't know them well enough? I suppose I have always maintained a kind of critical distance because we are accountable for our time and there's been little time for informality or conversation. But now . . .* (Final interview)

The co-ordinators also appeared to value the close relationships which developed with their linked researchers, for example one observed:

> *She* [the linked researcher] *enabled me to be honest about what hasn't worked . . . I have felt safe in seeking her advice. Early on, I think I was a bit worried about how it might look if I showed that I was finding it hard but this feeling was dispelled quite quickly.* (Interview)

Another, reflecting on the project overall, highlighted the importance of working in partnership; she perceived the shared national days provided a motor for her professional role and relished the potential challenges of taking the work even further:

> *I think, if we can do more work with others, with university folk and together encourage this sort of collaborative learning between schools, I think then practices like these will show impact. Schools will be more open. Because, as you say, it's not about us telling schools what to do. It's about those schools that are doing things that work – like these- finding out for themselves and sharing that in a wider way. . . . And really you know our role then becomes more challenging. We have to find ways of really working alongside and pushing people on from where they are and what they are finding out . . . which is what this project has been doing.* (Interview)

The opportunities afforded by the research developed the LA co-ordinators' understanding of the significance of strong open relationships within professional learning communities. They came to understand that collaboration and ongoing participation in a 'joint enterprise' can bring about profound changes in under- standing and practice (Crafton and Kaiser, 2011).

Learning about supporting teachers in constructing culturally responsive curricula

This aspect of the project work created challenges for the LA co-ordinators who were trying to help the practitioners consider how they could use their new knowledge – about themselves, the children and families – to change the way they planned for learning. In seeking to avoid the development of a tokenistic response, which merely paid lip service to the cultural practices or interests of the children, the LA co-ordinators felt somewhat daunted and voiced their concerns. Some had little knowledge of the teachers' planning and curriculum practices, while others knew that some of these were quite rigid and structured and they were concerned how best to enable the teachers to be more flexible, building a unit of work around the children's out-of-school learning. An extended email debate revealed different expectations, practices and worries about constructing curricula in a more respon- sive manner. The co-ordinators were also unsure how to give children more space to come into the classroom and open their 'virtual schoolbags' (Thomson, 2000). Many also discussed the perception that much of what the teachers had learnt was not limited to literacy, and they were even less confident about how to weave this knowledge into the broader curriculum.

Based on the teachers' hexagons of each child's home literacy practices, created into an asset blanket (see Figure 5.1), the teachers identified common themes on which they might build, while still seeking to respect individual differences. Building on the assets that the children showed in their home learning seemed partly to ease the LA co-ordinators' concerns and afforded new learning opportunities for them to engage with the teachers as 'co-learners'. Through such insider engagement they had the opportunity to evaluate their new ways of working:, 'I found that posing questions, modelling behaviour in relationships with children and offering a range of suggestions for consideration rather than [saying] "this is how you should do it" or "this is what I would do" was more effective.' For this LA co-ordinator there was a shift in positioning from a more hierarchical 'all knowing' stance to a more collegial position. Others came to conceive of curriculum more broadly, shifting from a perception of curriculum as the content to be covered to an understanding of curriculum as integrated with pedagogy and assessment and therefore related to the children's funds of knowledge and how these can be drawn into the way learning is designed. One co-ordinator revealed that for her, this last stage of the work had significantly shifted her thinking:

> I have moved from a deep belief that the school curriculum is 'right' to now reconsidering the 'rights' of children, families and communities to determine at least the starting points for learning.

> Getting out of deficit discourses lies at the heart of this project, and there are practical ways that this can be done to enable more equitable outcomes for pupils. Social justice is, in the end, what this project is about. (Final reports)

Working alongside a bilingual outreach worker: a case study

The case study which follows focuses on the work of a LA co-ordinator in partnership with professionals from other agencies. The case study describes how the co-ordinator, partners from other agencies, headteachers and teachers learned together about children's literacy and learning in the home, about teachers' professional learning, developing professional learning communities and the challenges in constructing a culturally sensitive pedagogy. It reflects the shifting perceptions of all the partners from other agencies as the project progressed.

From the outset, the multilingual nature of the local authority was recognised and valued as a rich context for uncovering children's and families' funds of knowledge. The involvement of Sofia as a bilingual outreach worker with the Portuguese-speaking community was the first step in recognising the need for someone who shared the language and culture of the local community. The significance of Sofia's role was highlighted in her final interview when she talked about the importance of providing the opportunity for parents to speak their mother tongue, for her contribution in terms of understanding the backgrounds of the families, and as she stated, 'being at ease' in her role. But, more importantly she provided a different perspective for the project: 'I am not so much into the school thoughts; the way that they see things is sometimes different.'

The complexities of these different ways of seeing things is presented here as a multi-layered case study reflecting the views of Sofia a bilingual outreach worker, Tess, the LA co-ordinator, Lyn an experienced specialist English as an Additional

Language (EAL) teacher and Laura, a classroom teacher. As Sofia noted at the outset: 'It's not that the Portuguese community cannot learn, I just think you need to have someone saying maybe you could do this.'

The first 'layer' is that the 'standards agenda' (a national agenda to raise standards in schools) can be problematic for teachers and schools, particularly in multilingual contexts and in schools where children are new to English. Tess illustrated this in her reflections on the pressure schools are under to present information on attainment:

> *Requirements for levels and sub-levels, and movement within sub-levels often remove us from the heart of it. The need to record a level for a new entrant EAL learner with little to no English presents schools with a difficulty in terms of numerical tracking.* (Interim report)

The denominational school St John's Primary is in an inner city borough with a high percentage of minority ethnic children. The school population reflects the wider cultural and linguistic nature of the area, with 89 per cent of the children bi/multilingual with Portuguese speakers as the largest, and underachieving, group. At the beginning of the project, the headteacher said: 'when children enter school with very low levels of English . . . many speak no English at all, it brings a lots of issues with it.'

The standards agenda may lead schools to take a deficit view of EAL learners. Sofia's statement that 'apparently children from Portuguese backgrounds weren't doing so well in terms of school achievement' is in sharp contrast to the central notion of the project which seeks to find out the funds of knowledge in the community. As Sofia stated at the end of the project, 'I think we need to challenge our own perceptions . . . looking at the positives, not the negatives'.

A key theme in Sofia's contribution to the research project related to her perceptions of the power relationship between home and school:

> *Parents will see that the school has got the power and . . . there is conflict because the parents still want to be part of the children's life . . . there is always going to be a conflict in the way that schools want things to be done and how they perceive parents should behave with their children.*

> *The school has been into the home environment, there's more of a friendly relationship . . . they're more on the same level.* (Final interviews)

Her view was that by moving into the home environment the project had made a difference: 'they're more like on the same level and they've shown what they can do at home.' However, both Lyn and Tess raised the issue of resistance from the school. Tess felt that this arose because the school believed, 'we can do this perfectly well, we know all about the Portuguese. It's fine'. And, in her final interview, Sofia high-lighted the constraints to bringing about change in relation to multilingual communities: 'I think personally it [the project] did have an impact, but whether that in translation means in practice anything will change, because it's up to who is higher, to make it happen.'

A key theme to arise in this local authority was a change in attitude to the Portuguese-speaking community and children are learning at home: 'because usually parents see schools like this are "their" territory, it's not my one; I'm not in power here. Some teachers use it as a powerful tool as well, their territory.'

Opening up a different view of learning

The second layer concerns the insights provided by the bilingual outreach worker, Sofia, who mediated between teachers and families and, because she had a different perspective, offered a different view of what was happening: 'The teachers could see that the families could open up a bit more with me, because I speak the language and understand where they are coming from.' Tess noticed this, recording in her spring term report that:

> *Her personal insight into the background of the families has allowed deeper layers of meaning to their* [the teachers'] *reflections on the interviews.* (Spring report)

The role of bilingual staff in English schools is documented in Drury's (2007) study of young bilingual learners at home and at school. The unique position of the Bilingual Teaching Assistant is highlighted here as a mediator of language and culture for young children entering an English speaking school setting. In *BC: RLL* the children were viewed as active participants in their learning at home, but as acknowledged throughout this text, these resources or 'funds of knowledge' of the child's world outside the classroom are rarely drawn on in school. Bilingual staff have an important role in mediating between the cultural and linguistic expectations of home and school and in this case Sofia's role was as a mediator bridging the LA co-ordinator, families, teachers and children's understandings and enabling new perspectives to be developed.

When making Learner Visits, the central importance of parents being able to use their mother tongue (even if they were competent in English) presented important messages about the project – the teachers were asking parents to talk about personal matters about their children's learning and the opportunity to share these thoughts in mother tongue meant that they could 'open up' more, as Sofia observed: 'The parents felt comfortable talking to me. They would switch from one language to another. Just to be able to express.'

The importance of finding out about children's multilingual literacies and use of mother tongue for learning is uncovered in the case study of Lyn and Vincente (aged seven) in the following section. This 'fund of knowledge' can be neglected by teachers who may, as Sofia commented, 'assume that this family, they don't do anything . . . it has probably given Lyn more information than she was expecting'. However, it is possible that here Sofia was expressing tacit assumptions about teachers too.

Initial views of home literacy and learning

Because of the multilingual nature of St John's Primary, understanding children's multilingual literacies, including their use of home languages, was a central theme in uncovering their funds of knowledge. However, during the first interview the headteacher commented:

> *EAL doesn't help. If our children are coming into school with no English, it means that often parents have very limited English. We try to address the EAL issues at school, but it's very hard for a Portuguese-speaking parent to read an English reading book at home with their children.* (Initial interview)

The view expressed by the headteacher and teachers may have an impact on how these funds of knowledge are viewed by parents and children in the school. Lyn was a very experienced specialist EAL teacher who worked across the school and had been involved in family reading. She commented about constraints:

> *It's been a very strictly run school . . . it's difficult to get parents to interact. The parents . . . are lovely really, they're very obedient somehow, they are not challenging at all, they don't have a lot of questions . . . they're very supportive.* (Initial interview)

Vincente was a 7-year-old Portuguese speaking boy, identified by Lyn as having '*poor reading skills*'. Her early assessment of Vincente was that '*he's a really clever boy, but has a very poor visual memory and problems with his reading*'. During an interview with Lyn at the beginning of the project she described his learning outside school as follows:

> *He doesn't read at home. I don't think he feels confident reading at home. He doesn't read Portuguese, but they speak Portuguese at home. He said he didn't read at home.* (Interview)

Lyn perceived Vincente as a mature boy who was 'keen to learn' at school, but her understanding of his learning at home was that his mother would not be able to help him, partly because the language used at home was Portuguese, and partly because she would not have the required knowledge or skills to support his school learning. Lyn reported that she had asked in school if his mum read at home, Vincente had immediately replied: 'Of course not!' This view of parental knowledge was reflected in her views on the family literacy sessions. She stated that as the children got older, they talked about things to her, but she said, 'from families, there's not an awful lot'. She ran workshops for the Portuguese-speaking parents, 'telling them how it's taught . . . so not an awful lots of relaxed chit chat', again reinforcing the view that parents' literacy knowledge was not valued as highly as the school's expectations in relation to literacy. Furthermore, in a discussion about how children use their funds of knowledge in the classroom, for example using their home languages, Lyn responded, 'they wouldn't'. It is widely documented (e.g. Kenner, 2012) that children in multilingual contexts construct multiple identities and develop their multilingual skills in their homes and communities and that mainstream schools rarely recognise and value community languages. Heller refers to these ideas as 'monolingualising ideologies' (1995: 374). It is interesting to note that, despite the knowledge and experience Lyn had accumulated as an EAL teacher, at the beginning of the project she expressed a somewhat deficit perspective. However, as she became a researcher and undertook Learner Visits she began to adopt a different position in relation to Vincente's learning.

Lessons from the Learner Visit: 'I wake them up with Beethoven'

The interview with Vincente's mother, Graca was a turning point in changing how Lyn viewed Vincente and his family. Graca welcomed the meeting and it was evident that the presence of Sofia, enabled a more open conversation in both English and Portuguese. Lyn's apprehension about the Learner Visit disappeared when Graca greeted them in a relaxed manner and when she began to describe how she talked to her son and explained things to him, so that he would grow up a calmer person. The first insight into Vincente's home experience was the family's shared love of music. (All conversations were in Portuguese, with Sofia translating, later the tapes were translated into English.)

> Graca: *He plays the guitar . . . sometimes he'll take the guitar to try to play . . . all day, all day, sometimes I have to say to him stop . . . I don't know how to play but I like to listen to music and we like to dance.*
> Sofia: *Do you usually do that?*
> Graca: *Yes, everyday, all the time.*
> Sofia: *Samba?*
> Graca: *Everything, samba, everything, we like to listen to everything.*
> Graca: *Sometimes my sister and I, cause she's separated as well, and she has a daughter as well and when we are home, we do a lot of parties with the children. Just us, and they love it we put music on and jump on the bed and they dance, Vincente dances a lot . . .*
> Sofia: *Does he like it?*
> Graca: *Oh he loves it.*
> Sofia: *What sort of music do you listen to?*
> Graca: *We listen to Brazilian music, but the more traditional ones, soft ones like Ton Jobin so that they don't get too excited. In the morning I wake them up with Beethoven to get them up but I think that it makes them sleepier they don't want to wake up.* (Transcription from home visit)

The picture of Vincente's home experiences was more complex than Lyn had anticipated. Of particular significance was the strong social interaction within the family: Graca lived with her sister, her niece, Vincente and his sister, Pietra. The sharing of roles within their cohesive family and strong spiritual and emotional connections were all aspects of Vincente's domains of knowledge which served as a foundation for learning. There was also the sadness and anxiety expressed about the fact that his father left them to return to Brazil: 'Sometimes he is sad and cries because of his dad . . . now he is older and he was really close to his dad and I think that he is suffering.' Graca explained how the links with his father were maintained through telephone conversations and Skype.

The second insight into Vincente's language and literacy experiences arose from conversations with Graca about the languages spoken, read and written in the home and wider community:

> Lyn: *So you speak Portuguese at home?*
> Graca: *Yes, only Portuguese, but between them just English . . . they mix it sometimes when they are so excited they just speak in English but with me and my sister they speak in Portuguese . . . with my family in Brazil . . . they speak well in Portuguese, very good. Some words they confuse, but they speak really well.* (Transcription from home visit)

Vincente's mother was proud of the fact that her children spoke their mother tongue, Portuguese, very well and communicated with the family (including their father) in Brazil. In addition, his mother commented on his literacy skills:

> Graca: *He tries to read in Portuguese. It is quite funny him reading. He doesn't know how to write, but Pietra doesn't know how to read, but she tries to read in Portuguese. But Vincente is curious and he wants to do things.*
> Sofia: *Can he read it?*
> Graca: *Yes . . . it's not perfect, but I know that he can do it . . . he's doing it by himself.* (Transcription from home visit)

This insight into Vincente's home learning illustrates the widely held view that families from language backgrounds other than English are generally assumed to be lacking in literacy – a view held by Lyn earlier in the project.

Developing knowledge of the social, linguistic and cultural context

In these conversations with Graca about her son, a richer picture of Vincente's linguistic abilities and multilingual literacies was developing. Contrary to the views held in school that Vincente did not read at home, his mother described in some detail a boy who was very keen to learn, and who was learning to read in Portuguese, as well as English (and also learning the guitar), with his mother, sister and extended family. A further aspect of Vincente's life was explored through a discussion of Graca's journey which brought her, and her children, to the community where they now lived and to the current school. Graca talked at length about the importance of a denominational school, and bringing up her children in a religious way:

> *The children in today's world, especially here, they grow up a lot of times without believing in God . . . I think that when you believe in God you are a calmer person, you are able to listen and think in a different way . . .*

> *We have to go to the church . . . and the priest knows them, he is a Brazilian priest . . . and our nun is Portuguese, she is really sweet . . .* (Transcription from home visit)

The religious texts read at home were written in Portuguese and Lyn reflected upon the fact that in answer to her question, 'does your mum read at home?' he had answered 'no, of course not!' She remembered that Vincente had said, 'well, she actually reads the bible', but the connection had not been made with the school's expectations of reading.

A third insight into Vincente's learning arose from Graca's frustration that she does not always know how to help her children with their school work, because the way of teaching is different to her experience of learning in Brazil. She gave an example of learning 'times tables': 'his teacher explained in a different way and Pietra's teacher explained a different way and Pietra understood the way Vincente explained to her, so Vincente is teaching his sister the English way.' Graca explained that her children were really keen to learn but she didn't have the knowledge of the English school system, and 'now because their dad is not around I am the person that needs to take over this, like the things his dad used to do'. Although the school's perception of the parents of EAL children was sometimes expressed in deficit terms, the picture emerging of Vincente's family was that education, and particularly literacy, was of the highest importance. In fact, Graca explained that, despite the opportunities offered to her to move area, to change job, she had chosen to keep her children at the same school for their stability and educational achievement.

Lyn's perception of Vincente's learning at home had changed over the course of her conversations with Graca, who played a key role as mediator in developing teachers' professional learning. At school, Vincente was viewed as a boy who was a poor reader; at home he was a keen learner, reading Portuguese books and working with his mother, using dictionaries and observing her reading of the bible. This was a family with strong spiritual and moral values with a strong mother who believed in the importance of being a 'calmer person' and waking up listening to Beethoven.

The layers of this case study give an insight into the complexities of understanding more about the social and cultural contexts for children's literacy learning. The strength of multi-professional collaboration and mediation is evident in the development of new professional learning communities. The opportunity to link with the bilingual outreach worker added a particular dimension to the research contributing to the emerging picture by offering a link between homes and school. This became particularly clear where the home language was not English. Not only did the teachers gain a great deal of knowledge from the Learner Visits but they were also able to capture ideas that might have been missed without translation (Anderson *et al.*, 2010). The first visits were to a home where it was perceived that there was not much support from the mother because of English not being her first language. However, both revealed valuable insights about the children's home literacy and learning experience. What may have begun as a deficit view of some homes and a more positive view of others emerged as being much more equivalent as the project developed, supported by the mediating roles of both Sofia in the homes (and in the meetings) and Tess in the LA. This mediation, alongside opportunities for discussion and reflection, led to a more nuanced view of homes, families and shared literacy experiences.

Conclusion

Fullan's (2005) formulation that change happens best when there is a balance between challenge and support holds good for the work of the LA co-ordinators and some partners from other agencies in this project. The role of mediation made professional and personal demands on the co-ordinators as they sought not only to take on a researcher stance themselves, but to support the teachers as they opened up their practice to new understandings. In LAs small teams of professionals, all of whom had been placed in the position of questioning their preconceptions and previous relationships with learners and their families learned together. Establishing a more open view based on the Learner Visits took time and effort. Evidence from the LA co-ordinators indicated the importance of developing a shared and open understanding of the social and culturally specific nature of literacy and forging good working partnerships if change is to happen (McLaughlin, 2005). As highlighted in the case study, the project developed a participatory perspective as teachers, LA co-ordinators, families and communities co-constructed their understandings.

The project design allowed the LA co-ordinators to consider, critique and change their professional practice. They found the project positioned them differently, and as a consequence subtly shifted their professional identities. The co-ordinators came to understand the significance of strong, open relationships within professional learning communities the value of 'not knowing' and not always leading, thus fostering the teachers' autonomy and agency. Like the teachers, the co-ordinators developed greater understanding of the social, cultural and context-specific nature of literacy, including a clearer sense of the range and complexity of multilingual experiences that the children demonstrated in the home.

10

CONCLUSION

Reflections and implications

Teresa Cremin and Marilyn Mottram

In the face of the rapidly changing nature of literacy and the persistence of deficit discourses in education which conceive of some families as lacking valuable literacy experiences, there is arguably an urgent need to establish new links between home and school which build on the practices and understandings that already exist in homes and communities. The *BC: RLL* project invited teachers to do just this: to position themselves as learners and researchers, reflect upon their assumptions constructed in part by the available discourse and open themselves up to new learning about children and families. The project enabled teachers to undertake Learner Visits to children's homes and to see the children they taught through a new research based lens. They were supported to become attentive observers and engaged listeners (Forsey, 2010), trying to understand children's everyday literacy lives, widen their understandings about twenty-first-century literacy identities, habits and cultures, and rethink the relationships between children's, families' and schools' practices. They were also supported as they began to unlock the children's and their families' funds of knowledge and make connections between these and their lives in school, such that new and more responsive classroom approaches could be created that recognised, validated and built on children's literacy lives and fostered positive literacy identities.

These demanding and diverse aims were differentially met. All the teachers undertook Learner Visits and as they shed the role and identity positions of teacher – of expert – and re-positioned themselves as learners and researchers they came to know some of the children and their families in new ways, and began to develop an understanding of the cultural, linguistic and social assets children bring to school from home. They also began to recognise that these cognitive resources can and should be used in the classroom and that they could develop responsive approaches that tapped into the young people's funds of knowledge. Through being able to locate children's literacy learning and through examining their own literacy histories and practices, many of the teachers in the project began to reconceptualise literacy in the twenty-first century and take on a wider view of literacy in school. They came to acknowledge that they were in a position of power in defining for parents and children what 'counts' as valid and valuable literacy and developed a wider view of the inseparable relationship between literacy and learning. They also came to recognise the variety and richness of children's funds of knowledge and that the system of 'school' stretched into children's homes – far beyond the school walls and in ways they had not known. Not all came to share their own home literacy practices or make personal connections in class-rooms, although in the context of the Learner Visits they often opened up with parents. Some teachers came to question their assumptions about particular children and their families or about parents more generally and began to build stronger, more reciprocal relationships with both parents and children. Some parents' perceptions of teachers also changed as a result of teachers' greater openness. While recognising the children's and families' diverse funds of knowledge, the teachers found it hard to create responsive pedagogical practice, school, cultural and time constraints made this difficult, and the consistency of this varied considerably. Some did, however, negotiate ways of working which built on the children's literacy lives and designed learning opportunities to connect home and school experience.

This UKLA research and development study, while drawing on the principles underpinning the seminal studies (Moll *et al.*, 1992; González *et al.*, 2005) and subsequent work in this area (see Hogg, 2011; Rodriquez, 2013 for recent reviews), focused more exclusively upon children's (and teachers') lived experience of literacy. The study was also differently contextualised in five areas of England (both urban and more rural.) This final chapter synthesises the project's findings, and offers a reflective critique of the work, highlighting the difficulties and tensions encountered and the lessons learned. In so doing it affords readers a more nuanced understanding of the teachers' and the wider team's journeys and makes recommendations for future work on building home–school communities.

Teachers as researchers

Central to the project's process were the teachers as researchers, conducting ethnographic case studies of selected children, entering into communities and families and holding up mirrors to their own perceptions and prejudices. In supporting the teachers as researchers, the project team deliberately chose not to visit the children's homes alongside them in order to explore a model for possible LA or school use, though it is clear methodological and theoretical support and sustained collegial engagement with other researchers was essential in this work. The same understandings and insights would not have been reached (nor the resultant pedagogic action or parental relations), if the university-based researchers had visited families and reported back to the teachers still located comfortably in their schools.

A core task of participatory research, as Kemmis and McTaggart (2005) acknowledge, is to include:

> widening groups of people in the task of making their own history, often in the face of established ways of doing things and often to overcome problems caused by living with the consequences of the histories others make for us.
>
> *(Kemmis and McTaggart, 2005: 598)*

The prevailing accountability culture in England has historically positioned teachers as knowledgeable experts; expected to lead, to know, and to impart their knowledge to children and parents in order to raise standards.

In stepping outside the school boundary and learning through enquiring, listening and observing, the teachers were radically repositioned. They were not in school with its security system offering 'staff only' access, they were not in their classrooms with the door closed, nor were they positioned as deputy headteachers, senior leaders, subject consultants or class teachers. Instead they were entering unknown territory – the children's homes – as learners. Furthermore, they were not arriving with information, critical feedback or advice about the school's agenda; rather they were visiting as interested professionals who wished to know more about the everyday lives, routines and literacy practices of the children. In this context, their professional knowledge, which related to curriculum, pedagogy and standards of attainment, was of considerably less value to them and of relatively little use. The teachers were not being called upon to instruct or manage, or to inform parents about their children's behaviour, achievements or targets. They were being asked to listen, to look and to learn without judging. By placing the teachers outside their comfort zones as professionals, it appeared they learned more. In reflecting upon the visits with the linked researchers (and later with other teachers and the LA co-ordinators), they were involved in the tracing out of what they had seen and heard which, through recounting orally and on paper, they began to analyse and interpret. The collaborative nature of this reflective enquiry process was crucial in helping all involved to recognise their own tacit assumptions, judgements and sometimes bias. Through valuing the children's funds of knowledge drawn from home, the teacher researchers forged not only different practices about literacy teaching but different professional identities. The teacher disposition began to make way for a more enquiring researcher disposition.

However, there were many challenges in inviting teachers to become not only researchers but a particular kind of researcher using an ethnographically styled approach, and crossing not only the physical boundaries of their schools, but also cultural and role boundaries. Many experienced anxiety and discomfort as they shed the expected social practices and dispositions of the teacher and negotiated the different disposition and perceptions of a researcher. This involved new actions, new perceptions and new appreciations. As researchers they were invited not only to observe and participate in Learner Visits, but in the classroom as well. As Hume and Mulcock (2004) argue, there is both tension and balance in research. It means being part of the context and to some degree being outside it; being part, in order to gain access and understanding, but stepping back both from the classroom and the homes visited in order to reflect upon and analyse new understandings. Maintaining both insider and outsider positions is particularly difficult for teachers whose roles as educators imply a certain kind of authority position in schools. Examining this duality and the value and dilemmas of both positions, Gregory and Ruby (2011) in their ethnographic studies connect to Bakhtin's ideas around the dialogic self, arguing that through 'double voicing' – 'a process of enrichment could take place, where both sides (teachers and researcher) joined in an inseparable dialogue' (171).This reflexive dialogue played a central role in the *BC: RLL* project; the teachers were reflective of their own literacy practices but at the same time they were in a position (and were enabled) to reflect upon imposed policy and practice – the 'game called literacy' that they were required to play as 'teachers' in the system. They were positioned to look inside themselves and outside at the system and were also invited to see the world of the child in the middle, straddling home and school. This enabled new understandings to emerge.

While Cochran-Smith and Lytle (1993) assert that the specific form that teacher research may take is less important than that it draws upon their intellectual engagement and experience, the project showed that if teachers are supported in learning to look and listen with an ethnographic eye and ear, this has the potential to afford new insights and can help them confront long-held assumptions and unquestioned 'knowledge' about children and their families. As González *et al.* observe, 'we learn ethnography by doing ethnography' (2005: 9) and this was evidenced as teachers sought to listen not judge, and adopt an emic perspective, understanding others' positions through being repositioned themselves. Research undertaken within the boundaries of their classrooms would not have afforded the same opportunities, nor might it have encouraged the same degree of discomfort, challenge and risk-taking.

> The real stuff of teacher research isn't 'safe.' It is radical and passionate, deeply personal and profoundly political-richly embedded in situations where the teacher's stance on her own practice and intellectual life matter, and where teachers' work lives, commitments, and relationships are complex and entangled.
>
> *(Lytle, 2008: 373)*

Through engaging in supported systematic inquiry and reflecting critically upon their perceptions and practices as educators, some of the teachers (and the LA co-ordinators) came to question the more traditionally conceived professional development in which their schools were involved. The core team recognised the difficulties experienced by the teachers in positioning themselves between the high profile 'what works' teaching agenda and the project's more open research agenda in which they gradually became involved. The high degree of tension between research and practice evidenced in *BC: RLL* developed in part because the teachers, working in the context of the English government's Literacy Strategy since 1998 (DfES, 1998), were used to the discourse of 'training', and saw this as involving the receipt of explicit guidance and practice expectations. The open endedness inherent in the research endeavour was not part of the educational culture in the schools involved; the teachers were used to working with prescribed and delineated outcomes, outcomes which were required. The discourse of research, particularly research involving visits beyond school to observe, enquire, and listen, put them in a position where no-one was telling them what to do and the outcome could not be predicted, it was unknown. This fostered insecurity.

While the teachers differentially took up and negotiated their identity positioning as researchers, and did not find the experience of being positioned as learners and researchers either accessible or comfortable, the spaces of discomfort that were opened up by the project led over time to more extended conversations – with themselves through reflection, with colleagues on the project and the wider research team and with the children and families who welcomed these researchers into their homes. The time set aside for communal reading, reflection and debate both in national and local meetings, as in the earlier 'study groups' (González *et al.*, 2005), was highly significant in fostering individual and collective understanding. These opportunities to talk not only helped the teachers understand more about research principles and processes, but also afforded them space to tentatively voice their hypotheses about the value and meaning of what they were experiencing. In the open spaces set aside for discussion, teachers, LA co-ordinators and university-based researchers took time to pause, to reflect, to connect, to conjecture and to question – together. Through the work the teachers became increasingly aware of the ceilings placed upon their professionalism, and of the new opportunities for exploration and enquiry that were afforded them through engaging in this way as researchers. A few, working in schools where support was forthcoming, sought to sustain this involvement through later project work on Master's courses for example or as part of their work in school. Many, recognising the value of working with uncertainty and adopting an enquiring stance, developed more open exploratory approaches that gave the children more space for collaborative enquiry in their classrooms.

University, local authority and school partnership research

The project *BC: RLL* was somewhat counter-cultural; it was not an 'intervention study', nor was it focused upon the prevailing standards agenda. It was a collaborative university, LA and school research and development partnership to enable all members to come together as learners; strong emphasis was given to the argument that all involved were journeying together, learning from and with one another as they travelled. The stance of partners in learning was sought in order to create collective understandings through developing learning communities, strengthened by the teachers' unique position as researchers visiting homes. The frame of the project incorporated features not always documented or analysed in practitioner research (Groundwater-Smith and Mockler, 2006), in particular the ongoing research relationship between the university researchers, the LA co-ordinators and the teacher researchers. Additionally, as noted above, rather than simply gathering information or offering views to university researchers (who then depart to analyse the data), the teachers were centrally placed and the LA co-ordinators played an important role. Inside the data gathering, the teachers took up positions as researchers and mediators between home and school. The university colleagues positioned more on the outside (as none visited homes), sought to support the teachers in gathering and analysing their data, while simultaneously researching the teachers' own journeys. Alongside the LA co-ordinators, they also took a mediating role serving as guides and collaborators, bridging different perspectives and developing their own understandings in the process. By asking questions to prompt reflection upon the teachers' observations, field notes, reflective records, the transcribed interviews and the wider home/community context, the university-based researchers and LA co-ordinators worked to support the teachers' emerging analyses and insights. These discussions and the ongoing debates about the research literature and methodological issues were central to the partnership and served to help the teachers question their descriptions and explanations and examine the theoretical assumptions which underpinned them, as well as enhance awareness of the value-oriented positions of all partners. As Kemmis (2006) acknowledges, participatory research requires a pluralistic outlook and awareness of one's own fallibility; this meant that the partnership between the teachers, the LA co-ordinators and the university-based researchers needed to be underpinned by openness and trust. This was required to share assumptions, discuss issues, debate perspectives, challenge points of view and develop new insights about one's own views and those of others. There was evidence of such rigour and trust in the school-based analysis meetings with the university researchers, in small groups on national days and in the open and lengthy email interchanges between and within the various sub-groups in the project, though it took time to develop and was not easy to foster across the multiple contexts of the work.

The identity positions of all involved in the partnership were at times challenged by the nature of the work, which was as much about teachers' and the LA co-ordinators' reflexivity in exploring changes in their own ideas and understandings, as was 'found out' through the Learner Visits and work with the case study children. The teachers found developing researcher dispositions within the ethnographic approach risky and demanding; in particular they noted difficulties in coping with the openness involved and knowing what to look for and what to record. The LA colleagues experienced similar tensions with regard to the risks involved: they felt they were being subversive in their attention to a project that was not overtly related to the standards agenda, and that the openness, lack of structure and the focus on finding out (and thus not knowing), was unusual and somewhat unsettling. Their commitment was unwavering however, and positioning themselves alongside the teachers as learners, the co-ordinators markedly developed their understanding of productive professional development. They came to perceive that dialogue, debate and challenge among equals was necessary for professional learning, and contrasted this with what they perceived was the conception of professional training reflected in the National Strategy (DfES, 2007). This they came to view as prescriptive and transmission-focused, a series of packages delivered to raise literacy standards, which were neither cognisant of teachers' needs or funds of knowledge nor able to be responsive to them.

The research model employed in the *BC: RLL* project, while drawing on the work of Moll *et al.* (1992), additionally afforded a critical role to these LA co-ordinators. This was both innovative and potentially influential, since they too developed their understandings of literacy, of children's and families' practices and of professional learning. The application of these insights has potential in their future work, which altered significantly as the project drew to a close, since the National Strategy infrastructure was dismantled and four of the five LA co-ordinators took new posts as senior leaders in primary schools. The involvement of the partners from other agencies, while not fully developed within the project, indicated that potential exists for new and alternative collaborations, particularly for example with colleagues from the local community services, such as the Minority Communities Achievement Service and Family Liaison Officers. In sum, the model suggests there is scope for multi-agency partnerships of teachers (from individual schools or as members of school federations or Teaching Schools) working with university colleagues, local education personnel and other agencies to build new home–school communities based around wider recognition of children and families' funds of knowledge.

Teacher development

Despite the difficulties inherent in undertaking collaborative partnership research, the teachers' unique positions as educators, looking inwards to themselves and outwards to the school and the wider contexts of children's lives were undoubtedly an asset to the project. There were clear benefits for many; for professional understanding and pedagogic practice, for relationships and in some instances for the wider school community. There were examples of 'awakenings' (Greenan and Dieckmann, 2004) as teachers through researching learners' lives and exploring new concepts, reconstructed their understanding of learning, enabling them to envisage and plan for alternative approaches. For some, transformative learning took place, resulting in altered perspectives, understandings and visions of selves, relationships, power and positioning (O'Sullivan, 2003). The overall picture, while very varied, suggests that as teachers developed researcher dispositions and learned about the children and their literacy practices they also became increasingly aware of their own literacy identities and over time began to reconceptualise literacy. This prompted many to question the limitations of school literacy and to realise their authority as educators in shaping ideas about the nature of literacy learning in school. New pedagogic practices were developed as teachers sought to respond to and encompass the children's literacy and learning experiences beyond school. In addition, many new relationships with parents were made and some teachers came to challenge their assumptions about perceived deficits in children's and families' learning and literacy. Each of these elements of teacher development is now considered.

Teachers' knowledge of children and their literacy practices

The teachers began the project with a highly restricted knowledge of the children's everyday lives and practices and scant awareness of their interests, passions and pleasures beyond school. Through exploring these, both by working with and through their classes and by undertaking Learner Visits to homes, they became aware of the diverse social, cultural and linguistic practices in the children's homes and communities. They were surprised by the breadth and depth of the children's funds of knowledge and came to appreciate that children experience a wide range of learning and literacy practices outside school that are neither recognised nor replicated inside it. These included specific cultural and religious practices alongside other social practices in different families and communities. The teachers also found out more about the children as rounded individuals and as family members and came to appreciate their active, agentic and independent engagement as learners outside school and not just within the home. Significantly too, they came to appreciate the children's proficiencies with different literacy practices that emerged from their funds of knowledge, in particular their extensive knowledge of popular cultural texts and the range of digital technologies that they were familiar with and could use. However, some teachers demonstrated a degree of 'digital blindness' and had to be helped to notice the presence of digital media in children's homes. Commonly their new knowledge significantly altered the teachers' perceptions and expectations of the learners. In large part the teachers' initial knowledge of children was 'thin and single stranded' related mainly to the standards agenda, but through the Learner Visits they came to appreciate the young learners' 'multidimensional depth and breadth' (Gonzalez *et al.*, 2005). Their newly informed and more mindful stance towards the children they visited, reflected a more nuanced understanding of them as unique individuals with their own personal interests, emotional lives and complex histories.

Initially operating with a narrow conception of literacy, defined by the English education system and its attendant assessment framework, over time the project teachers came to expand their understandings. They were encouraged to think about what they valued and what they measured in school in relation to literacy as well as what was missing from what they were expected to measure. The data show that multiple insights were derived from the project teachers' explorations in classrooms, along with a new depth of knowledge acquired through the Learner Visits. The teachers' observations highlighted the diverse nature of literacy practices which their pupils engaged in on a daily basis. Simultaneously, and significantly, they also turned in on themselves to reflect upon their own literacy identities and the relationship of both to dominant discourses and the concept of multiple literacies. Through examining their literacy identities, practices and associated biases and through their observations and reflections, many teachers began to recognise that individuals learn about literacy through their relationships and that the multiple sets of social practices that comprise literacy differ according to context. Recognising this plurality of literacies across the different realms of life, home, work and school and the significance of identity in literacy practices was significant for the teachers. While reading and debating research papers served to inform and extend their knowledge, for most of the teachers this understanding developed through the personal process of introspection regarding their own literacy practices and observation of the children's everyday uses of reading and writing in their homes and communities.

The teachers were also encouraged to share their own literacy practices with the children and use themselves as a resource for teaching, though many felt vulnerable at the thought of this and were unsure of its value. Straying into this new unrehearsed and undeveloped area challenged the ways in which some of the teachers constructed their professional identities, and several were disquieted by a possible reduction in professional distance. There were recurring threads here about the teachers' insecurities, both in developing researcher dispositions and in blurring personal and professional boundaries by sharing more of their lives and literacy practices in school. These anxiety-generating threads included risk taking, openness, and departure from the 'safety net' of the known. Initially teachers tended to share their book-based preferences, but while this expanded as their understanding of literacies developed, there was little evidence of the teachers sharing their digital practices and preferences in the classroom.

Connecting their developing conceptualisations of literacy with their widening understanding of the uses of literacy in the children's lives, served as an influential catalyst which helped practitioners recognise the limitations of school literacy and their own roles as educators in framing, sustaining or if they chose to, widening school definitions of literacy. In considering their own literate identities and the ways in which their conceptualisations of literacy and literate identities might serve to position young learners in the classroom, the teachers began to recognise that they were in a position of power in offering a definition of valid and valuable literacy for parents and children. In this position they could demystify the dominance of 'school literacy' as the most powerful genre/only genre of value, though they were also conscious of needing to work within the system. The teachers sought to distinguish between the reality of what children need to know and be able to do in order to succeed in the 'school system' and the social and cultural worlds of children's literacy of which they were now more aware. Discussions focused on the limitations of schooled notions of literacy, of levels, targets and tests which atomise literacy, reducing it to a set of discrete sub-skills underpinned by a pre-conceived trajectory of development. This 'autonomous' model of literacy (Street, 1984; 2008) was questioned by the teachers who began, in the words of the project evaluator, 'to start to view literacy as a rich and complex tapestry rather than a ladder of levels' (Durrant, 2011: 21). The diversity of the children's literacy practices which the teachers had witnessed in their homes involving different activities, different media and multiple modes, made a marked impact upon these professionals, as did the extensive involvement of siblings, friends and other family members. This, combined with their reflections on their own literacy histories, identities and practices enabled many of the teachers to see literacy as embedded in social and cultural interaction.

Pedagogical consequences and challenges

As a consequence of reconceptualising literacy in a manner more aligned with Street's (1984, 2008) 'ideological model', and learning about the children's funds of knowledge, the practitioners sought ways to reflect this enriched and more diverse conception in school. They worked to validate the children's everyday literacy lives, personal passions and popular cultural interests, significantly widening the textual diversity available for independent reading for example and seeking to create more responsive and flexible curricula. They developed more 'hybrid pedagogical spaces' (Hicks, 2000) in which children's out-of-school interests were afforded recognition in the curriculum; their pursuits, passions and practices from home were no longer marginalised. In recognising that the children's literacy practices beyond school were often interconnected, child-initiated and directed, some of the teachers began to shift from more performative oriented pedagogies to more competence oriented pedagogies (Bernstein, 1996). These encompassed more space for learner self-regulation and enabled children to use their literacy and learning assets in school. As a result of the teachers' more open stance and inclusive practice, they noticed an immediate and marked increase in the children's motivation, engagement and commitment in school. This may also have been influenced by some of the teachers using their own literacy lives as teaching resources in order to make personal connections and enable the children to do likewise. These kinds of practices, placed alongside increased choice in reading and writing, which was itself prompted by the marked degree of choice-driven independent activity (observed in children's homes) also had an impact. They teachers perceived more conversational engagement developed when they allowed children's out-of-school experiences to enter and enrich the official school literacy curriculum. They sought to enable the children to use the 'texts of their lives' (Fecho, 2011) as a resource to retell, reinterpret, or remake in multiple ways, as in the memory boxes work for example. Critiquing the lack of personal authorship opportunities in classrooms, Fecho (2011: 4) argues that such opportunities enable young people to 'use writing to explore who they are becoming and how they relate to the larger culture around them'. In summarising this, Thomson and Clifton (2013: 56) describe it as: 'an extended ongoing conversation which brings together the intersections of the personal and academic in ways that help children and young people – and their teachers – build understandings of themselves and their worlds'.

In some classrooms, teachers wrote alongside children using the texts of their own lives too, which reduced professional distance and also prompted conversation.

In these various ways, the curriculum in the project teachers' classrooms became, at least at times, somewhat more permeable, with children drawing upon their home knowledge and concrete lived experience in school.

However, while the practitioners came to recognise that the ways in which they conceptualised literacy and positioned themselves as literate individuals in their classrooms was important, this was not always easy or even feasible to translate into changed practice. For example, the teachers reflected a lack of confidence about integrating and extending the children's digital competencies which were frequently well in advance of the ICT curriculum on offer. Many were acutely aware they were not in a position to offer digital text-production opportunities and felt unable to build on the young people's evident technological expertise. Additionally, developing new more responsive pedagogical practices in the year-long timeframe of the project was difficult. Some, although keen to expand the permeability of their literacy classrooms, struggled; they were concerned that they did not know how to plan a locally tailored curriculum. The younger teachers in particular found this difficult as they were more used to relying upon packages, and as a consequence they turned to the LA co-ordinators and sought directional advice, requesting techniques and lesson plans. These were not forthcoming; instead the co-ordinators worked alongside the teachers in their classrooms exploring ways forward, conscious that these young committed practitioners had experienced few opportunities to plan extended units of work that were not related to the prescribed literacy curricula. Other teachers were concerned that by extrapolating from or connecting to particular children's funds of knowledge this would privilege some and 'disadvantage' others. This concern is aligned to a recent critique of the pedagogical consequences of a funds of knowledge approach by Rodriquez (2013). She posits that since teachers are ultimately in charge of selecting what is legitimate knowledge in schooling, the approach may still reflect traditional power relations. Teachers, Rodriquez asserts are likely to select those funds of knowledge which afford the richest alignment with the given curriculum, and are thus 'positioned to deemphasize' other aspects of their students' lives (ibid.: 94). In *BC: RLL* this was also evidenced as 'convenient' choices tended to be made which enriched the official school literacy curriculum but did not substantially transform it. As the project was positioned in opposition to/in competition with the dominant discourse of performativity, difficulties were inevitable; these constrained professional practice.

Thus while the metaphor of teachers 'turning around' (Comber and Kamler, 2005) to children and developing 'turn around pedagogies' to connect to their literacy lives usefully characterises the work of some of the project teachers, these difficulties meant that for others, this operated more as a 'turn around' in their heads. Nonetheless, this 'turned around' mindset encompassed the realisation that the children's interest in, attitudes towards literacy, and their literate competence in school was only part of a much broader richer picture. It also recognised the value of sustained enquiry since local communities and neighbourhoods change, as do children and their families; funds of knowledge do not remain static.

School-centric perspectives

At the start of the project, the school system, laden with organisational rules and structures, left little time for building relationships between children, parents and families that were not consciously organised and driven by the institutional agenda. In England, as in many accountability cultures, this agenda was, and has remained, focused on pupil attainment: on raising individual children's literacy and numeracy standards as measured by test scores. Influenced by international comparisons, the performative (Ball, 1998) nature of this agenda dominates educational discourse and as the project evidenced, frames and shapes, not only pedagogic practice, but home–school relationships. From the outset the prevailing view of learning and literacy in the schools was locked into this school agenda; it was limited, limiting and school-centric in nature.

Additionally, the evidence suggests that the majority of teachers' and head-teachers' perceptions of the children and families were framed by the standards agenda: this was the lens through which they viewed families and children. Their perspectives were thus 'school-centric' in orientation; and focused upon what parents could and in some cases 'should' do to support children's school literacy. A school-centric view is located within a view of 'pro-fessional expertise' which seeks to implies that 'teachers know best' and 'parents need to learn from them'. A some-what 'moated castle' view, this suggests that once parents and children cross the drawbridge, school rules apply. The project also revealed that a range of assumptions were held by the teachers and headteachers about children and parents, and parents' capacities to support children's school literacy. These were often related to class and ethnicity, and included assumptions based on children's behaviour, attainment and the presumed degree of parental involvement. The teachers in this study were not, as in most of the previous studies in this area (e.g. Moll *et al.*, 1992; Comber and Kamler, 2004; Rosemberg *et al.*, 2013), only visiting the homes of traditionally marginalised young people. The Learner Visits were undertaken in a wide range of homes and the teachers sought information from all the children in their classes. However, despite this broader than usual focus, this did not reduce the breadth and number of tacitly held assumptions about children and their families; these appeared to be held regardless of economic, social and cultural differences. Thus the project data affirms other lamentable evidence that deficit discourse persists in schools (e.g. Anderson *et al.*, 2010), it also reveals a highly school-centric perspective prevails.

One of the dangers of schools adopting a purely school-centric view is that they are likely to ignore whatever else is happening in children's lives. In which case everything will be measured by the agenda set by and for the school. As Brice-Heath (1983: 290) observed when studying the language, life and work of different families in North Carolina, 'those who measure themselves by themselves are not wise'. In an increasingly diverse society, such a position will surely become even more problematic. However, in *BC: RLL,* as the teachers worked to adopt researcher dispositions and undertook the pivotal Learner Visits, they relinquished the power inherent in traditionally framed school–centric relationships with families and were instead positioned as learners, seeking to know and to understand more about the children's everyday literacy lives. Positioned thus the teachers had both to face and to accommodate the 'complexities, contradictions, tensions and richness' (Gregory and Ruby, 2011: 164) involved in research which acknowledges 'disparities of power between teachers and families and families and researchers'. As researchers they had to make relationships with the research participants – the parents – and found that as they stepped out from the safe context of the school into the community and children's homes this involved taking risks, though their desire to find out about the children and build new home–school relations carried them through. Nonetheless, as Whitehouse and Colvin (2001) note, teacher research that seeks to understand through dialogue involves:

> opening ourselves up to families, a position that puts us, as educators and researchers, into a vulnerable stance as we are forced to relate to families as people and not objects.
>
> *(Whitehouse and Colvin, 2001: 218)*

When teachers reached out to parents in this way, not in order to inform and instruct them on educational issues regarding their child, but in order to learn more about the child, and their family and community, opportunities for relationship building emerged. Visiting homes fostered the teachers' awareness of parents as interested and interesting people; people with expertise and hopes and dreams for themselves and their children. As the teachers shared more of their own identities as parents and family members, as interested and interesting adults too, conversations between teachers and parents opened up and new connections were made. In drawing on their own diverse funds of knowledge, teachers often found common ground with parents and reported increased communication and ease in communicating, not just when engaged in Learner Visits but more broadly. Many voiced a new respect for parents and were prompted to ponder upon and question previously held perceptions about the families. In part this occurred though the process of visiting, but also through the process of critical reflection engendered through the local and national meetings and the time set aside for meeting with their linked researcher. These research activities allowed teachers the opportunity to deconstruct their taken-for-granted assumptions and previously unquestioned positions. During the course of the project some teachers and schools began to recognise the limitations of their positioning and came to adopt a less school-centric approach, although their views were sometimes still constrained by this dominant discourse. The picture remains complex.

In seeking to characterise the nature of school-centricity, the project team sought to conceptualise schools' and teachers' positioning in relation to parents and families (see Figure 10.1). This conceptualisation, whilst recognising that the characteristics listed represent tendencies not absolutes, suggests that schools and teachers who adopt more open and less school-centric orientations tend to question and challenge the dominant discourse around the standards agenda. They see standard-ised literacy tests as just one part of a much wider and richer set of literacy achieve-ments and interests pertaining to each child. While these institutions and individuals recognise the need to attend to school literacy they do not perceive this is sufficient, and also seek to find out about children's concrete experiences of literacy and funds of knowledge, valuing and legitimising these in school. In contrast, the evidence suggests, schools and individuals with more school-centric perspectives tend to reify school literacy and legitimate only what the system recognises and assesses; teaching the prescribed curriculum but not more than this, they do not afford much if any attention to children's literacy lives beyond the school gate. As Figure 10.1

Schools and teachers with more school-centric perspectives and orientations tend to . . .	Schools and teachers with more open/less school-centric perspectives and orientations tend to . . .
Be framed by the standards/performance-based agenda.	Challenge the standards agenda and work to a set of broader outcomes.
Measure literacy attainment through performance in standardised tests.	See standardised literacy tests as part of a wider set of literacy achievements and interests.
Conceive of learning as school-based.	Recognise that learning happens in multiple contexts in and out-of-school.
Focus on school literacy.	Focus on school and everyday literacies.
Provide families with information about school literacy.	Find out about children's everyday literacy practices and funds of knowledge.
Legitimate what the system recognises alone.	Value and legitimate students' out-of-school experience.
Construct one-way traffic between school and home.	Foster and value two-way traffic between home and school.
Teach the prescribed curriculum.	Tailor the prescribed curriculum in responsive ways and draw on children's funds of knowledge.
Focus on teaching.	Focus on teaching and learning.
Retain professional distance and more hierarchical positions.	Build close professional and more equivalent teacher–parent–child relationships.

FIGURE 10.1 A conceptualisation of school positioning in relation to parents and families

exemplifies, those with more school-centric orientations are likely to foreground teaching, and the control and authority of the teacher is likely to be more overtly maintained though exercising the hierarchical position of the expert. This expert is likely to retain professional distance and inform and instruct parents on what and how they 'should' support their children in order to ensure success in school literacy. In contrast, in schools with more open and less school-centric perspectives, teaching and learning will both be afforded attention and it is more likely determined efforts will be made to establish two-way traffic and more equivalent and close professional teacher–parent–child relationships.

The findings suggest that while a persistent language of evaluation appears to exist in schools, alongside some entrenched and largely unquestioned assumptions about children and communities, where teachers and schools come to appreciate children's and families' funds of knowledge, they may begin to view literacy – and education – differently, challenging existing boundaries between home and school and adopting less school-centric perspectives. However schools need support to sustain and embed ways of working that encompass broader outcomes, reposition the standards agenda and redefine what counts as literacy.

Ways forward and implications

Instead of promoting school-centric views of improvement, where schools with a perceived monopoly on learning reach outwards to draw families and communities in, but only to support the school's purposes, the *BC: RLL* project suggests it is important to explore and build upon teachers', families' and children's individual and collective knowledge, experiences and resources in order to initiate new learning and nourish, sustain and evaluate learning that is *already happening*. This requires a new strategic emphasis that places the locus of control in communities, where schools work with families in shared spaces, with participants as co-learners, using a wider range of cultural resources to support literacy and learning. This could support the small steps and awakenings of teachers in England and other countries who may be shaking off a culture of dependency. The project evidence suggests that in order to make this work in day-to-day practice, teachers need to be challenged and supported to develop enquiring mindsets and invest in cultural change, repositioning them-selves, and developing new professional identities on the journey. In the context of per-vasive external accountability judgements, teachers cannot enter this new profes-sional territory easily without the understanding and advocacy of school leaders and the advice, support and critical friendship of others from local organisations.

Developing an enquiring mindset

The project's evidence suggests that initially, the teachers' work was based on established views of what counts as literacy, assumptions about children's interests and approaches to learning and in some cases deficit models of children and families, all of which were conditioned by a policy agenda which foregrounds standards and performativity. The project encouraged a more balanced and inclusive approach, where the lives and literacies of teachers, children and families all become *part of* the curriculum. However, to achieve this, all participants – children, teachers, parents and others – must be learners. Learners that can let go of their preconceptions, share control, take risks, give of themselves and open themselves up to learning with and from one another. This will not happen unless teachers are given the space to be learners or are able to collectively forge such spaces, perhaps through brokering new partnerships for learning. If schools wish to move forward to build home–school communities, then teachers need to be given the authority and support to value relationships, people and communities above standards and levels of attainment; selves over statistics; being alongside knowing. Education is not about knowing all the answers – even before the question has been asked – but about continuing to be a learner. To develop a society that values learning and education, the education profession needs to assert what is known about conditions for learning building on research evidence and experience to enable teachers as well as parents, and children as well as adults, to feel confident enough to take risks, raise questions and work together in new ways. Formulaic approaches and simplistic standalone activities that seek to make home–school connections are not the solution. Instead, open-ended ways that foreground enquiry, exploration and co-participation offer more potential for building reciprocal relationships and the construction of multifaceted home–school communities.

In the project *BC: RLL* through committed collaborative enquiry, the teachers became secure enough to question the way literacy is defined in education in England, and to reflect upon their own implicit assumptions about children and their families. As professionals they were willing and enabled to learn. To foster such professional learning requires education policies that facilitate cultures of openness and trust within school communities and professional development that is non-directive and less judgemental against criteria and competences, enabling teachers to be leaders, learners, investigators, thinkers and developers. This is not about training and implementation but about living and learning.

Investing in cultural change

If schools are to introduce this mindset and invest in cultural change and the development of curriculum and pedagogy that builds upon children's everyday literacy lives and funds of knowledge, senior managers need insight and some strength of mind to recognise the value of projects which seem distanced from the imperative to provide hard data. When schools take up innovations, they do so in ways that reflect their own values and visions. The approach to learning underlying this project, premised on the significance of relationships, is only likely to take full effect if the school as a learning community itself, enables teachers to take an attentive and reflective view of how pedagogy and curriculum work to restrict or expand the potential of learners both the children and the professionals. In schools determined to adopt a less school-centric perspective, collaborative space and time will need to be created for teachers and support staff to build relationships with children and families and the nature of relationships revisited to explore the role of trust, respect and reciprocity. Too much emphasis on teachers however may neglect the valuable 'insider' knowledge of, for example, teaching assistants who live within the community and other members of the wider school community as well as outside agencies. In England, where ostensibly schools have been granted increased autonomy over how the National Curriculum (DfE, 2014) is enacted, teachers have the opportunity to create a localised curriculum, building upon the children's assets as learners. This represents a possible way forward. Much will depend upon the school's vision. If learning is foregrounded then self-evidently knowledge about the children's out-of-school literacy and learning practices will be needed to enable them to use their tools for thinking in school.

Taking full account of home literacies and witnessing the funds of knowledge in homes and communities is not an 'add on' to everyday practice; it is a transformational process that has to be experienced and embraced by the professionals involved. The project suggests that where assumptions and pre-conceived notions about children's and family literacy are replaced by evidence and reflection there will be gains both for schools and for learners. More enlightened approaches to external accountability are thus needed to enable open and investigative mindsets, recognition of diverse funds of knowledge and leadership of learning.

The evidence suggests that it is timely to explore again what 'being a professional' means, particularly in relation to the need to develop stronger more equivalent professional relationships with parents and children built on mutual respect and two-way home–school traffic. Schools working towards this goal may need to be aware of and prepared for the emotional implications of bringing teachers' and children's lives into school and into their learning, and new professional protocols may be needed to safeguard teachers, children and families where boundaries of place and space are crossed and shared activity is taking place. The project has highlighted that professionals' humanity, passion and intellectual understanding contribute to children's learning once they are given 'permission' to value and develop these aspects. Yet as Fielding (2006) argues, schools are operating in an instrumental and audit-driven manner in an increasingly dehumanised context. If teachers are positioned as little more than technicists they may not feel able to develop person-centred relational education. Where 'teacher-student and student-student relationships are merely a means to league-tabled ends' (Thomson *et al.*, 2012: 12), the enhanced professionalism developed and personal connections shared in this project with children and parents are unlikely to flourish.

The project also suggests that the professional development led by the National Strategy (DfEE, 1988; DfES, 2006) in England has been bound by top-down approaches, oriented towards training and telling, with a focus on aspects for which teachers are accountable in terms of standards, and related to outcomes and impact against national and international benchmarks. Unsurprisingly perhaps, this has been mirrored in classrooms where an emphasis on delivering the given curriculum, not developing learning or learners has been documented (e.g. Burns and Myhill,

2004; Goodwyn and Fuller, 2011). The training appears to have fostered professional risk-aversion, a concern to 'get things right', and has conditioned professionals to make judgements about others. The project suggests that the concept of professional development should by contrast recognise the importance of building professional communities who research and travel together, building in space for enquiry, reading and critical reflection, the raising of questions, uncertainties and disagreements. Such communities will foster risk-taking and have potential for learning. As the project's evaluator argues, cultural shifts can be achieved 'through small moments of insight, through individual conversations, realisations and nudges of understanding', and the policy-driven assumption that this can only happen 'through national reform and centralised approaches to school improvement' is erroneous (Durrant, 2011: 22).

Additionally, consideration needs to be given to how this kind of work might be supported and embedded across larger numbers of schools. Increased support for and commitment to teacher research is one way forward here:

> If we want to see teacher research become central and commonplace to literacy teachers' everyday practice, globally, then changes to existing policy, pre-service and continuing teacher education is timely and paramount... A further step would be to reform teacher credentialing to ensure teacher research and inquiry were viewed as essential and necessary across the life span of the profession.
>
> *(Walsh and Kamler, 2013: 508–9)*

Such reform would significantly expand the scope for teachers to develop new insights and understandings in context and for new collaborative home–school projects with university-based researchers and local communities to develop, affording opportunities for partnerships of learners to advance educational knowledge and practice.

Building communities

The concept of communities as fluid, involving complex intersections of practice and multiple connections and relationships between people, reflected the way communities grew within the *BC: RLL* project – from many different directions and between many different sets of people. Different kinds of relational dialogue slowly opened up in the project's communities. In the school-based data analysis, LA and national meetings, issues were discussed and debated and trust was gradually built. Openness was key, as was the space to think aloud, and voice disagreements, hesitant thoughts and views and to continually re-examine these, it was as though 'assumptions and preconceptions' were placed 'in parenthesis' (Luca, 2009: 22) alongside the data accumulated from the teachers' ethnographic enquiries and other learning. For the teachers and parents, as the evaluator noted 'the locus of control had started to shift by mid-way through the year, away from the mutual disinterest, suspicion and lack of confidence that might be engendered, however subconsciously, by school-centred approaches, towards valuing family and community, mutual dialogue and more reciprocal relationships' (Durrant, 2011: 11). Over time, what González *et al.* (2005) describe as *confianza* developed. While this term has multiple meanings in Spanish, it translates approximately to an amalgam of 'trust' and 'confidence', which teachers, parents, children, the LA co-ordinators and university-based researchers began to hold, albeit differently, in relation to one another. The dual meaning of *confianza* highlights the close connection between 'being confident' as a quality of the individual, and trust in a relationship. It serves as a reminder of the deep significance of personal relationships in education, between children and children, teachers and children and teachers and parents.

To very different degrees and starting from very different positions, the eighteen teachers all made 'shifts' along a community continuum undergirded at one end by Gesellschaft and at the other by Gemeinschaft. Initially it appeared that framed by the system, the teachers were operating in a form of 'commercial contract' (based on Gesellschaft) with parents and schools. By mutual (and unconscious) consent, this rational agreement related to children's literacy development within the system and for the system – the school system of standards. As the teachers learned more about the children's literacy and learning lives beyond school and visited homes, often several times, they brokered new kinds of relationships with parents; shared more of themselves and found that personal/professional boundaries blurred. In this way they shifted towards a more social notion of community (based on Gemeinschaft) which had a stronger sense of shared connections, shared ties, values and affect.

While situated views of learning have led to an understanding of the concept of communities of practice (Lave and Wenger, 1991), the project suggests that there should be a closer focus on where the communities of practice of schools and homes intersect and overlap. If, as Wenger argues, communities of practice develop through 'the sustained pursuit of a shared enterprise' (Wenger, 1998: 45) then the classroom needs to become a site which fosters the mutual exchange of children's and adults' funds of knowledge and the basis for the development of newly forged communities of practice. Furthermore, the concept of 'sociality', as articulated by Thomson *et al.* (2012: 13) has some value here; they describe this as 'the ways in which people live together and find a place in a community', at the heart of which is a deep sense of the personal, of interaction and *confianza*, of 'becoming somebody', somebody who has a growing sense of their own strengths and resources and is enabled to use them.

Recommendations

The project *BC: RLL* indicates that in order to avoid children experiencing a debilitating gap between literacy and learning inside and outside school, the profession needs to reconceptualise literacy in the twenty-first century and to build on children's everyday literacy experiences and funds of knowledge. In particular, teachers need to recognise that they are key agents in maintaining and/or contesting what constitutes literacy for children and parents. It reveals that through examining their own literacy histories and practices as well as those rooted in children's everyday experiences, teachers can expand their understanding of literacy, recognising and validating this in school. Particular support, however, may be required to help teachers embrace, integrate and extend children's digital competencies and take account of learners' identities, interests and wider of funds of knowledge. Local, national and global conversations that not only foreground children's home literacy practices in this new media age, but recognise the myriad ways in which home–school–community practices are changing, may help to challenge the dominant conception of literacy as a school-defined construct framed by the standards agenda. Teachers with wider conceptions of literacy and a richer understanding of children's social, cultural and linguistic assets can contribute richly to such critical conversations.

It is also recommended that schools, teachers and student teachers are supported to examine their perceptions and orientations, individually and institutionally, in the light of the wider policy agenda and to consider their values, and the ways in which they view children, parents and communities as homogenous or heterogeneous groups. They may need support in acknowledging and disrupting any taken-for-granted assumptions about individual children, parents or families, in discovering their funds of knowledge and building new more reciprocal relationships. In order to foreground learning, teachers will need to take responsibility for developing their understanding of children's strengths and resources, their ways of learning outside school and explore ways to build on these to foster deeper and more connected learning. Thus training schools, initial teacher education institutions, and organisations offering professional development, need to consider how they can sensitively respond to this agenda. In particular, offering support to help practitioners find out about and respond to children's funds of knowledge and the new possibilities for meaning-making and learning that arise from children's experiences of literacies, particularly their digital literacies.

The project *Building Communities: Researching Literacy Lives* has provided new insights about the possibilities and challenges involved in developing an evidence-informed, less school-centric view of parents and families, one which acknowledges assets rather than identifies deficits, sees difference and diversity as strength and the children and their parents as individuals. It has highlighted that regardless of curriculum change and policy dictat, in order to broaden what is recognised, valued and validated as literacy in school, there is an urgent need to align professional understanding of literacy in the twenty-first century with the lived experience of young learners.

REFERENCES

Abrams, S. and Merchant, G. (2013) 'The digital challenge', in K. Hall, T. Cremin, B. Comber and L. Moll, *The Wiley Blackwell international research handbook of children's literacy, learning and culture* (pp. 319–332), Oxford: Wiley Blackwell.

Alexander, R. (2000) *Culture and pedagogy: International comparisons in primary education*, Oxford: Blackwells.

Alper, M. (2013) Developmentally appropriate new media literacies, supporting cultural competencies and social skills in early childhood education, *Journal of Early Childhood Literacy*, 1(2): 175–196.

Alsup, J. (2005) *Teacher identity discourses: Negotiating personal and professional spaces*, London: Routledge.

Anderson J., Anderson A., Friedrich, N. and Kim, J. (2010) Taking stock of family literacy: some contemporary perspectives, *Journal of Early Childhood Literacy*, 10(1): 33–53.

Andrews, J. and Yee, W.C. (2006) Children's 'funds of knowledge' and their real life activities: Two minority ethnic children learning in out-of-school contexts in the UK, *Educational Review*, 58(4): 435–449.

Andrews, J., Yee, W.C., Greenhough, P., Hughes, M. and Winter, J. (2005) Teachers funds of knowledge and the teaching and learning of mathematics in multi-ethnic, primary school classrooms: 'Two teachers' views of linking home and school, *Zentrablatt fur Didaktik der Mathematick*, 37(2): 72–80.

Angelides, P., Theophanous, L. and Leigh, J. (2006) Understanding teacher–parent relationships for improving pre-primary schools in Cyprus, *Educational Review*, 58(3): 303–316.

Archer, L. (2010) *The minority ethnic middle-classes and education. Final report*, London: British Academy and King's College.

Atkinson, M., Jones, M. and Lamont, E. (2007) *Multi-agency working and its implications for practice: A review of the literature*, Slough, Berks: CfBT Education Trust/National Foundation for Educational Research.

Atkinson, M., Wilkin, A., Stott, A., Doherty, P. and Kinder, K. (2002) *Multi-agency working: A detailed study*, Slough, Berks: National Foundation for Educational Research.

Au, K.H. (1993) *Literacy instruction in multicultural settings*, Fort Worth, TX: Harcourt Brace Jovanich.

Auerbach, E. (1990) 'Which way for family literacy: Intervention or empowerment?', in L.M. Morrow (ed.) *Family literacy: Connections in schools and communities*, Newark, DE: International Reading Association.

Auerbach, E.R. (1995) 'Which way for family literacy: Intervention or empowerment?', in L.M. Morrow (ed.), *Family literacy: Connections in schools and communities* (pp. 11–28), Newark, DE: International Reading Association.

Auge, M. (1995) *Non-places. Introduction to an anthropology of supermodernity* (J. Howe, trans.). London and New York: Verso.

Australian Curriculum Assessment and Reporting Authority (ACARA) (2014) Australian Curriculum: English. www.australiancurriculum.edu.au/English/Aims (accessed 14 January 2014)

Ball, S.J. (1998) 'Performativity and fragmentation in "Postmodern Schooling"', in J. Carter, (ed.), *Postmodernity and fragmentation of welfare* (pp. 187–203), London: Routledge.

Ball, S.J., Rollock, N., Vincent, C. and Gillborn, D. (2011) Social mix, schooling and intersectionality: identity and risk for Black middle class families, *Research Papers in Education*, pp. 1–24, iFirst Article Published online at: http://dx.doi.org/10.1080/0267152 2.2011.641998_Routledge Taylor and Francis.

Barnes, D. (1988) 'Knowledge as action', in M. Lightfoot and N. Martin, *The word for teaching is learning*, essays for James Britton, Portsmouth Heinemann.

Barton, D. (1991) *Literacy: An introduction to the ecology of written language*, Oxford: Blackwell.

Barton, D. and Hamilton, M. (1998) *Local literacies: Reading and writing in one community*, London: Routledge.

Barton, D., Hamilton, M. and Ivanič, R. (eds) (2000) *Situated literacies: Reading and writing in context*, London, Routledge.

Bearne, E. (2009) Multimodality literacy, and texts: Developing a discourse, *Journal of Early Childhood Literacy*, 9(2): 156–187.

Bearne, E. and Kennedy, R. (2009) Primary Languages Action Research Group 2008–2009: Evaluation Report. (unpublished report) Birmingham Local Authority in partnership with Coventry Local Authority.

Bearne, E. and Kennedy, R. (2012) *Literacy and community: Developing a primary curriculum through partnerships*, Leicester: United Kingdom Literacy Association.

Bearne, E., Clark, C., Johnson, A., Manford, P., Mottram, M. and Wolstencroft, H. (2007) *Reading on screen*, Leicester: United Kingdom Literacy Association.

Belenky, M., Bond L.A. and Weinstock, A. (1997) 'Otherness', in M. Belensky, L.A. Bond and A. Weinstock (eds), *a tradition that has no name: Nurturing the development of families and communities*, New York: Basic.

BERA (2011) Revised Ethical Guidelines for Educational Research (2011). British Educational Research Association. www.bera.ac.uk.

Bernstein, B. (1990) *The structuring of pedagogic discourse, volume IV: Class, Codes and control*, London: Routledge.

Bernstein, B. (1996) *Pedagogy, symbolic control and identity: Theory, research, critique*, New York: Rowman and Littlefield.

Berthoff, A. (1987) 'The teachers as researcher', in D. Goswami and P. Stillman (eds), *Reclaiming the classroom: Teacher research as an agency for change* (pp. 28–39), Portsmouth, NH: Boynton Cook-Heinemann.

Bourdieu, P. (1977) *Outline of a theory of practice*, Cambridge: Cambridge University Press.

Bourdieu, P. (1990) *The logic of practice*, Oxford: Blackwell.

Bourdieu, P. (2008) *Political interventions: Social science and political action*, London: Verso.

Brenden M. (2005) 'Funds of knowledge and team ethnography: Reciprocal approaches', in N. Gonzalez, L. Moll and C. Amanti (eds), *Funds of knowledge: Theorizing practices in households, communities and classrooms* (pp. 199–212), Mahwah, NJ: Erlbaum.

Brice-Heath, S. (1983) *Ways with words: Language, life and work in communities and classrooms*, Cambridge: Cambridge University Press.

Brooker, L. (2002) *Starting school: Young children learning cultures*, Buckingham: Open University Press.

Bruner, J. (1986) *Actual minds, possible worlds*, Cambridge, MA: Harvard University Press.

Burnett, C. (2011) Pre-service teachers' digital literacy practices, *Language and Education*, 25(5): 433–449.

Burns, C. and Myhill, D. (2004) Interactive or Inactive? A consideration of the nature of interaction in whole class teaching, *Cambridge Journal of Education*, 34(1): 35–49.

Cairney, T. (1995) *Pathways to literacy*, London: Cassell.

Cairney, T.H. (1997) Acknowledging diversity in home literacy practices, *Early Child Development and Care*, 127(1): 61–73.

Cairney, T.H. (2002) Bridging home and school literacy, *Early Child Development and Care*, 172(2): 153–172.

Cairney, T.H. (2003) 'Literacy within family life', in *Handbook of early childhood literacy*, London: Sage, pp. 85–98.

Carr, W. and Kemmis, S. (1986) *Becoming critical: Education knowledge and action research*, London: RoutledgeFalmer.

Carrington, V. (2007) 'Social inclusion and digital literacies', in E. Bearne and J. Marsh, *Literacy and social inclusion: Closing the gap* (pp. 103–114), Stoke on Trent: Trentham Books.

Carspecken, P. (1996) *Critical ethnography in educational research: A theoretical and practical guide*, New York: Routledge.

Clark, M. (1975) *Young fluent readers*, London: Heinemann.

Clarke, M. (2008) The ethico-politics of teacher identity, *Educational Philosophy and Theory*, 1–16.

Cliff-Hodges, G. (2010) Rivers of reading: Using critical incident collages to learn about adolescent readers and their readership, *English in Education*, 44(3): 180–199.

Clough, P. and Nutbrown, C. (2012) *A student's guide to methodology*, 3rd edn, London: Sage.

Cochran-Smith, M. and Lytle, S. (1993) *Inside-outside: Teacher research and knowledge*, New York: Teachers College Press.

Cochran-Smith, M. and Lytle, S. (2009) 'Teacher research as stance', in B. Somekh and S. Noffke (eds), *Handbook of educational action research* (pp. 39–49), London: Sage.

Coffey, A. and Atkinson, P. (1996) *Making sense of qualitative data analysis: Complementary strategies*, Thousand Oaks, CA: Sage.

Comber, B. (1997) Literacy, poverty and schooling: Working against deficit equations, *English in Australia, 119–120*, 22–34.

Comber, B. (1998) The problem of 'background' in researching the student subject, *The Australian Educational Researcher*, 25(3): 1–21.

Comber, B. (2007) 'Assembling dynamic repertoires of literate practices: Teaching that makes a difference', in E. Bearne and J. Marsh (eds), *Literacy and social inclusion: Closing the gap*, Stoke on Trent: Trentham Books.

Comber, B. and Kamler, B. (2004) Getting out of deficit: Pedagogies of reconnection, *Teaching Education*, 15(3): 293–310.

Comber, B. and Kamler, B. (2005) *Turn around pedagogies: Literacy interventions for at-risk students*, Sydney: Primary English Teaching Association.

Comber, B., Nixon, H. and Reid, J.A. (2007) *Literacies in place: Teaching environmental communications*, Sydney: Primary English Teaching Association.

Commeyras, M., Bisplinhoff, B.S. and Olson, J. (2003) *Teachers as readers: Perspectives on the importance of reading in teachers' classrooms and lives*, Newark, NJ: International Reading Association.

Compton-Lily, Rogers, C. and Lewis, T. (2012) Analyzing epistemological considerations related to diversity: An integrative critical literature review of family literacy scholarship, *Reading Research Quarterly*, 47(1): 33–60.

Conrad, B. (2012) New conceptions on the dispositions of culturally responsive teachers: The three domains of culturally responsive teaching. Paper presented at the *Conference of the American Education Research Association*, Vancouver.

Cope, B. and Kalantzis, M. (2000) 'Multiliteracies: The beginning of an idea' in B. Cope and M. Kalantzis (eds), *Multiliteracies: Literacy learning and the design of social futures* (pp. 3–8). London: Routledge.

Cordingley, P. (2011) Professional practitioner use of research. Paper presented at the *Conference of the American Educational Research Association* (AERA), April 2011.

Cordingley, P., M., Bell, Rundell, B., Evans, D. and Curtis, A. (2003) *The impact of collaborative CDP on classroom teaching and learning. How does collaborative Continuing Professional Development (CPD) for teachers of the 5–16 age range affect teaching and learning?* London: EPPI Centre.

Cox, R. and Durrant, C. (2012) 'An introduction to the Australian curriculum: English', in R. Cox, *Primary English teaching: An introduction to language, literacy and learning. The Australian version*, Melbourne: Hawker Brownlow.

Crafton, L. and Kaiser, E. (2011) The language of collaboration: Dialogue and identity in teacher professional development, *Improving Schools*, 14(2): 104–116.

Crago, M. and Crago, H. (1983) *Prelude to literacy: A preschool child's encounter with picture and story*, Carbondale, IL: Southern Illinois University Press.

Cremin, T. (2006) Creativity, uncertainty and discomfort: teachers as writers, *Cambridge Journal of Education*, 36(3) 415–433.

Cremin, T. (2009) with contributions from Bearne, E. Dombey, H. and Lewis, M., *Teaching English Creatively*, London: Routledge.

Cremin, T. (2010a) 'Reconceptualising reading in the 21st century', in T. McCannon (ed.), *Reading in the 21st Century*, Dublin: Reading Association of Ireland.

Cremin, T. (2010b) 'Poetry teachers: Teachers who read and readers who teach poetry', in M. Styles and M. Rosen (eds), *Poetry and Childhood* (pp. 219–227), London: Trentham.

Cremin, T. (2010c) 'Motivating children to read through literature', in G. Gillon, J. Fletcher and F. Parkhill (eds), *Motivating literacy learners in today's world*, Wellington: New Zealand Council for Educational Research.

Cremin, T (2013a) 'Teachers researching literacy lives', in A. Goodwyn, L. Reid and C. Durrant (eds), *International perspectives on teaching English in a globalised world*, London: Taylor and Francis/Routledge.

Cremin, T. (2013b) 'Exploring teachers' positions and practices', in S. Dymoke, A. Lambirth and A. Wilson, *Making poetry matter: International research on poetry pedagogy* (pp. 9–19), London: Bloomsbury.

Cremin, T. and Baker, S. (2010) Exploring teacher-writer identities in the classroom: Conceptualising the struggle, *English Teaching: Practice and Critique*, 9(3): 8–25.

Cremin, T., Bearne, E., Mottram, M. and Goodwin, P. (2008a) Primary teachers as readers, *English in Education*, 42(1): 1–16.

Cremin, T., Bearne, E., Mottram, M. and Goodwin, P. (2008b) Exploring teachers' knowledge of children's literature, *Cambridge Journal of Education*, 38(4): 449–464.

Cremin, T., Mottram, M., Collins, F., Powell, S. and Drury, R. (2011) Executive summary: Building Communities: Researching literacy lives www.ukla.org/research/previous_ukla_funded_research/_uklaou_building_communities_researching_literacy_lives_/ (accessed 5 May 2014).

Cremin, T., Mottram, M., Collins, F., Powell, S. and Drury, R. (2012) Building communities: Teachers researching literacy lives, *Improving Schools*, 15(2): 101–115.

Cremin, T., Mottram, M., Collins, F., Powell, S. and Safford, K. (2009) Teachers as readers: Building communities of readers, *Literacy*, 43(1): 11–19.

Cremin, T., Mottram, M., Collins, F., Powell, S. and Safford, K. (2014) *Building communities of engaged readers: Reading for pleasure*, London and NY: Routledge.

Crozier, G. (2000) *Parents and schools. Partners or protagonists?* Stoke on Trent: Trentham Books. www.bera.ac.uk/resources/researching-parent-school-relationships (accessed 6 January 2014).

Crozier, G. (2012) *Researching parent-school relationships,* British Educational Research Association online resource. www.bera.ac.uk/resources/researching-parent-school-relationships (accessed 6 January 2014).

Crozier, G. and Davies, J. (2007) Hard to reach parents or hard to reach schools? A discussion of home-school relations, with particular reference to Bangladeshi and Pakistani parents, *British Educational Research Journal*, 33(3): 295–313.

Department for Education (DfE) (2010) *The Importance of Teaching: The Schools White Paper 2010*, London: DfE Publications.

Department for Education (DfE) (2012) *Teachers Standards*, London: Crown Copyright.

Department for Education (DfE) (2013) *The National Curriculum for England: Framework document*, London: DfE Publications.

Department for Education (DfE) (2014) *The National Curriculum in England 2014.* www.gov.uk/government/collections/national-curriculum (accessed 12 January 2014).

Department for Education and Employment (DfEE) (1998) *The National Literacy Strategy Framework for Teachers*, London: DfEE Publications.

Department of Education and Science (1976) *A language for life*, London: Her Majesty's Stationery Office.

Department for Education and Skills (DfES) (2004) *Aiming high: Understanding the educational needs of minority ethnic pupils in mainly white schools*, London: DfES.

Department for Education and Skills (DfES) (2004) *Every child matters: Change for children*, London: Department for Education and Skills.

Department for Education and Skills (DfES) (2006) *Primary National Strategy: Primary Framework for literacy and mathematics*, London: Her Majesty's Stationery Office.

Department for Education and Skills (DfES) (2007) *Primary Framework for literacy and mathematics*, Nottingham: DfES Publications.

Denscombe, M. (2008) Communities of practice: A research paradigm for the mixed methods approach, *Journal of Mixed Methods Research*, 2: 270–283.

Denzin, N.K. (1997) *Interpretive ethnography: Ethnographic practices for the 21st century*, Thousand Oaks, CA: Sage.

Denzin, N.K. and Lincoln, Y.S. (2000) *Handbook of qualitative research*, 2nd edn, Thousand Oaks, CA: Sage.

Desforges, C. and Abouchaar, A. (2003) *The impact of parental involvement, parental support and family education on pupil achievement. Report Number 433.* London: Department of Education and Skills.

Desimone, L.M. (2009) Improving impact studies of teachers' professional development: toward better conceptualizations and measures, *Educational Researcher*, April 2009, 38(3): 181–199.

Dewey, J. ([1933] 1985) *How we think, a restatement of the relation of reflective thinking to the educative process*, Boston, MA: Heath.

Diez, M.E. (2007) Looking back and moving forward: Three tensions in the teacher dispositions discourse, *Journal of Teacher Education*, 58(5): 388–396.

Dombey, H. (1998) 'Changing literacy in the early years of school', in B. Cox (ed.), *Literacy is not enough. Essays on the importance of reading* (pp. 125–132), Manchester: Manchester University Press and Book Trust.

Dowdall, C. (2009) Impressions, improvisations and compositions: Reframing children's text production in social network sites, *Literacy*, 43(2): 91–99.

Drury, R. (2007) *Young bilingual learners at home and school*, Stoke-on-Trent: Trentham.

Dunsmore, K. and Fisher, D. (2010) (eds) *Bringing Literacy Home*, Newark, NJ: International Reading Association.

Durrant, J. (2008) *Evaluation of teachers as readers: Building communities of readers.* Report submitted to the Esmee Fairbairn Foundation www.ukla.org/research/previous_ukla_funded_research/ukla_research_on_teachers_as_readers/ (accessed on 10 October 2013).

Durrant, J. (2011) *Building communities: Researching literacy lives teachers as readers Phase III, 2009–10 External Evaluation*, Canterbury: Christ Church University.

Dwyer, B. (2013) 'Developing online reading comprehension: Changes, challenges and consequences', in K. Hall, T. Cremin, B. Comber and L. Moll, *The Wiley Blackwell international research handbook of children's literacy, learning and culture* (pp. 344–358), Oxford: Wiley Blackwell.

Dwyer, B. and Harrison, C. (2008) 'There's no rabbits on the Internet: Scaffolding the development of effective search strategies for struggling readers during Internet inquiry' in Y. Kim and V.J. Risko (eds), *57th Yearbook of the National Reading Conference* (pp. 187–202), Oak Creek, WI: National Reading Conference.

Dyrness A. (2007) 'Confianza is where I can be myself': Latina mothers' constructions of community in education reform, *Ethnography and Education*, 2(2): 257–271.

Dyson, A.H. (1997) *Writing superheroes. Contemporary childhood, popular culture, and classroom Literacy*, New York and London: Teachers' College Press.

Dyson, A. and Robson, E. (1999) *School, family, community: Mapping school inclusion in the UK*, Leicester: Youth Work Press for the Joseph Rowntree Foundation.

Edwards, P. (2010) 'The role of family literacy programs in the school success or Failure of African American families and children', in K. Dunsmore and D. Fischer (eds), *Bringing literacy home*, Newark, DE: International Reading Association.

Elliott, J. (2005) Becoming critical: The failure to connect, *Educational Action Research*, 13(3): 359–374.

Erickson, F. (1984) What makes school ethnography 'ethnographic'? *Anthropology and Education Quarterly*, 15: 51–66.

Fan, X. and Chen, M. (2001) Parental involvement and students' academic achievement: A meta-analysis, *Educational Psychology Review*, 13, 1–22.

Fecho, B. (2011) *Writing in the dialogical classroom. Students and teachers responding to the texts of their lives*, Urbana, IL: National Council of Teachers of English.

Feiler, A., Greenhough, P., Winter, J., Salway, L. and Scanlan, M. (2006) Getting engaged: possibilities and problems for home-school knowledge exchange, *Educational Review*, 58(4): 451–469.

Fender, L. (2004) Praxis and agency in Foucault's historiography, *Studies in Philosophy and Education*, 23(5): 445–466.

Fielding, M. (2006) Leadership, radical student engagement and the necessity of person-centred education, *International Journal of Leadership in Education*, 9(4): 299–313.

Finders, M. (2005) Hybridisation of literacy practices: A review of 'What they don't learn in school: Literacy in the lives of urban youth.' *Reading Research Quarterly*, 40(3): 388–397.

Finlay, L. (2002) Negotiating the swamp: The opportunity and challenge of reflexivity in research practice, *Qualitative Research*, 2: 209–230.

Fishman, S. and McCarthy, J. (2000) *Unplayed tapes: A personal history of collaborative teacher research*, New York: Teachers College Press.

Forsey, M.G. (2010) 'Ethnography and the myth of participant observation', in S. Hillyard (ed), *New frontiers in ethnography (studies in qualitative methodology, Volume 11* (pp. 65–79), Emerald Group Publishing Limited.

Fox, C. (2004) 'Playing the Storyteller', in N. Hall, J. Larson and J. Marsh, *Handbook of Early Childhood Literacy* (pp. 189–198), London: Sage.

Frater, G. (2000) Observed in practice, English in the National Literacy Strategy: Some reflections, *Reading*, 34(3): 107–112.

Freedman, B. (2004) Instructional visibility: Principals facilitating in an age of accountability, *The Australian Association for Research in Education*. www.aare.educ.au/04pap/freoH066.pdf (accessed January 2009).

Freire, P. (1972) *Pedagogy of the oppressed*, New York: Herder and Herder.

Frey, N. (2010) 'Home is not where you live but where they understand you', in K. Dunsmore, and D. Fisher (2010) (eds), *Bringing literacy home* (pp. 42–52), Newark, NJ: International Reading Association.

Fullan, M. (2005) 'The meaning of educational change: A quarter of a century of learning', in A. Lieberman, *The roots of educational change: International handbook of educational change* (pp. 202–216), New York: Springer.

Gannon, G. and Davies, C. (2007) For the love of the word: English teaching, affect and writing, *Changing English*, 14(1): 87–98.

Gee, J.P. (1996) *Social linguistics and literacies: Ideology in discourses*, 2nd edn, London: Taylor and Francis.

Geertz, C. (1973) *The interpretation of cultures: Selected essays*, New York: Basic Books.

Gewirtz, S. (2001) Cloning the Blairs: New Labour's programme for the re-socialization of working class parents, *Journal of Education Policy*, 16(4): 365–378.

Glazier, J.A. (2005) Talking and teaching through a positional lens: Recognizing what and who we privilege in our practice, *Teaching Education*, 16(3): 231–243.

Goldman, T. (2009) DCSF Presentation at the Schools Analysis and Research Division (SARD) policy meeting with the research community. Westminster, London.

González, N. (2006) Testimonios of border identities: 'Una mujer acomedida donde quiera cabe', in D. Delgado Bernal, C.A. Elenes, F.E. Godinez and S. Villenas (eds), *Chicana/Latina education in everyday life: Feminista perspectives on pedagogy and epistemology* (pp. 197–213), Albany, NY: State University of New York Press.

González, N. and Moll, L. (2002) Cruzanda el puente: Building bridges to funds of knowledge, *Educational Policy*, 16(4): 623–641.

González, N., Moll, L. and Amanti, C. (2005) *Funds of knowledge: Theorizing practices in households, communities and classrooms*, London: Lawrence Erlbaum.

González, N., Moll, L., Floyd-Tenery, M., Rivera, A., Rendon, P. and Gonzales, R. and Amanti, C. (1993) Teacher research on funds of knowledge: Learning from households. National Centre for Research on Cultural Diversity and Second Language Learning. http://ncbe.gwu.edu/miscpubs/ncrcdsll/epr6.html

González, N., Moll, L., Floyd-Tenery, M., Rivera, A., Rendon, P., Gonzales, R. and Amanti, C. (1995) Funds of knowledge for teaching in Latino households, *Urban Education*, 29: 444–471.

Goodwyn, A. and Fuller, C. (2011) *The great literacy debate: A critical response to the literacy strategy and the framework for english*, London: Routledge.

Graham, L. (2008) Teachers are digikids too: The digital histories and digital lives of young teachers in English primary schools, *Literacy*, 42(1): 10–18.

Grainger, T. Goouch, K. and Lambirth, A. (2005) *Creativity and writing: Developing voice and verve in the classroom*, London: Routledge.

Greenan, N.P. and Dieckmann, J.A. (2004) Considering criticality and culture as pivotal in transformative teacher education, *Journal of Teacher Education*, 55(3): 240–255

Greenhough, P., Scanlon, M., Feiter, A., Johnson, D., Yee, W., Andrews, J., Price, A., Smithson, M., and Hughes, M. (2003) Boxing clever: Using shoeboxes to support home school knowledge exchange, *Literacy*, 39(2): 97–103.

Gregory, E. (2001) Sisters and brothers as language and literacy teachers: Synergy between siblings playing and working together, *Journal of Early Childhood Literacy*, 1(3): 301–322.

Gregory, E. (2007) 'What counts as reading outside school? and with whom? how? and where?', in Bearne, E. and Marsh, J. (eds), *Literacy and social inclusion: Closing the gap* (pp. 41–52), Stoke on Trent: Trentham Books.

Gregory, E. and Kenner, C. (2003) 'The out of school schooling of literacy', in *Handbook of Early Childhood Literacy* (pp. 75–84), London: Sage.

Gregory, E., S. Long and D. Volk (2004) 'Syncretic Literacy Studies: starting points', in E. Gregory, S. Long and D. Volk (eds), *Many pathways to literacy*, London: RoutledgeFalmer.

Gregory, E. and Ruby, M. (2011) The 'insider/outsider' dilemma of ethnography: Working with young children and their families in cross cultural contexts, *Journal of Early Childhood Research*, 9(2): 162–164.

Gregory, E. and Williams, A. (2000) *City literacies: Learning to read across generation and cultures*, London: Routledge.

Grieshaber, S., Shield, P., Luke, A. and Macdonald, S. (2012) Family literacy practices and home literacy resources: An Australian pilot study, *Journal of Early Childhood Literacy*, 12(1): 131–138.

Griffith, A. and Smith, D. (2005) *Mothering for schooling*, New York: RoutledgeFalmer.

Groundwater-Smith, S. and Mockler, N. (2006) Research that counts: Practitioner research and the academy. Counterpoints on the quality and impact of educational research, *Special Edition of Review of Australian Research in Education*, 6: 105–117.

Grugeon, E. (2005) Listening to learning outside the classroom: Student teachers study playground literacies, *Literacy*, 39(3): 3–9.

Gutiérrez, K.D. (2008) Developing a sociocritical literacy in the third space, *Reading Research Quarterly*, 43(2): 148–164.

Gutiérrez, K. and Rogoff, B. (2003) Cultural ways of learning: individual traits or repertoires of practice, *Educational Researcher*, 32(5):19–25.

Hall, K. (2008) 'Leaving middle childhood and moving into teenhood: Small stories revealing identity and agency' in K. Hall, P. Murphy and J. Soler (2008) *Pedagogy and practice: Culture and identities* (pp. 87–104), London: The Open University and Sage.

Hall, L., Johnson, A., Juzwik, M., Stanton, E., Wortham, F. and Mosley, M. (2010) Teacher identity in the context of literacy teaching: Three explorations of classroom positioning and interaction in secondary schools, *Teaching and Teacher Education*, 26: 234–243.

Hall, C., Thomson, P. and Russell, L. (2007) Teaching like an artist: the pedagogic identities and practices of artists in schools, *British Journal of Sociology of Education*, 28 (5): 605–619.

Hallgarten, J. and Edwards, L. (2000) *Parents as partners. Findings of a programme of consultation with Wednesbury parents. Wednesbury education action zone*. London: Institute for Public Policy Research.

Hammersley, M. (1995) *The politics of social research*, London: Sage.

Hammersley, M. (2012) Methodological paradigms in educational research, British Educational Research Association on-line resource. www.bera.ac.uk. Last accessed 31 December 2013.

Hammersley, M. and Atkinson, P. (1995) *Ethnography. Principles in practice*, 2nd edn, London: Routledge.

Hammett, R. (2009) 'New literacies and teacher education', in A. Burke and R.F. Hammett (eds), *Assessing new literacie* (pp. 177–192), Bern & New York: Peter Lang.

Hannon, P. (1995) 'Literacy, home and school: Research and practice', *Teaching Literacy with Parents,* London: Falmer Press.

Harris, A. and Goodall, J. (2007) Engaging parents in raising achievement – do parents know they matter? Department for Children, Schools and Families. http://webarchive. nationalarchives.gov.uk/20130401151715/https://www.education.gov.uk/publications/ eOrderingDownload/DCSF-RBW004.pdf.

Harris, A. and Goodall, J. (2008) Do parents know they matter? Engaging all parents in learning, *Educational Research*, 50(3): 277–289.

Hattam, R., Brennan, M., Zipin, L. and Comber, B. (2009) Researching for social justice: contextual, conceptual and methodological challenges, *Discourse: Studies in the Cultural Politics of Education*, 30(3): 303–316.

Heath, S.B. (1983) *Ways with words: Language, life and work in communities and classrooms*, Cambridge: Cambridge University Press.

Hedges, H. (2011) Rethinking SpongeBob and Ninja Turtles: Popular culture as funds of knowledge for curriculum co-construction, *Australian Journal of Early Childhood*, 36(1): 25–29.

Heller, M. (1995) Language choice, social institutions, and symbolic domination, *Language in Society*, 24: 373–405.

Hempel-Jorgensen, A. (2009) The construction of the 'ideal pupil' and pupils' perceptions of 'misbehaviour' and discipline: contrasting experiences from a low and a high socio-economic primary school, *British Journal of Sociology of Education*, 30(4), 435–448.

Hibbert, K. Heydon, R. and Rich, S.J. (2008) Beacons of light, rays or sun catchers? A case study of the positioning of literacy teachers and their knowledge in neoliberal times, *Teaching and Teacher Education*, 24(2): 303–315.

Hill, S. (2010) The millennium generation: Teacher-researchers exploring new forms of literacy, *Journal of Early Childhood Literacy*, 10(3): 314–340.

Hogg, L. (2011) Funds of knowledge: An investigation of coherence within the literature, *Teaching and Teacher Education*, 27: 666–677.

Holland, D., Lachicotte, W., Skinner, D. and Cain, C. (1998) *Identity and agency in cultural worlds*, Cambridge, MA: Harvard.

Holland, D. and Lave, J. (2001) 'History in person', in *Enduring struggles: Contentious practice, intimate identities* (1–32), Sante Fe, NM: School of American Research Press.

Holliday, A. (1999) Small cultures, *Applied Linguistics*, 20(2): 237–264.

Homan, R. (2001) The principle of assumed consent: The ethics of gatekeeping, *Journal of Philosophy of Education*, 35(3): 329–343.

Hopkins, D. (1983) *A teachers' guide to classroom research*, 2nd edn, Buckingham: Open University.

Hughes, M. and Greenhough, P. (2006) Boxes, bags and videotape: enhancing home-school communication through knowledge exchange activities, *Educational Review*, 58(4): 471–487.

Hughes, J. and Kwok, O. (2007) Influence of student–teacher and parent–teacher relationships on lower achieving readers' engagement and achievement in the primary grades, *Journal of Educational Psychology*, 99(1): 39–51.

Hughes, M. and Pollard, A. (2006) Home-school knowledge exchange in context, *Educational Review*, 58(4): 385–395.

Hume, M. and Mulcock, J. (2004) *Anthropologists in the field: Cases in participant observation*, New York: Columbia University Press.

Jackson, K. and Remillard, J. (2005) Rethinking parent involvement: African American mothers construct their roles in the mathematics education of their children, *School Community Journal*, 15(1): 51–73.

Jarrett P. (2010) *BC: LL* unpublished. Steering Committee Mimetas, April 2010.

Jeffrey, B. and Troman, G. (2004) Time for ethnography, *British Educational Research Journal*, 30(4): 535–548.

Jenkins, H. (2006) *Confronting the challenges of participatory culture: Media education for the 21st century*, Chicago, IL: The John D. and Catherine T. MacArthur Foundation.

Jenkins, R. (1992) *Pierre Bourdieu*, London: Routledge.

Johnston, P.H. (2004) *Choice words: How our language affects children's learning*, York, ME: Stenhouse Publishers.

Kagan, D.M. (1992) Implications of research on teacher belief, *Educational Psychologist*, 21(1): 65–90.

Kamler, B. and Comber, B. (2008) Making a difference: Early career English teachers research their practice, *Changing English: Studies in Culture and Education*, 15(1): 65–76.

Kemmis, S. (2006) Participatory action research and the public sphere, *Educational Action research*, 14(4): 459–476.

Kemmis, S. and McTaggart, R. (2005) 'Participatory action research: Communicative action and the public sphere', in N. Denzin and Y. Lincoln (eds), *The Sage Handbook of Qualitative Research* (pp. 559–604), London: Sage.

Kennedy, R. and Bearne, E. (2009) Summer reading Challenge 2009 Impact Research Report. www.readingagency.org.uk/children/summer-reading-challenge/ (accessed 28 July 2014).

Kenner, C. (2000) *Home pages: Literacy links for bilingual children*, Stoke on Trent: Trentham Books.

Kenner, C. (2005) Bilingual families as literacy eco-systems, *Early Years*, (3): 283–298.

Kenner, C. and Mahera, R. (2012) *Interconnecting worlds: Teacher partnerships for bilingual learning*. Stoke-on-Trent: Trentham.

Kincheloe, J. (2003) *Teachers as researchers: Qualitative inquiry as a path to empowerment*, 2nd edn, New York: Falmer.

Kinder, M. (1991) *Playing with power in movies, television, and video games: From Muppet Babies to Teenage Mutant Ninja Turtles*, Oakland, CA: University of California Press.

Krashen, S. (2004) *The power of reading: Insights from research*, Portsmouth, NH: Heinemann.

Kress, G. (2005) Interview with Gunther Kress, *Discourse: Studies in the cultural politics of education*, 26(3): 287–300.

Kwek, D., Albright, J. and Kramer-Dahl, A. (2007) Building teachers creative capabilities in Singapore's English classrooms: a way of contesting pedagogical instrumentality, *Literacy*, 42(1): 71–78.

Ladson-Billings, G. (1992) Liberatory consequences of literacy: A case of culturally relevant instruction for African American students, *The Journal of Negro Education*, 61(3): 378–390.

Lambirth, A. (2003) 'They get enough of that at home': understanding aversion to popular culture in schools, *Reading, Literacy and Language*, 37(1): 9–13.

Lankshear, C. and Knobel, M. (eds) (2006) *New literacies: Everyday practices and classroom learning*, 2nd edn, Maidenhead: Open University Press.

Lareau, A. (1987) Social class differences in family-school relationships: The importance of cultural capital, *Sociology of Education*, 60: 73–85.

Lareau, A. (2000) *Home Advantage: Social class and parental intervention in elementary education*, 2nd edn, Lanham, MO: Rowman & Littlefield.

Larson, J. and Marsh, J. (2005) *Making literacy real*, London: Sage.

Lave, J. (2008) 'Everyday life and learning', in P. Murphy and R. McCormick (eds), *Knowledge and practice: Representations and identities* (pp. 3–14), London: SAGE.

Lave, J. and Wenger, E. (1990) *Situated learning: Legitimate peripheral participation*, Cambridge: Cambridge University Press.

Lave, J. and Wenger, E. (1991) *Situated learning: Legitimate peripheral participation*, Cambridge: University of Cambridge Press.

Lawson, M.A. (2003) School–family relations in context. Parent and teacher perceptions of parent involvement, *Urban Education*, 38(1): 77–133.

Leander, K. and Sheehy, M. (2004) (eds) *Spatializing literacy research and practice*, New York: Peter Lang.

Lee, C. (1995) A culturally based cognitive apprenticeship: Teaching African American High School student skills in literary interpretation, *Reading Research Quarterly*, 30(4): 608–630.

Levy, R. (2008) Third Spaces are interesting places: Applying 'third spacetheory' to nursery-age children's constructions of themselves as readers, *Journal of Early Childhood Literacy*, 8(1): 43–66.

Levy, R. (2009) 'You have to understand words … but not read them': young children becoming readers in a digital age, *Journal of Research in Reading*, 32(1): 75–91.

Levy, R., Yamada Rice, D. and Marsh, J. (2013) 'Digital literacies in the primary classroom', in K. Hall, T, Cremin, B. Comber and L. Moll, *The Wiley Blackwell international research handbook of children's literacy, learning and culture* (pp. 333–343), Oxford: Wiley Blackwell.

Lingard, B. and Keddie, A. (2013) Redistribution, recognition and representation: working against pedagogies of indifference, *Pedagogy, Culture & Society*, 21(3): 427–447.

Livingstone, S. and Helsper, E. (2007) Gradations in digital inclusion: Children, young people and the digital divide, *New Media and Society*, 9(4): 671–696.

Lortie, D. (1975) *Schoolteacher: A sociological study*, London: University of Chicago Press.

Luca, M. (2009) *Embodied research and grounded theory*, Cardiff: University of Wales: www.wales.ac.uk/en/featuredcontent/articles/staffarticles/EmbodiedResearchandGroundedTheory.aspx.

Luke, A. (1988) *Literacy, textbooks and ideology: Postwar literacy instruction and the mythology of Dick and Jane*, London: Falmer.

Luke, A. (1997) 'Genres of power: Literacy education and the production of capital', in: R. Hasan and G. Williams (eds), *Literacy in society* (pp. 308–338), London: Longmen.

Luke, A. (2010) Documenting reproduction and inequality: Revisiting Jean Anyon's 'Social class and school knowledge', *Curriculum Inquiry*, 40(1): 167–182.

Lyons, N. (2010) 'Reflection and reflective inquiry: Critical issues, evolving conceptualisations, contemporary claims and future possibilities', in N. Lyons (ed.), *Handbook of Reflective Inquiry* (pp. 3–22), New York: Springer.

Lytle, S. (2008) At last: Practitioner inquiry and the practice of teaching: Some thoughts on better, *Journal of Research in Teaching*, 42(3): 373–379.

Lytle, S. and Cochran-Smith, M. (1990) Learning from teacher research: A working typology, *Teachers College Record*, 92: 83–103.

Marsh, J. (2000) Teletubby tales: Popular culture in the early years language and literacy curriculum, *Contemporary Issues in Early Childhood*, 1: 119–133.

Marsh, J. (2003) One way traffic? Connections between literacy practices at home and in the nursery, *British Educational Research Journal*, 29(3): 369–382.

Marsh, J (2003a) 'Early childhood literacy and popular culture', in N. Hall, J. Larson and J. Marsh (2003) *Handbook of early childhood literacy* (pp. 112–125), London: Sage.

Marsh, J. (2003b) One way traffic? Connections between literacy practices at home and in the nursery, *British Educational Research Journal*, 29(3): 369–382.

Marsh, J. (2004) The techno-literacy practices of young children, *Journal of Early Childhood Research*, 2(1): 51–66.

Marsh, J. (ed.) (2005) *Popular culture, new media and digital literacy in early childhood*, London: RoutledgeFalmer.

Marsh, M.M. (2002) The shaping of Ms. Nicholi: The discursive fashioning of teacher identities, *Qualitative Studies in Education*, 15: 333–347

Marsh, J. and Bearne. E. (2008) *Moving literacy on: Evaluation of the BFI lead practitioner scheme for moving image media literacy*, Leicester: United Kingdom Literacy Association.

Marsh, J., Brooks, G., Highes, J., Ristchie, L., Roeberts, S. and Wright, K. (2005) Digital beginnings: Young children's use of popular culture, media and new technologies. Sheffield: University of Sheffield. www.digitalbeginnings.shef.ac.uk.

Martin, T. (2003) Minimum and maximum entitlements: Literature at Key Stage 2, *Reading Literacy and Language*, 37(1): 14–17.

Mayall, B. (2002) *Towards a sociology for childhood: Thinking from children's lives*, Buckingham: Open University Press.

Mayall, B. (2007) *Children's lives outside school and their educational impact* (Primary Review Research Survey 8/1), Cambridge: University of Cambridge Faculty of Education.

Maylor, U. and Williams, K. (2009) *Black middle-class parents' accounts of managing their children's education*. Paper presented to the British Educational Research Conference. University of Manchester.

McCarthey, S. (1997) Connecting home and school literacy practices in classrooms with diverse populations, *Journal of Literacy*, 29(2): 145–182.

McCarthey, S.J. and Moje, E.B. (2002) Identity matters, *Reading Research Quarterly*, 37(2): 228–238.

McDougall, J. (2009) A crisis of professional identity: How primary teachers are coming to terms with changing views of literacy, *Teaching and Teacher Education*, 24: 1–9.

McIntyre, E., Rosebery, A. and González, N. (eds) (2001) *Classroom diversity: Connecting curriculum to students' lives*, Portsmouth, NH: Heinemann.

McKinney, M. and Giorgis, C. (2009) Narrating and performing identity: Literacy specialists' writing identities, *Journal of literacy research*, 41(1): 104–149.

McLaughlin, M.W. (2005) 'Listening and learning from the field: Tales of policy implementation and situated practice', in A. Lieberman, *The roots of educational change: International handbook of educational change* (pp. 58–72), New York: Springer.

McNaughton, S. (1995) *The patterns of emergent literacy*, Oxford: Oxford University Press.

McNiff, J. (2010) *Action research for professional development*, Poole: September Books.

McNiff, J., Lomax, P. and Whitehead, J. (1996) *You and your action research project*, London: Routledge.

Meek, M. (1991) *On being literate*, London: Bodley Head.

Meek, M. (2001) 'Preface', in M. Barrs and V. Cork (eds), *The reader in the writer*, London: Centre for Literacy in Primary Education.

Mercer, N. (2000) *Words and minds: How we use language to think together*, London: Routledge.

Minns, H. (1997) *Read it to me now!: Learning at home and at school*, 2nd edn, Buckingham: Open University Press.

Moje, E.B. and Luke, A. (2009) Literacy and identity: Examining the metaphors in history and contemporary research, *Reading Research Quarterly*, 44(4): 415–437.

Moje, E., McIntosh Ciechanowski, K., Kramer, K., Ellis, L., Carrillo, R. and Collazzo, T. (2004) Working towards third space in content area literacy: An examination of everyday funds of knowledge and Discourse, *Reading Research Quarterly*, 39(1): 38–70.

Moll, L. (1992) 'Literacy research in community and classrooms: A sociocultural approach', in R. Beach, J. Green, M. Kamil and T. Shanahan, *Multidisciplinary perspectives on literacy research*, Urbana, IL: National Council of Teachers Of English.

Moll, L., Amanti, C., Neff, D. and González, N. (1992) Funds of knowledge for teaching: Using a qualitative approach to connect homes and classrooms, *Theory into Practice*, 31: 132–141.

Moll, L. and Cammarota, C. (2010) 'Cultivating new funds of knowledge through research and practice', in K. Dunsmore, and D. Fisher (eds), *Bringing literacy home* (pp. 289–305), Newark, NJ: International Reading Association.

Moll, L. and Greenberg, J. (1990) 'Creating zones of possibly combining social context for instruction', in L. Moll (ed.), *Vygotsky in education* (pp. 319–348), Cambridge: Cambridge University Press.

Moll, L., Soto-Santiago, S.L. and Schwatrtz, L. (2013) 'Funds of knowledge in changing communities' in K. Hall, T. Cremin, B. Comber and L. Moll (eds), *The Wiley Blackwell international research handbook of children's literacy, learning and culture* (pp. 172–183), Oxford: Wiley Blackwell.

Moll, L., Tapia, J. and Whitmore, K. (1993) 'Living knowledge: The social distribution of cultural resources for thinking', in G. Salomon (ed.), Distributed cognitions (pp. 139–163), Cambridge: Cambridge University Press.

Moreau, S. and Sharrad, N. (2005) 'Enticing reluctant boys into peer writing communities', in B. Comber and B. Kamler (eds), *Turn around pedagogies: Literacy Interventions for at risk students* (pp. 31–46), Sydney: PETA.

Morgenstern, C. (1918) Stufen eine entwickelung in aphorismen und tagebuch-notizen. Project Gutenberg e-book www.gutenberg.org/etext/15898.

Mottram, M. and Hall, C. (2009) Diversions and diversity: Does the personalisation agenda offer real opportunities for taking children's home literacies seriously? *English in Education*, 43(2): 98–112.

Munn, P. (ed.) (1993) *Parents and schools: customers, managers or partners?* London: Routledge.

Murphy, P. and Wolfenden, F. (2013) Developing a pedagogy of mutuality in a capability approach: Teachers' experiences of using the Open Educational Resources (OER) of the teacher education in sub-Saharan Africa (TESSA) programme, *International Journal of Educational Development*, 33: 263–271.

Muschamp, Y., Wikeley, F., Ridge T. and Balarin M. (2007) *Parenting, caring and education: Primary Review Research Survey 7/1, Interim Report*, Cambridge: University of Cambridge.

Muschamp, Y., Wikeley, F., Ridge T. and Balarin M. (2010) 'Parenting, caring and education: Primary review research survey', in R. Alexander, with C. Doddington, J. Gray, L. Hargreaves and R. Kershner, R. (eds), *The Cambridge primary review research surveys*, London: Routledge.

Nash (1990) Bourdieu on educational, social and cultural reproduction, *British Journal of Sociology of Education*, 11: 431–447.

Navarro, Z. (2006) In search of a cultural interpretation of power: The contribution of Pierre Bourdieu, *Institute of Development Studies Bulletin*, 37(6): 11–22. doi: 10.1111/j.1759-5436.2006.tb00319.x

Nespor, J. (1997) *Tangled up in school: Politics, space, bodies and signs in the educational process*, Mahwah, NJ: Lawrence Erlbaum Associates.

New London Group (NLG) (2000) 'A pedagogy of multiliteracies: Designing social futures', in B. Cope and M. Kalantzis (eds), *Multiliteracies: Literacy learning and the design of social futures* (pp. 9–37), Melbourne: Macmillan.

New Zealand Ministry of Education (2014) New Zealand Curriculum Online: English Available on: http://nzcurriculum.tki.org.nz/The-New-Zealand-Curriculum/Learning-areas/English (accessed 14 January 2014).

Nichols, S., Nixon, H. and Rowsell, J. (2009) The 'good' parent in relation to early childhood literacy: symbolic terrain and lived practice, *Literacy*, 43(2): 65–74.

Nias, J. (1989) *Primary teachers talking: A study of teaching as work*, London: Routledge.

Nutbrown, C., Hannon, P. and Morgan, A. (2005) *Early literacy work with families: Policy, practice and research*, London: Sage.

Oja, S.N. and Reiman, A.J. (2007) 'A constructivist developmental perspective', in M.E. Diez and J. Raths (eds), *Dispositions in teacher education* (pp. 93–117), Charlotte, NC: Information Age Publishing.

Onwuegbuzie, A.J., Johnson, R.B. and Collins, K.M.T. (2009) Call for mixed analysis. A philosophical framework for combining qualitative and quantitative approaches, *International Journal of Multiple Research Approaches*, 3(2): 114–139.

O'Sullivan, E. (2003) Bringing a perspective of transformative learning to globalised consumption, *International Journal of Consumer Studies*, 27(4): 326–330.

Pahl, K. (2002) Ephemera, mess and miscellaneous piles: Texts and practices in families, *Journal of Early Childhood Literacy*, 2(2): 145–166.

Peel, R. (2000) 'Beliefs about "English" in England', in R. Peel, A. Patterson and K. Gerlach (eds), *Questions of English: Ethics, aesthetics, rhetoric and the formation of the subject in England, Australia and the United States* (pp. 116–188), London: RoutledgeFalmer.

Peters, M., Seeds, K., Goldstein, A. and Coleman, M. (2007) *Parental involvement in children's education 2007*, London: BRB International for the DCSF.

Peterson, S.S. and Heywood, D. (2007) Contributions of families' linguistic, social, and cultural capital to minority-language children's literacy: Parents', teachers', and principals' perspectives, *Canadian Modern language Review*, 63(4): 517–538.

Pollard, A. (1996) 'Playing the system: pupil perspectives of curriculum, assessments and pedagogy', in P. Croll (ed.), *Teachers, pupils and primary schooling: Continuity and change*, London: Cassell.

Prensky, M. (2001) Digital narratives: Digital immigrants, *On the Horizon*, 9(5): 1–6.

Pugh, A. (2009) *Longing and belonging: Parents, children and consumer culture*, Berkley: University of California Press.

Reese, L. and Gallimore, R. (2000) Immigrant Latinos' cultural model of literacy development: An evolving perspective on home-school discontinuities, *American Journal of Education*, 108(2): 103–134.

Reeves, J. (2008) Teacher investment in learner identity, *Teaching and Teacher Education*, 25: 34–41. doi:10.1016/j.tate.2008.06.003

Ren, L. and Hu, G. (2011) The comparative study of family social capital and literacy practices in Singapore, *Journal of Early Childhood Literacy*, 13(1): 98–130.

Robertson, L.H. (2004) 'Multilingual flexibility and literacy learning in an Urdu community school', in E. Gregory, S. Long and D. Volk (eds), *Many pathways to literacy*, London: RoutledgeFalmer.

Robinson, M. and Turnbull, B. (2005) 'Verónica: An asset model of becoming literate', in J. Marsh (ed.), *Popular culture, new media and digital technology in early childhood*, London: Routledge Falmer.

Rodriguez, G. (2013) Power and agency in education: Exploring the pedagogical dimensions of funds of knowledge, *Review of Research in Education*, 37: 87.

Rogoff, B. (1990) *Apprenticeship in thinking: Cognitive development in social Contexts*, New York: Oxford University Press.

Rogoff, B. (1993) 'Children's guided participation and participatory appropriation in sociocultural activity', in R. Wozniak and K. Fisher (eds), *Development in context* (pp. 121–153), Hilldale, NJ: Erlbaum.

Rogoff, B. (1995) 'Observing sociocultural activity on three planes: Participatory appropriation, guided participation and apprenticeship', in K. Hall, P. Murphy and J. Soler (eds), *Pedagogy and practice: Culture and identities*, London: Open University Press/ SAGE.

Rogoff, B. (2003) *The cultural nature of human development*, New York: Oxford University Press.

Rose, J. (2006) *Independent review of the teaching of early reading*, London: Department for Education and Skills.

Rosemberg, C.N., Stein, A. and Alam, F. (2013) 'At home and at school: Bridging literacy to children from poor rural or marginalized urban communities', in K. Hall, T. Cremin, B. Comber and L. Moll, *The Wiley Blackwell international research handbook of children's literacy, learning and culture* (pp. 67–82), Oxford: Wiley Blackwell.

Schieffelin, B.B. and Cochran-Smith, M. (1984) 'Learning to read culturally: Literacy before schooling, in H. Goelman, A. Oberg, and F. Smith (eds), *Awakening to literacy*, Victoria: Heinemann Educational.

Schön, D. (1987) *Educating the reflective practitioner*, San Francisco, CA: Josey Bass.

Scribner, S. and Cole, M. (1981) *The psychology of literacy*, Cambridge, MA: Harvard University Press.

Selwyn, N., Banaji, S., Hadjithoma-Garstka, C. and Carlk, W. (2011) Providing a platform for parents? Exploring the nature of parental engagement with school learning platforms, *Journal of Computer Assisted Learning*, 27(4): 314–323.

Solvasson, C. (2013) Embedding ethicality within student practice-approaches and dilemmas. *TACTYC Reflections*, November 2013. www.tactyc.org.uk/reflections.

Somekh, B. (2006) *Action research: A methodology for change and development*, Maidenhead: Open University Press.

Stein, P. (2004) Reconfiguring the past and the present: Performing literacy histories in a Johannesburg classroom, *TESOL Quarterly*, 517–528.

Stenhouse, L. (1975) *An introduction to curriculum research and development*, London: Heinemann.

Stooke, R. (2005) OP-ED Many hands make light work' but 'too many cooks spoil the broth': representing literacy teaching as a 'job for experts' undermines efforts to involve parents, *Journal of Curriculum Studies*, 37(1): 3–10.

Street, B. (1998) New literacies in theory and practice: What are the implications for language in education?, *Linguistics and Education*, 10(1) 1–24.

Street, B.V. (1984) *Literacy in theory and practice*, Cambridge: Cambridge University Press.

Street, B.V. (2008) 'New literacies, new times: developments in literacy studies', in B.V. Street, and N. Hornberger (eds), *Encyclopedia of language and education, Vol 2: Literacy* (pp. 3–14), New York: Springer.

Street, C. (2003) Pre-service teachers' attitudes about writing and learning to teach writing: implications for teacher educators, *Teacher Education Quarterly*, 30(3): 33–50.

Talmy, S. (2011) The interview as collaborative achievement: Interaction, identity and ideology in a speech event, *Applied Linguistics*, 32(1): 25–42.

Taylor, D. and Dorsey-Gains, C. (1988) *Growing up literate: Learning from inner-city families*, Portsmouth, NH: Heinemann.

Tenery, M.F. (2005) 'La Visita' in N. González, L. Moll, and C. Amanti (eds), *Funds of knowledge: Theorizing practices in households, communities and classrooms* (pp. 119–130), London: Lawrence Erlbaum.

Thomson, P. (2002) *Schooling the rustbelt kids. Making the difference in changing times*, Sydney: Allen & Unwin.

Thomson, P. and Clifton, J. (2013) 'Connecting parents and the community in an urban primary school', in K. Hall, T. Cremin, B. Comber and L. Moll, *The Wiley Blackwell international research handbook of children's literacy, learning and culture* (pp. 54–66), Oxford: Wiley Blackwell.

Thomson, P. and Hall, C. (2008) Opportunities missed and/or thwarted? 'Funds of Knowledge' meet the English national curriculum, *The Curriculum Journal*, 19(2): 87–103.

Thomson, P., Hall, C., Jones, K. and Sefton-Green, J. (2012) *The signature pedagogies project: The final report*, London: Culture, Creativity and Education.

Tveit, A.D. (2009) A parental voice: parents as equal and dependent – rhetoric about parents, teachers, and their conversations, *Educational Review*, 61(3): 289–300.

Unsworth, L. (2001) *Teaching multiliteracies across the curriculum*, Buckingham: Open University Press.

Vasquez, V.M. (2005) 'Resistance, power-tricky and colourless energy: What engagement with everyday popular cultural texts can tell us about learning, and literacy', in J. Marsh (ed.), *Popular culture, new media and digital literacy in early childhood*, London: RoutledgeFalmer.

Vélez-Ibáñez, C.G. and Greenberg, J.B. (1992) Formation and transformation of funds of knowledge among U.S.-Mexican households, *Anthropology and Education Quarterly*, 23: 313–335.

Vincent, C. (1996) *Parents and teachers*, London: Falmer Press.

Volk, D. (2004) 'Mediating networks for literacy learning', in E. Gregory, S. Long and D. Volk (eds), *Many pathways to literacy*, London: Routledge Falmer.

Volk, D. and de Acosta, M. (2004) 'Mediating networks for literacy learning: the role of Puerto Rican siblings', in E. Gregory, S. Long and D. Volk (eds), *Many pathways to literacy. Young children learning with siblings, grandparents, peers and communities*, New York: Routledge Falmer.

Walsh, C. (2007) Creativity as capital in the literacy classroom: youth as multimodal designers *Literacy*, 41(2): 74–80.

Walsh C. and Kamler, B. (2013) 'Teacher Research on Literacy: Turning around to students and technology', in K. Hall, T. Cremin, B. Comber and L. Moll, *The Wiley Blackwell international research handbook of children's literacy, learning and culture* (pp. 499–500), Oxford: Wiley Blackwell.

Watson, C. (2004) Effective professional learning communities, *British Educational Research Journal*, 40(1): 18–29.

Watson, C. (2014) Effective professional learning communities, *British Educational Research Journal*, 40(1): 18–29.

Watts, J. (2006) 'The outsider within': Dilemmas of qualitative feminist research within a culture of resistance, *Qualitative Research*, (6: 3) 385–402.

Weber, C.M. and Raphael, T. (2013) 'Constructing a collective identity: professional development for twenty first century pedagogy', in K. Hall, T. Cremin, B. Comber and L. Moll, *The Wiley Blackwell international research handbook of children's literacy, learning and culture* (pp. 169–184), Oxford: Wiley Blackwell.

Weigel, D.J., Martin, S.S. and Bennett, K.K. (2005) Ecological influences of the home and the child-care center on preschool-age children's literacy development, *Reading Research Quarterly*, 40(2): 204–233.

Wells, G. (1987) *The meaning makers: Children learning language and using language to learn*, London: Hodder and Stoughton.

Wenger, E. (1998) *Communities of practice: Learning, meaning and identity*, Cambridge: Cambridge University Press.

Whalley, M. (2007) *Involving parents in their children's learning*, 2nd edn, Thousand Oaks, CA: Sage.

Whitehouse, M. and Colvin, C. (2001) 'Reading families': Deficit discourse and family literacy, *Theory Into Practice*, 40(3): 212–219.

Willett, R., Robinson, M. and Marsh, J. (2008) *Play, creativity and digital cultures*, London: Routledge.

Williams, R. (1976) *Keywords: A vocabulary of culture and society*, London: Fontana.

Williams, R. (1982) *The sociology of culture*, New York: Schocken.

Williams, T.J. (2009) *Save our children: The struggle between Black parents and schools*, New York: African American Images.

Woods, P., Boyle, M. and Hubbard, N. (1999) *Multicultural children in the early years: Creative teaching, meaningful learning*, Clevedon: Multilingual Matters.

Wyse, D. and Styles, M. (2007) 'Synthetic phonics and the teaching of reading: The debate surrounding England's "Rose Report"', *Literacy*, 41(1): 35–42.

Yamada Rice, D. (2010) New media, evolving multimodal literacy practices and the potential impact of increased use of the visual mode in the urban classroom on young children's learning, *Literacy*, 45(1): 32–43.

Yeo, M. (2007) New literacies, alternative texts: teachers' conceptualisations of composition and literacy, *English Teaching: Practice and Critique*, 6(1): 113–131.

Yoon, K.S., Duncan, T., Lee, S.W.-Y., Scarloss, B. and Shapley, K.L. (2007) *Reviewing the evidence on how teacher professional development affects student achievement*, Institute of Educational Sciences: U.S. Department of Education.

Zammit, K.P. (2010) The New Learning Environments framework: scaffolding the development of multiliterate students, *Pedagogies*, 5(4): 325–337.

Zammit, K.P. (2011) Connecting multiliteracies and engagement of students from low socio-economic backgrounds: Using Bernstein's pedagogic discourse as a bridge, *Language and Education*, 25(3): 203–220.

INDEX

Andrews, J. 23, 67, 74, 87
'asset blanket' 75, 88, 160
Atkinson, M. 153
attentiveness, flexibility and openness 94–6
Auge, M. 114
'autonomous' and 'ideological' models of
    literacy 12, 177–8

Barton, D. 12
Bearne, E. 23, 70, 93
'behaviour problems' 90, 118–19
Bernstein, B. 68–9, 90
bilingual learners 13–14 bilingual outreach
    worker 58, 153, 161–7
bilingual staff 163
Bourdieu, P. 49–50
Brice-Heath, S. 15–16, 17–18, 180
Bruner, J. 11
*Building Communities: Researching Literacy
    Lives (BC:RLL)* project 2–8; ways
    forward and implications 183–8;
    recommendations 188–9
*Building Communities: Researching Literacy
    Lives (BC:RLL)* project methodology:
    aims and rationale 28–31; children and
    families 33–5; data sources and analysis
    40–2; design 37–40; ethics 42–4;
    headteachers and teachers 33; local
    authorities and project co-ordinators 32;
    organisational challenges 44–5;
    participants 31–2; partners from external
    agencies 35; philosophical challenges
    45–6; professional development activities

35–7; schools 33; structure and
    organisation 31
Bullock Report 81

Cairney, T. 7, 16
case studies: bilingual outreach worker
    161–7; Carol and Cole 76–80; Freda and
    Molly 60–4; St Mary's School 138–46;
    Sophie and Jo and family 117–26, 133–4;
    Viv and Razia 99–104
children and families, project methodology
    33–5; funds of knowledge 18, 74–6,
    88–90, 103–4
children, developing knowledge of 66–7,
    176–8; beginning the journey 67–9;
    beyond the school gate 69–71; case study:
    Carol and Cole 76–80
children's interests: home literacy
    practices and classroom activity 84–6;
    nature and country pursuits 77–8,
    79–80, 83; *see also* digital and multimodal
    literacy
choice and independence 90–1
Clark, M. 78
co-partners in research 50–1, 173–5
Cochran-Smith, M. 50
Comber, B. 6–7, 24, 25, 26, 51, 83, 157,
    179
communities: building 186–8; concepts of 7,
    9–11; initial knowledge of families and
    129–30; of practice 46, 103, 152, 187–8;
    professional learning 157–60
Cremin, T. 5, 7, 22, 35, 43, 106